the **game** cookbook

clarissa dickson wright and johnny scott

the game cookbook

clarissa dickson wright and johnny scott

with food photography by gus filgate

kyle cathie limited

This edition published in 2005 by Kyle Books
An imprint of Kyle Cathie Limited
general.enquiries@kyle-cathie.com
www.kylecathie.com

Distributed by National Book Network
4501 Forbes Blvd., Suite 200
Lanham, MD 20706
Phone: (301) 459 3366   Fax: (301) 429 5746

First published in 2004 by Kyle Cathie Limited

Text copyright © 2004 Clarissa Dickson Wright and Johnny Scott
Photography copyright © 2004 Gus Filgate
Book design © 2004 Kyle Cathie Limited
ISBN 1 904920 21 7

The Library of Congress Cataloging-in-Publication Data

The Game Cookbook/ Clarissa Dickson Wright and Johnny Scott.

ISBN 1 904920 21 7
1. Cookery, International. 2. Game - Description.

2005926309

Senior Editor Kyle Cathie
Design and art direction Geoff Hayes
Photography Gus Filgate
Home Economist David Morgan
Food Stylist Penny Markham
Americaniser Delora Jones
Indexer Alex Corrin
Production Sha Huxtable and Alice Holloway
Color reproduction by Sang Choy, Singapore
Printed and bound by Tien Wah Press, Singapore

1 2 3 4 5   01 02 03 04 05

Dedication:

To Sam Scott in the hope that he and all his generation may enjoy the
fruits of the chase for his life and for the centuries to come.

Acknowledgments:

CDW: Thanks go to my butcher and friend Colin Peat of Haddington,
England, for supplying most of the game for these recipes. To Kyle Cathie
for having the foresight to publish this book. To gamekeepers, stalkers,
ghillies, and waterbalifs everywhere and to all who keep faith with the
Countryside.

JS: British Association of Shooting and Conservation
Countryside Alliance
Federation of Fieldsports Associations of the European Union
The Game Conservancy Trust
Colin McElvie
Colin Woolf

**Most recipes serve 4. Game birds, with the exception of
pheasant, serve 1 per head, pheasant serves 2–3 people. A
1–pound pie serves 2 people.**

**The bold line in the text indicates the division between
Johnny Scott's text and Clarissa Dickson Wright's.**

contents

introduction   **6**

game birds   **8**
partridge   10
pheasant   22
quail   36
grouse   42
dove   54
american woodcock   64
snipe   70

wildfowl   **74**
duck   80
goose   92

cloven hoof   **96**
venison   102
white-tail   110
wapeti   116
moose   121
antelope   121
caribou   125
wild boar   128

hares & rabbits   **132**
hare (jackrabbit)   134
rabbit   142

game fish   **154**
salmon   160
trout   166
sea trout   170
zander (pike perch)   173
pike   174
carp   175

**composite dishes,
sauces, & stock**   **180**

meat suppliers   196

cooking glossary   198

website addresses   202

index   206

acknowledgements   208

introduction

To sportsmen all over the world, the very word "Game" evokes vivid memories of sights, sounds, scents, and flurries of sudden adrenaline-pumping action—midges and the glorious colors of maple leaves; birch and aspen trees and the sound of running water; a raven croaking above a highland corrie; an elk bugling; a ruffed grouse exploding from a forest floor. A bell tinkling on a Brittany spaniels's collar; the iodine smell of the sea; dawn and skeins of geese honking overhead; the russet plumage of a woodcock blending with the golden colors of dead bracken; numb feet and thin, wintry sunlight glinting on the phoenix plumage of a pheasant; the graceful movement of a white-tail buck; the earthy smell of wet dog; the exquisite sensation of hot water on frozen limbs, log fires, and in all its different forms, the most delicious food.

The preservation and possession of game is entwined in the antiquity and histories of the Old and New Worlds. As a vital food source, its value influenced constitutions and the laws of European land ownership. Our manners are directly attributable to the glorification of game and the complicated ceremonies and traditions that evolved during the Age of Chivalry.

Game was the subject of the earliest art form and continued to be the inspiration for a major part of the heritage of our art, music, and literature. Game was responsible for the most dramatic advancement in firearm evolution in 400 years. Percussion detonation, invented by a Scottish wildfowling Minister of the Kirk and developed by an American landscape artist, is the ignition mechanism that propels every shell, bullet, or cartridge anywhere in the world today.

Perhaps the most significant role that game has filled in the last hundred years is in the conservation of other wildlife species. During the eighteenth century, game in Europe and America came under pressure from a number of directions. A rapidly escalating urban population made enormous demands on what everyone had accepted for centuries as an historic, harvestable natural food source. Revolutionary advances in gun making facilitated these demands. Railways made game more accessible, but it was habitat destruction caused by agricultural expansion that probably did more damage than all the hunters put together. Efforts to conserve game in America started as long ago as 1791, when the heath hen became endangered, and these efforts continued sporadically throughout the nineteenth century, but the problem was a lack of cohesion nation-wide. Towards the end of the century and in the beginning of the next, Theodore Roosevelt, assisted by other visionary sporting naturalists, instigated far-reaching wildlife conservation initiatives that have been strengthened and advanced with each generation.

Across Britain and Europe, game conservation became an essential part of land management and was recognized as providing habitats that have led to the increase in all bird species and to creating a whole biodiversity of animal and insect life. An ethos that was best described by King George VI when he remarked, "The wildlife of today is not ours to dispose of as we please. We have it on trust for those who come after."

As the world advances into the twenty-first century, game in Britain generates in excess of £4 million by direct expenditure from shooting and stalking alone, to say nothing of that generated by the 3^1/2 million fishermen, plus another £250 million from ancillary businesses connected with it. These figures and their significance to wildlife conservation are an impressive part of Britain's economy, but tiny when compared internationally. The Federation of Fieldsports Associations of the European Union, which represents seven million sportsmen from the 15 member countries, recently commissioned a study by the Institut National Agronomique in Paris to evaluate the expenditure on fieldsports in Europe. Money spent on habitat preservation ran to well over €10 billion and generated 100,000 jobs, not including sporting tourism in Africa, Canada, and South America. A similar survey in the US, by the Congressional Sportsmen's Foundation, produced figures in tens of billions of dollars.

Forty million hunters and anglers in the US have spent $70 billion every year on their sport, which creates $179 billion in a ripple effect to ancillary businesses, supporting more jobs than America's largest employer, Wal-Mart. Sportsmen spend nearly $2 billion annually on conservation and pay more than 65 percent of all state fish and wildlife agency budgets—money that funds fisheries, wildlife, and recreational projects.

Since 1934 when the first Duck Stamp was purchased, more than $650 million has gone towards the purchase and conservation of wildlife habitat, totaling an area larger in size than the state of Massachusetts, providing natural environment to countless wildfowl and wetland birds. $360 million from money raised from taxes goes towards educating young sportsmen about wildlife. $4 billion in excise taxes has been raised from hunters since 1939, and $3 billion from fishermen since 1952. American hunters and anglers hold 36 percent of the voting potential, and sportsmen internationally are the financial backbone of the management of fish and wildlife (in every country other than Britain) wielding great influence over public opinion and voting behavior.

Where consumer demand for a particular wild species exceeds available supplies, game farming becomes an option for diversification from standard agriculture. There is a historical precedent of farming certain species of game, particularly deer. The Chinese were at it 2,000 years ago, primarily for medicinal purposes. The Romans brought with them a culture of living larders—hares, pheasants, and possibly fallow deer and rabbits, which they had inherited from earlier civilizations. The Normans did the same, bringing with them the ancient practice of fish farming and a form of deer farming not that different from what is practiced today. The purpose of living larders was to provide a readily available food source and the practice has persisted in one form or another into the modern age.

Deer farming is by far the biggest industry, with well over four million red deer, reindeer, wapiti, sika, elk, fallow, rusa, and musk deer being farmed in the USA, Russia, China, Korea, Australia, New Zealand, and across Europe. Fish farming also has a long history, with the controversial intensive farming of salmon created by the destruction of wild salmon stocks and an increased consumer demand for fish as world resources diminished. Wild boar, bison, quail, pheasants, partridges, and, more recently, mallard are farmed worldwide to a greater or lesser degree, depending upon the requirements of different countries. Some species, like grouse, migratory wildfowl, and wetland birds can never be domesticated.

Unfortunately, farmed game, because of the nature of modern farming, will never have quite the same wonderful flavour as its wild counterpart. Domesticated animals do not run free or eat the same natural herbage that makes wild game so sought-after. However,

farmed game does provide those without access to wild game a chance to experience the next best thing.

Game is healthy, low in fat, high in protein, and easy to cook. If you like the good things in life, it holds its head among the best. I hope our book will remind those who have forgotten, and inspire those who have yet to experience eating the world's most wonderful produce.

game birds

partridge

The two species of partridge that are such a familiar sight of the North American countryside—the chubby gray (or Hungarian) partridge, (*Perdix perdix*) with his orange face and distinctive inverted horseshoe mark on his light gray breast, and the slightly larger, white-faced, red-legged chukar (*Alectoris chukar*)—were originally strangers to the New World. Their place in the history of shooting and conservation on both sides of the Atlantic, and in the development of the sporting shotgun, is so important that it is worth recording.

Hungarian or gray partridges are a bird of northern Europe and their cousin, the red-legged (or French) partridge, of which the chukar is a subspecies, are birds of the arid south Mediterranean and Eurasia. The ideal habitat for partridges is open spaces on the edges of woods and scrubland, with plenty of good ground cover, which provides seeds and insects to eat and shelter to nest and rear their broods, safe from hawks and other aerial predators. For many centuries, partridges were the principal game bird in Europe. They became such a major part of the diet in the early Middle Ages that "toujours perdix," indicating a monotony in food, became a common expression and still is to the present day.

Under the rigid Norman Forest Laws (which applied both to Britain and France) partridges, rabbits, hares, and pheasants were classified as beasts of Free Warren. All game belonged to the King, but the right to hunt game in either forest, chase (open parkland), or warren was handed out as bribes or rewards to the nobility or clergy. The right of Free Warren was a fairly minor perk that was often granted to monastic houses, and so during the Middle Ages, partridges became synonymous with a privileged and increasingly decadent priesthood. The connection between partridges and the scandal of excess among the clergy persisted to the extent that when Henry IV

of France sentenced the Bishop of Dijon to life imprisonment, part of the sentence dictated that the Bishop should never be fed anything other than partridges.

Not only were partridges prolific, but their behavioral pattern made them obligingly easy to catch. Until they separate to mate in winter, partridges stick together in family groups (as do quail), and their harsh rasping call is as familiar a sound in the American countryside as it is in Britain and other parts of Europe. At the first

sign of danger they scuttle together, crouching, not moving, until danger passes or they are forced into the air. To rout them out, a setting dog—the ancestor of our pointers and setters—was used, a dog trained to locate the partridges and approach stealthily, holding their attention while at the same time diverting it from the net being drawn over them. To force the partridges into the air, a falconer would release a bird of prey to persue the partridges and bring them down. As techniques in falconry improved with knowledge acquired in the Middle East during the crusades, partridges flushed from cover became the falconer's popular game bird.

Gunpowder was first used in European warfare in the thirteenth century. By the 1500s, primitive military matchlocks and delicate sporting wheellocks, firing solid lumps of lead, were being used on deer and the occasional unsuspecting, flightless bustard. The shotgun came into being with the invention of small shot in the second half of the sixteenth century and the potential for bagging quantities of birds was instantly recognized and immediately condemned. However, to actually get a shot at game birds was difficult. Most early firearms weighed over 20 pounds, had barrels at least six feet long, and had to be fired from a gun stand. With impossibly unwieldy guns like these, birds could only be shot on the ground—not in flight—following an elaborate stalk, often involving a "stalking horse," a retired farm horse, its ears blocked with wool, behind which the gunner hid. Despite these difficulties and the sport's notoriety, shooting with hail shot began to grow in popularity, something which infuriated the hawking community. Gunmaking in the seventeenth century was more advanced in Europe, with the best sporting guns made in Italy and France. These were lighter and more maneuverable, enabling European sportsmen to shoot partridges "on the wing" as coveys (families of partridges) took to the air. This innovation in shooting was brought to Britain by those who had witnessed it while on the Grand Tour—an adventure very much in vogue among wealthy eighteenth-century Britons. At the same time, an expansion in cereal production in the 1780s, and the introduction of turnips as winter stock feed, led to an increase in the gray partridge population. Tall, hand-scythed wheat and broad-leaved winter root crops were all perfect habitat for partridges, providing deep cover and a plentiful feed source.

Partridges were shot immediately after harvest, with the aid of pointers, originally imported from Spain. These large, hound-like, slow working dogs had phenomenal noses. Trained to quarter the ground searching for coveys, they stood "on point" as soon as one was scented. This enabled sportsmen to cock their flintlocks, check their priming, and creep forward, ready to fire the moment the covey took to the air. "Shooting flying" became the fashion and inspired the British gun trade—gunmakers like Manton, Egg, and Twigg—to make quality guns along European lines.

Richard Bache, an immigrant from England who was to marry Benjamin Franklin's daughter, Sarah, in 1767, made several attempts to establish gray partridges, imported from Britain, at his estate on the banks of the Delaware River. He would almost certainly have imported a brace or more of the new Spanish pointing dogs, introducing to America a breed that has been one of its most popular and useful gun dogs ever since. Despite the similarity between farming in Britain and farming on the East Coast of America at that time, Bache's partridges did not survive and it was many decades before partridges were to become part of the American landscape.

Red-legged partridges became established in Britain towards the end of the eighteenth century. The Marquis of Hertford imported several pairs, and thousands of eggs, from the south of France. This foundation stock soon spread into the neighboring counties but, from a shooting point of view, these new birds looked like they would be a failure. Instead of obligingly keeping still when marked by pointers, and taking to the wing only when guns were cocked and sportsmen ready to shoot, red-legs continually crept ahead of dogs and took to the wing when they were well out of range. However, the red-

legged's potential was recognized. A new method of igniting the main charge in a firearm had been invented by the Rev. Alexander Forsyth, Minister of the parish of Belhelvie in Aberdeenshire, Scotland. His experiments with sulphate of mercury, which explodes when struck, led to the first breakthrough in four hundred years of firearm manufacturing. Forsyth's percussion detonation of 1807, refined in America by an immigrant named Joshua Shaw ten years later, had replaced the weather-sensitive, flintlock, open firing mechanism by 1820. Now sportsmen on both sides of the Atlantic could shoot in any weather and at any angle, without the risk of the ignition charge getting damp, or falling out of the pan.

Gray partridges were still shot over pointers while the new, red-legged birds continued to induce apoplexy and xenophobic eruptions of rage by creeping ahead of dogs and only flying if they came to an obstacle like a hedge. Someone, presumably out of sheer frustration, eventually had the idea of positioning themselves behind such a barrier and firing as partridges flew over him. The novelty caught on, and driving coveys over forward-standing guns concealed behind high hedges was experimented with widely. The value of red-legs as a driven bird could now be appreciated. Unlike gray partridges that flew in coveys and were soon over guns, reds came over in ones and twos, providing a continuity of sporting shots. The first organized driven partridge shoot, involving an army of beaters and some of the crack shots of the day, took place in 1845 at Heveningham Hall in Suffolk, England, the seat of Lord Huntingfield. The day was considered a huge success. The bag was impressive and his Lordship, who is reputed to have practiced for weeks beforehand on potatoes lobbed over the high-walled kitchen gardens by his servants, shot well. There was one obvious drawback—guns were still loaded at the muzzle, and keeping pace with driven partridge necessitated a relay of four guns per person and as many loaders. The whole performance of trying to pour powder and shot into a muzzle loader in the heat of the moment, with birds whizzing over, and an impatient employer yelling for a fresh gun was, as one loader put it so succinctly in the Huntingfield Arms Inn that night, bloody dangerous.

Two innovations in engineering, exhibited at the Great Exhibition at Crystal Palace in London in 1851, revolutionized shooting worldwide, and partridge shooting in Britain. The first was another leap forward in gunmaking technology by the French gunmakers, Casimir Lefaucheux. The second was a mechanical corn reaper, invented by the American father and son, Robert and Cyrus McCormick—founders of the giant US agricultural engineering works, whose name is known to farmers anywhere in the world. Lefaucheux's gun hinged opened at the breech to be loaded with a cartridge containing powder, shot, and its own percussion cap. By 1860, gunmakers on both sides of the Atlantic had improved Lefaucheux's breech loader so that sportsmen were now able to shoot as fast as they could load Eley's new composite cartridge. The McCormic reaper reduced stubble cover to the level where both gray and red-legged partridges now ran ahead of guns, making walking-up over pointers hopelessly unproductive. Driven partridges, pheasant, and grouse became all the rage across the UK, and British gunmakers like Purdey, Holland and Holland, Boss, and Westley-Richards, and in the US, Stevens, Winchester, Ithica, Marlin, Harrington and Richardson, Smith, and Savage, competed to build better handling guns. The next fifty years, up until WW1, was the era of the great British shooting house parties, with

landowners devoting enormous sums to creating habitat that suited partridges and pheasants; this not only shaped the landscape, but provided a conservation legacy that has benefited all wildlife. Royalty led the way, with Queen Victoria developing the shoot at Windsor and where royalty led, the nobility and gentry followed. In Europe Bohemia and Hungary were the main attractions and in particular, the estate of Baron Hirsch at St. Johann in Hungary, where partridges swarmed in an open landscape of corn strips and stubble fields. Baron Hirsch, whose New York-based Jewish Colonial Fund, assisted thousands of Eastern European Jews to resettle in the New World, was an authority on gray partridges. He advised the future King Edward VII on partridge rearing and, after a series of disastrously wet springs, in the late 1870s, when partridge chicks died of cold, sent over thousands of young birds to replace lost stock on the Prince's estate at Sandringham.

Britain became a mecca for wealthy American and Canadian sportsmen, who came over to experience driven partridges and pheasants in England, and the red deer stalking, salmon fishing, and driven grouse in Scotland. It was only a matter of time before a second attempt to establish gray partridges in North America got under way. Several dozen pairs were imported to estates on the Eastern seaboard in 1899. Their survival heralded large scale importations over the next thirty years, with gray partridges being introduced all the way from Portland, Maine, and northern New York to South Carolina and other southeastern states. Gray partridges prefer large, open fields away from woodland, above one thousand feet and with a cool, dry climate. For example, it came as a surprise that partridges released in the wooded Willamette Valley in Oregon, where pheasants were proving so successful, quickly disappeared but a similar

release in northeastern Oregon and southeastern Washington, thrived and rapidly increased. Northern Iowa and southern Minnesota also provided particularly favorable gray partridge habitat. Importations to Canada proved remarkably successful, with the first pairs arriving in Nova Scotia in 1908. Additional stocks arrived the following year, and quickly became established south of Calgary, with the Northern Alberta Game and Fish Protection League liberating more birds near Edmonton. During the first quarter of the twentieth century, gray partridge became established across Canada from subarctic regions to the international boundary and are now by far the most common upland game bird.

Gray partridges are not only habitat sensitive, but they are also self-destructive. The cock birds, like British red grouse, are extremely aggressive and territorial. Old birds, unless shot, will continually extend their mating territory as they drive young cock birds away. The result is a high proportion of barren hen birds, infertile eggs, and a rapid localized drop in population. In the 1930s, sportsmen in those states less suited to gray partridges decided to experiment with establishing red-legged or chukar partridge. These natives of Eurasia have a distribution from the Mediterranean to Greece, Turkey, Iran, southeastern Russia, India, and China, and are larger, less habitat-specific, and hardier than gray partridges. Chukar were quickly established in all the western US states and up into Canada. Idaho, Nevada, and Oregon have the highest populations, with strong stocks in eastern California, Utah, Texas, Montana, Wyoming, and Colorado. They have also been sighted in New Mexico, South Dakota, and across the border in southern Alberta. Introductions of chukar to New Zealand and the Hawaiian Islands have been equally successful. Chukars thrive in high desert regions, like the

Great Basin, using the rocky terrain for protection against heat and predators, huddling together in flocks for warmth during winter. This type of habitat provides them with an abundance of weed seed species, forbs, and green shoots to feed on and enough cover to nest and rear their broods. During the 1960s and 70s, all wildlife suffered as a result of habitat disturbance caused by intensified farming and the use of pesticides. Gray partridges were particularly vulnerable and their numbers dropped dramatically. Wildlife conservation bodies were quick to react to the crisis in the uplands, and world famous organizations like Pheasants Forever, Quails Unlimited, and Game Conservancy USA, raised millions of dollars towards habitat preservation. These organizations and the government Conservation Research Program (offering farmers subsidies to take land out of production to create wildlife habitat to benefit all species) have ensured a future for these temperamental, sporting little birds. Chukar partridge have a long season, roughly October 1st to April 30th depending upon which state you shoot in, with bag limits of about eight birds a day. The season for grays starts and finishes earlier, with a similar bag limit. Both are hunted in the traditional manner, walked-up over pointers and retrievers. Faster out of cover than pheasants but not as quick as quail, both species of partridge provide tremendous sport and delicious eating.

I yearn for partridge during the intervening months, gray partridge that is, although the red-legged described by the poet, Robert Browning as "plump as bishops" repays the attention you may lavish on it. I feel partridge should feature in the meal I eat before they hang me. If you have a young gray partridge roast it, otherwise here, on the following pages, are some ideas for you.

Aging

It is easy to age a young gray partridge at the beginning of the season as the legs will be yellowish, the beak dark, and the bones soft, while adults are gray beaked, gray legged, and hard boned. As winter starts, I use the flight feather test as the two primaries will be pointed; if the primary feathers are pointed but bedraggled and faded, they denote a bird born later in the previous season which has not yet molted, but it will be obvious. In the Bursa test (see page 24) a toothpick will go up a half-inch in a young bird. With red-legged partridges, the primaries are tipped with cream-colored plumage in a young bird.

Hanging

Young grays have such a delicate flavor that they shouldn't be hung for more than 3–5 days according to temperature; older birds should be given 5–7 days to tenderize. If you are lucky enough to have young grays, promise me you will simply roast them, all the complicated recipes are for the more tasteless and now common red-legged Frenchman as they are often called.

Plucking and drawing

As for pheasant (see pages 24–25).

Roasting

Insert a piece of seasoned butter in the bird's cavity and cover the breast with barding fat, rather than bacon, to keep the delicate flavor. Cook in a very hot oven at 425°F for 30 minutes, removing the fat for the last 10 minutes to brown. Baste frequently but, if you don't have time for this, cook the birds on their breasts and turn upright to brown at the end. Serve with thin gravy, bread sauce, and fried bread crumbs. Allow 1 roasted partridge per person.

partridge with lentils and pickled lemons

I think I could eat partridge every day. I invented this dish having received some red-legged partridges whilst reading Freya Stark and dreaming of Araby. I think it's rather good.

12 ounces green or brown lentils (about 2 cups)
1/4 cup olive oil
2 cloves garlic, chopped
2 partridges, cut in half
2 large Swiss chard leaves (remove the stems and cut them into
  small pieces, then slice the leaves diagonally into narrow strips)
1 1/4 cups water
2 pickled lemons, cut into pieces, or 1 tablespoon fresh
  lemon juice
salt and pepper

Cook the lentils in lightly salted, boiling water for 20 minutes, drain them, and keep the liquid. Heat the oil in a heavy frying pan, which has a lid you can later use. Fry the garlic for a few minutes, then remove and discard it. Brown the partridges all over in the oil and then set them aside.

Wilt the green chard strips in the hot oil for 2 minutes, remove, drain on paper towels, and set aside. Return the partridges to the pan along with the lentils, chard stalks, pickled lemon pieces or juice, and a little of the lentil water; cover and simmer for 20 minutes or until the partridges are tender. Add the wilted chard strips, heat through, and serve with a fresh crisp green salad.

broiled partridge with garlic, oil, lemon, and cayenne

This is a very simple way of cooking tender young red-legs that don't have a great deal of flavor of their own, but respond very well to broiling. It makes a quick dish for hungry shots. You need to cut the partridge through the back and flatten them out. It is also a dish that can be cooked over the embers of an open fire out of doors.

1/4 cup olive oil
4 cloves garlic, crushed
juice of 1 lemon
4 partridges, spatchcocked
1 tablespoon cayenne pepper
salt and pepper

Mix the oil, garlic, and lemon juice together and marinate the partridges in it for 1–3 hours.

Take them from the marinade, season, and sprinkle the cayenne over them. Broil, turning from time to time for about 15–20 minutes. Be careful not to overcook, and baste them with the marinade from time to time.

partridge in a pilaf

6 partridges

1 medium onion, peeled

3 whole cloves

1 cinnamon stick

2^1/$_2$ cups stock made from pheasant, chicken, or partridge

2 tablespoons olive oil

4 ounces blanched almonds (about 1 cup)

4 ounces pine nuts (about 1 cup)

2 tablespoons clarified butter

1 pound long-grain rice—if it's not quick cook, soak the rice for
  30 minutes and drain well (about 2^2/$_3$ cups)

^{1}/$_2$ teaspoon ground cinnamon

^{1}/$_2$ teaspoon ground allspice

salt and pepper

Season the partridges with salt and pepper and put them in a large
pan along with the onion (into which you have stuck the cloves),
the cinnamon stick, and the stock; add water to cover. Bring to a
boil and simmer gently for 15–20 minutes. Drain, saving the stock,
and cut the birds into halves down the back. Keep warm.

Heat the oil in a frying pan and cook the almonds until golden,
then set aside; do the same with the pine nuts.

In a pan which has a tight-fitting lid, melt the clarified butter, add
the rice, and stir until it is all coated with the butter. Add about 2
cups of the reserved stock, cover, bring to a boil, and cook until
the rice is tender—about 15–20 minutes; add the ground
cinnamon and allspice, and more stock if necessary.

Turn the rice onto a dish and mix in the nuts. Lay the partridge
pieces on top, and serve with Arab flatbread and yogurt.

partridges stuffed with chestnuts

**Chestnuts always remind me of partridges; they have the
same appealing shape and smallness. I tend to buy mine
ready-peeled but, if you have a chestnut tree and children,
the fresh ones will repay the extra effort.**

^{1}/$_4$ cup (^{1}/$_2$ stick) butter

2 shallots, chopped (if unavailable, use 2 tablespoons chopped
  mild onions)

4 partridges (livers reserved if possible, otherwise use other game
  bird livers or chicken livers)

1 pound peeled chestnuts (about 2^1/$_2$–3 cups)

^{2}/$_3$ cups whole milk

barding bacon

a little stock

salt and pepper

Heat the butter in a frying pan and soften the shallots in the butter.
Cut the livers in half, add them, and cook a little longer. Add the
chestnuts and cook gently for about 5 minutes. Remove to a bowl
and pour the milk over them; let stand and infuse for 30 minutes.

Preheat the oven to 425°F.

Either by hand or in a food processor, mash the chestnut mixture,
leaving the nuts quite textured—so not puréed but a bit lumpy!
Stuff the partridges with this mixture, truss and season them, and
then bard them with bacon and cook in the oven for about 20
minutes. Remove the bacon and return the partridges to the oven
to brown the breasts for another 10 minutes.

There will be some stuffing left over, so purée it finely and add to
the pan juices, stir it in, and add a little stock to make a sauce.

la mancha

The plains of La Mancha are home to thousands of Spanish partridge. I like to think of Don Quixote sitting by his fire eating partridge done in the same manner. The earthenware dish of water causes the jucies inside the dish to rise and fall back, moistening the braise to give a good flavor. The method of cooking, and the fried bread accompaniment, gives the recipe a date of four hundred years, and it has survived the test of time.

4 partridges
1 cup strong red wine (Spanish of course)
1 tablespoon oil
1 ounce unsmoked bacon, chopped (about 1/4 cup)
1 head garlic, cloves peeled
3 1/2 ounces raw Spanish ham, sliced (about 1 cup)
1 bouquet garni or 2 whole cloves
8 peppercorns, crushed
1/2 cinnamon stick
thyme
2 slices bread, fried in olive oil
salt

Marinate the partridges in the red wine for 1 hour. Heat the oil in a large pan and sauté the bacon and garlic cloves. When they begin to color, drain the partridges, pat them dry with paper towels, add them to the pan, and brown all over. Add the ham, bouquet garni, peppercorns, cinnamon stick, and a sprig or two of thyme and 2 tablespoons of the marinade wine. Cook for 5 minutes, season with salt, and reduce the heat. Cover with tinfoil and place on top of an earthenware dish of warm water. Cook over very low heat for 1 1/2 hours, turning the partridges a couple of times during cooking. When the birds are tender, remove to a dish and arrange the ham around them. Discard the bouquet garni, strain the sauce and pour it over the birds. Serve with sippets of fried bread.

partridges with peppers and tomato

This is a dish that came about because I had made some *Marmouma*, a Tunisian dish from Claudia Roden's brilliant *Book of Jewish Food*. I was called away so didn't have it for lunch and fancied something meatier for my dinner, so I threw in the partridge and some lemon juice. I hope you enjoy it.

1/4 cup olive oil
4 partridges
4 red peppers
3 cloves garlic, mashed with salt
1 1/2 pounds tomatoes, peeled and roughly chopped
  (about 2 1/2–3 cups)
pinch of sugar
juice of 1/2 lemon
salt and pepper

Heat the oil in a heavy pan, season the partridges with salt and pepper, and brown them all over. Remove them from the pan and set aside.

Core and seed the peppers, and cut them into strips. Cook them in the oil, slowly turning as you go, for about 10 minutes. Add the garlic and cook until the peppers are beginning to soften. Add the tomatoes, sugar, and lemon juice, and season. Return the partridges to the pan and simmer uncovered for about 25–30 minutes, until the partridges are done and the sauce is jammy.

partridges for lady lucy

Gerry Bramley asked me to cook a dinner for the Prince of Wales Trust once, and he chose as the venue James Percy's stylish Lodge at Linhope, in the middle of England's Northumbrian Hills. James joined us in the kitchen for scraps and told me that this is how his wife treats partidge breasts, and an excellent idea it is, too. The sauce I offer here is my own.

4 partridge breasts
1 egg, beaten
1/4 cup bread crumbs, made with stale bread

Cut the breasts from the partridges, trim, and press them flat. Place each flattened breast between 2 pieces of plastic wrap and gently beat flatter until they are as thin as you think they will go. Dip them in egg and then bread crumbs and fry quickly in butter.

For the sauce:
A quantity of ratatouille (a good bottled one will do)
14 1/2-ounce can of chopped tomatoes
dash of Tabasco sauce
fresh basil or cilantro/coriander leaves
salt and pepper

Put all the sauce ingredients in a blender and pulverize for a few seconds. Transfer in a small saucepan, heat, and season to taste. Serve with the partridges.

partridges with cockles in a cataplana

This is a Portuguese recipe which Johnny gave me. It's an unusual dish but surprisingly good. A *cataplana* for those of you who don't know is a Portuguese double saucepan which locks closed, and which you can turn over to apply heat to either side. It is reputed to be the precursor to the pressure-cooker and is particular to the Algarve coast, so you may have picked one up on vacation; otherwise use a heavy pan for which you have a tight-fitting lid. *Piri piri* is a Portuguese hot sauce readily available in supermarkets.

2 ounces cockles, without their shells (about 1/2 cup)
1/4 cup (1/2 stick) butter
3 cloves garlic, crushed
2 partridges, cut in half
piri piri, to taste
a scant cup dry port wine
1 1/4 cups dry white wine
1 bay leaf
1 bunch of parsley, chopped
salt

Wash the cockles well in salted water to remove any grit—unsalted water will kill them. Put the *cataplana* or heavy pan on the heat, and put in the butter and the garlic cloves.

Brown the partridges in the melted butter. Season with some salt and *piri piri*, and then add the wines and bay leaf. Close the *cataplana* and cook until the partridges are done—about 15–20 minutes. Add the cockles and continue to cook for another 5 minutes to just cook them through. Don't overcook the cockles or they will be tough. Sprinkle with parsley.

hungarian **bartash** with eggplant

The original Hungarian recipe was, I thought, rather bland. At the Bodega Toston in Fuengerola (arguably the best tapas restaurant in Spain), I had red peppers stuffed with partridge which were very good but lacked a dimension, so I have combined the two. It is an excellent dish for a buffet or a supper table and also makes a very nice appetizer. It can also be made with cold pheasant. The technique of putting your hot broiled peppers into a plastic bag makes them so much easier to peel—the skin just flakes off. Rinse them under a faucet to remove any lingering black specks.

the meat from 4 roast partridges or 1 pheasant, finely chopped
3 large eggplants
5 small red peppers
2 cloves garlic
1/2 teaspoon salt
1 1/4 cups thick, whole milk yogurt
fresh mint

Broil the eggplants, turning as you go, until they are well blackened and the pulp is soft. This will take about 15 minutes. Remove the eggplants from the broiler and place them in a plastic bag to let cool. Put the peppers on a tray to catch any oil that may run and place them in the broiler. Broil the peppers, turning as is necessary until they, too, are well blackened; place in a plastic bag to cool, when they will be easy to peel.

Once cooled, scrape the pulp from the eggplants and let drain. Mash the garlic cloves with the salt, stir in the yogurt and fresh chopped mint, and fold in the eggplant pulp. Add the meat. Peel the red peppers and remove the core carefully so as not to break them. Stuff them with the partridge-eggplant mixture and serve at room temperature.

partridge with belgian endive

I love the bitterness of Belgian endive and the fact that it sprouts happily in your garage in mid-winter, and I have always cooked it like this. One day having a handy partridge I decided to add it, and was most pleased with the result, as I hope you will be. If you look at the base of the Belgian endive head you will see a little round core, excise it with a knife and the plant loses its unacceptable bitterness.

1/2 cup (1 stick) butter
2 partridges
2 slices bacon
3 heads Belgian endive
juice of 1/2 lemon
salt and pepper

Heat half the butter in a pan for which you have a tight-fitting lid and brown the birds evenly, and then season them with salt and pepper. If the birds are not young, continue cooking them gently in the butter for another 5 minutes.

Chop the bacon and carefully slice the Belgian endive heads in half, removing the little core at the base of the heads that causes the bitterness. Melt the rest of the butter in a heavy pan and sauté the bacon for a few minutes, then toss in the Belgian endive. Add the partridges with any remaining butter, and the lemon juice. Cover tightly and cook for 10–15 minutes over low heat or until the partridges are tender.

pheasant

No other bird has become quite so synonymous with the British and American countryside as a cock pheasant and yet, this state bird of South Dakota, is an immigrant to both. *Phasianus colchicus* has come a long way from the marshy, rush-covered banks of the sluggish River Phasis, in what is today the country of Georgia (in the former Soviet Union). The species known as the Old English black-necked pheasant was, according to Greek legend, brought back to Greece by Jason and the Argonauts, and received with as much rapture and amazement as the Golden Fleece itself. Mythology aside, the historian Aeschylus left records of these wondrous creatures adorning the stockyards of ancient Greece, a culture that was subsequently acquired by the Romans. Roman chefs loved anything exotic and pheasants were soon appearing at patrician banquets, dressed for the table in all their plumage. Philladius wrote an account of the elaborate feeding process involved in fattening pheasants. Chicks were fed for the first two weeks on boiled grain sprinkled with wine; thereafter, on a more robust diet of locusts and ants' eggs mixed with flour and olive oil, lovingly rolled into bite-sized balls.

The Romans, who liked to travel with life's little luxuries, brought pheasants across the English Channel during their colonization of Britain, and for the next five hundred years, the ancestors of our modern pheasant lived in pampered domesticity. The collapse of the Roman Empire and the evacuation of the Romans from the British Isles must have come as a shock to pheasants that were left behind but somehow, enough survived scratching for seeds in the ruined gardens of their former homes to breed a nucleus of a feral population. The later invasions by the Saxons and Danes do not enlighten us as to the pheasant's progress as these invaders were hopeless historians. The earliest documentation of the naturalization of pheasants is in ancient manuscripts belonging to Waltham Abbey in Essex in which there is an entry referring to a regulation of King Harold in 1059, granting the canons an option to chose between a brace of partridges or a single pheasant as a gift for one of their feast days. Following the Norman Conquest, the Normans brought to England from France more pheasants of Roman origin. The bird appears regularly thereafter, in the statistics of nobility and clergy permitted by the monarch to kill them, or as highly prized delicacies in historical records of elaborate medieval feasting.

Vain, supercilious, and quarrelsome, these immaculate creatures strut across the centuries, insouciantly rubbing shoulders with the great and the good. Under Norman Forest Laws, all game belonged to the crown, and pheasants were classified as Fowls of Warren and in the King's gift. The right to take pheasants was doled out as a privilege to the clergy and nobility. Even as semi-domesticated birds, living in the protection of warrens, their rarity ensured what must be a documentation unique to pheasants. Thus we know that Henry I granted the Abbot of Amesbury a licence to take pheasants and that Thomas à Becket had just dined off one on 29th December, when Henry II's heavies dropped by Canterbury Cathedral for a little chat. Prices were scrupulously recorded—4d (a couple of cents) in 1299 had risen to 12d (about fifty cents) by 1512 with a massive leap to sixteen shillings (2 dollars) in 1560. Henry VIII had his own personal pheasant breeder, a French monk, who was considered so important that Henry paid him out of his own privy purse. In France, pheasants were even more revered. In 1453, after a particularly emotional banquet, Phillip Duke of Burgundy, who was obsessed by pheasants, swore a solemn oath over the carcass of a roast bird that, on the following day, he would lead all who cared to join him, to liberate Christian Greece from the infidel Turks. This outburst was enormously well received. It was a big party and the flower of French nobility were all present. To a man they agreed to follow him and to a man, failed to turn up at the departure point. Undeterred by what a lesser person might have felt a humiliating setback, Phillip founded the Order of the Pheasant in 1455. The nobility, who were expected to become initiates, invoked the name of God, the Virgin, and the Pheasant before making some chivalrous knightly vow.

The volume of literature on how to catch pheasants during that period is another indication of their esteem. Britain was still largely covered in forest and the pheasant's preferred habitat of young woodland on the edge of cultivated land was relatively scarce. When feeding in the open and suddenly startled into flight, pheasants gave falconers an exciting alternative to partridges, with their tremendous turn of speed and habit of rapidly gaining height between cover. They were flown at with peregrines and sparrow hawks or sometimes driven out of woodland by little beagly brachets and sacrificed to fast, savage goshawks. Apart from some taken by hawks and a few by primitive firearms, most pheasants were trapped by liming, snaring, and netting. I have a copy of *The Gentleman's Recreation*, written in 1676 by Nicholas Cox and the field sports bible of the time, in which he lists the various options that had been in use for several centuries. Netting ensured the biggest bag, but required immense skill. An Eye (the cock, hen, and poults) had first to be located in some secluded area of open woodland. The netter had to conceal himself for several days where he could listen and memorize

the different calls used by adult birds to warn the young of danger, summon them to new feeding areas, or chide them when they straggled too far. Then came the painstaking business of softly imitating the different calls to draw pheasants into the open where a net could be thrown over them. The same skills would have been used by early settlers to trap a whole range of indigenous American birds.

By the middle of the eighteenth century, agricultural improvements and an ever-increasing demand for timber was changing the British landscape. A mosaic pattern of woods, pasture, and grain evolved, creating an increase in habitat for pheasants. Shotguns, built along European lines, were becoming lighter and more efficient. Pheasants started to compete with partridges as the principal game bird. The first introduction of pheasants to North America was apparently as early as 1733, when a dozen pairs were released on Governor's Island in New York Harbor, of which none survived. British immigrant Richard Bache, who was to become

Benjamin Franklin's son in law and Controller of the US Postal Service, attempted to establish a breeding nucleus on the mainland in 1760. Wishing to replicate the style of shooting he was familiar with in England, Bache released a quantity of black-necked pheasants and some gray partridges at his estate on the Delaware River. Although these descendents of Roman and Norman stock would have found the agricultural landscape in Pennsylvania not dissimilar to the habitat they had left behind, Bache's experiment failed, probably due to a combination of predators and extremely harsh weather in their first season.

In T.B. Johnson's 1831 edition of the *Sportsman's Cyclopedia*, he mentions that pheasants were unknown in America, although there were several unsuccessful attempts to establish them in the United States and Canada soon after that date. However, in 1881, a breed was introduced which was to thrive across virtually the whole continent. Judge Owen Denny, the United States Consul General in Shanghai,

sent thirty birds to the United States of which twenty-one survived the long sea journey, to be released into woodland on his brother's estate at Willamette in Oregon. These hardy, resilient birds quickly adapted to the surrounding countryside and another hundred pairs were sent out from China. So rapidly did this initial population increase and spread across the county, that twenty-one years later, on the opening day of Oregon's first official pheasant season in November 1892, fifty thousand cock pheasants were shot. These gorgeous creatures, with the distinctive ring of white feathers around their neck, once referred to as living flowers, were soon to become a bird for "everyman" in the United States.

Pheasants began to move outwards across the continent from Oregon. As in Britain, the need to feed an expanding urban population had led to the reclamation of huge acreages of forest and swamp. These were replaced by the wooded, small-field mixed-farming policy of the time, creating an artificial pheasant habitat with a perfect mix of cover and food. This environment had another advantage. Although pheasants roost for much of the year, the hens are ground nesters, making a shallow nest on the edge of cover. They and their brood are vulnerable to predators for at least two months over the gestation and rearing period, before the poults are able to fly properly. Nature compensates for this by making hen pheasants prolific layers—clutches of up to fifteen eggs are average and the agrarian world they found themselves in during the late nineteenth and early twentieth century, was one where predators were rigorously culled to protect livestock. Pheasants flourished and numbers soared. State wildlife departments were quick to appreciate the potential for the sporting recreation industry and rapidly set up their own breeding units, releasing pheasants across America wherever there was suitable habitat. They were introduced to Washington, D.C. and the northeastern states within five years, to South Dakota in 1898, and Ohio had a breeding stock of 200 pairs by 1899, with Michigan opening a state pheasant farm in 1917. In Canada in Nova Scotia, where attempts to establish pheasants had first been tried in 1856, King's County Fish and Game Association acquired 1,000 eggs in 1935. Eighty-five hatched and survived to become the foundation stock for a highly successful breeding program.

The early twentieth century was the heyday of great country house shooting parties in Britain at which many wealthy Americans were guests. Some tried to emulate the driven pheasant shooting they experienced in Britain on their east coast estates, but for the majority of American sportsmen, pheasants were shot walked-up over pointers in the traditional manner. Such was the popularity of the sport and prolificacy of pheasants that, in Michigan alone, more than a million birds found their way to the table each year, until the 1960s. The pheasant populations in both America and Britain went into a rapid decline through the 1970s and 80s for exactly the same reasons: massive intensification of farming that led to arable monoculture; hedgerow to hedgerow plowing that destroyed wide, weedy field margins; elimination of food and shelter through pesticides and herbicides; loss and disruption of habitat through urban expansion and highway construction. As pheasant numbers plummeted, some states endeavored to maintain shooting revenues by rearing pheasants right through until the beginning of the season, before turning them out. The countryside became infested with lethargic, overweight birds that had no idea how to cope in the wild and were reluctant to fly. The shooting community scorned them, and their lack of self-preservation led to an increase in predators.

Such was the concern of conservation loving sportsmen, that Pheasants Forever was set up in 1981. The non-profit making organization is dedicated to the protection and enhancement of pheasants and other wildlife in North America, through habitat improvement, land management, public awareness, and education. In the last twenty-four years, a grass route membership of 100,000 have developed more than 3 million acres of pheasant and other wildlife habitat. They have built up 600 chapters across the USA, developing 25,000 conservation projects, and they have more than 4,000 educators promoting conservation through the Leopold Trust, and a vast network of corporate and individual contributors. Through their help, Pheasants Forever have purchased 65,000 acres on which 600 conservation sights are permanent fixtures of the landscape. In 1985, the US Department of Agriculture, in an about-face on policy, started the Conservation Reserve Program, paying farmers not to cultivate marginal land and establish long-term, resource conserving covers on eligible land. Some 40 million acres have come out of production nationwide to be replaced by woodland, which in its early stage of growth, does not suit ring-necks. State game managers embarked on an experiment to find a species better suited to young woodland, importing eggs off small, wild birds from the Szechuan province of Manchuria. These, crossed with domestic stock have produced a hardy, phenomenally fast flying bird, full of hybrid vigor. "Michigan bluebacks" have put pheasants back at the top of American sportsmen's list of upland game birds.

Until you have been around pheasant shoots you will not comprehend quite how many pheasants you have to deal with, and what a variety of ages and conditions you will find them in. I once worked on a large family shoot at Danehill in Sussex, and quite understood the story of the small boy arriving late at his boarding school and on being offered something to eat, replying, "Oh nothing that's any trouble, just some cold pheasant will do." In my grandmother's day your social standing was determined by how many brace you were given for Christmas, curiously a doctor only received one pheasant. There is nothing lovelier at the start of the season than a young roast pheasant with all the trimmings: game chips, bread sauce, thin gravy, red currant jelly, and nothing nastier than a dried–out old pheasant (unless you take care to prepare the old pheasant properly).

Aging

The first thing is to age your pheasant, which if you have seen a lot of pheasant, becomes a matter of common sense. Julia Drysdale in her excellent book in association with the Game Conservancy in 1975, waxes eloquently on the Bursa Test. The Bursa is a blind vent above the anus, the purpose of which is still really unknown; it closes completely when the bird reaches sexual maturity, so a toothpick inserted will tell all. I have to say in heaven knows how many years of aging pheasants I have never tried this. For me the main test is the foot; as with humans, old pheasant have old feet, long spurs and horny beaks and feet. Although some young pheasants have long spurs, they are still much more pliable than the old ones. The plumage of the younger birds is brighter and the beaks less horny. If in doubt, ask a keeper or your butcher for advice. When buying pheasant don't let the butcher chop the feet off, ask him to pull them as this will take the tendons out of the legs and make them easier to eat.

Hanging

This is a matter of personal taste and weather conditions. A lot of people are put off the thought of game by stories of pheasants crawling with maggots, as relished by our Victorian and Edwardian forebears. In the days before refrigeration, people were much more used to strong flavors and even today, the Swedes yearn for Surstumming (rotten herring) and the Japanese and Finns for fermented fish; the Icelanders still eat shark rotted in the permafrost and there are gentlemen who like their Stilton just short of the maggot stage. How ripe you eat your pheasant is a matter for you, but hang it you must, even if only for as little as three days, for all meat must be allowed to rest and mature. The game larder should be well aired and protected from flies and other insects. People will hang pheasant in pairs, but ideally they should be hung singly so the air can circulate. Hang them by the neck, in feather, with the innards intact. I don't like mine very high so I usually hang them until I can easily pull out the longest tail feather—about 7–10 days in cold weather.

Plucking

Start at the neck, pulling against the way the feathers grow and taking particular care over the breast, so as not to tear the skin. Once you have plucked 2–3 birds you will find it comes easily to you. If the weather is fine, pluck outdoors. I have it to such an art I tend to sit down and pluck into a garbage bag, but then I've had years of practice. Break the leg at the knee joint and twist it to loosen the tendons, then put the foot over a suitable hook and pull gently, twisting as you pull. All the tendons will pull out with the foot, and the meat on the legs will be totally edible. Singe a hairy bird by lighting a taper and running it over the skin.

Drawing

Cut off the head just where the neck starts and discard. Pull out the crop, which will reveal the pheasant's last meal, and discard. Cut off the neck where it joins the pheasant's body and keep for stock. Make a slight slit at the vent and insert your first two fingers—the entrails will pull out quite easily. Retain the liver, the heart, and the gizzards which you will need to cut open and clean out, and discard the rest. If the liver is discolored, cut out the damaged part.

Roasting

1 young pheasant
1/2 apple or 1/2 small onion
2 tablespoons butter
4 slices bacon or barding fat
salt and pepper

Season the bird inside and out. Place a piece of apple, cored and skinned, or half a small onion inside the bird along with half the butter. Rub the outside of the bird with the remaining butter and cover the breast with bacon or barding fat. Or, omit the pork and wrap in tinfoil. Roast at 375°F for 45 minutes, if it's not wrapped in tinfoil, baste from time to time. Remove the bacon or peel back the tinfoil for the final 10 minutes to brown the breast. Make a thin gravy with the roasting juices and serve on a warm dish.

Carving

Basically, follow the same procedure as for carving a chicken. Remove any trussing, and position the pheasant with the drumsticks pointing away from you. Insert your carving fork into the thick upper part of the left hand drumstick with the prongs straddling the bone, and lever away from the body. Cut down between body and thigh until the joint is exposed. Lever again and separate joint by probing with the knife's point. Cut around the

curvature of the body on either side of the joint and, if the thigh has still not separated, twist free by hand. Remove the wing by cutting through the joint where it is attached to the body, without touching the breast meat. Now turn the bird so the pheasant's equivalent of the parson's nose is facing you. Insert the fork to the left of the breastbone and carve the first slice from the breast where the body curves around to the point of the wing joint. Continue carving slices in towards the breastbone a quarter-inch thick. If the slices are too thin, the delicate flavor will be lost. When one side is finished, repeat process. Serve the thigh and a drumstick as one portion.

One pheasant is enough for 2–3 people, and the cock bird is more generous than the hen.

pheasant terrine with pickled walnuts

pheasant with saffron and bread soup

When I worked for Rebeka Hardy (the best boss I ever had) at Danehill, she also ran a successful family shoot so I had a great deal of pheasant to work with. I bitterly resented buying forcemeat for terrines and so I made this. Press down well when making it or it may crumble, but I am delighted with it.

2 pheasants
1 cup sweet red vermouth
2 pounds bacon, or fat
8 ounces pickled walnuts, each cut into about 3 slices
 (about 1 1/2–2 cups)
salt and pepper

Cut both the light and dark meat from the pheasants and then cut it into strips the thickness of, and half the length of, your little finger. Soak overnight in the vermouth in the refrigerator. Line a greased terrine or loaf pan with bacon slices making sure there are no gaps, but reserving enough bacon to later cover the terrine.

Preheat oven to 350°F.

Remove the pheasant from the marinade, shake dry, and season with salt and pepper. Half-fill the dish with pheasant strips and press down well. Place as many walnut slices as you need to make a single layer along the top of the pheasant. Fill the top half of the dish with pheasant, again pressing down well. Cover with the rest of the bacon.

Prepare a water bath, place the terrine in the pan of hot water, and bake in the oven for 45 minutes. Leave to cool slightly and turn out of the terrine.

This is a Middle Eastern dish and very good for using up badly shot birds. It is very heartening on a winter's night and a little different from ordinary game soup.

1 pheasant, quartered
2 ounces cooked chickpeas, drained (about 1/3 cup)
1/4 cup (1/2 stick) butter
1 celery stalk and 6 sprigs parsley, tied together
5 cups water
pinch of cinnamon
pinch of saffron
2 eggs
juice of 1 lemon
2 tablespoons olive oil
1/2 loaf stale white country bread
salt and pepper

Put the pheasant, chickpeas, butter, celery and parsley, salt and pepper into a large pot, and add the water. Bring to a boil and simmer for 1 hour. Remove the celery and parsley. Take the pheasant out and either remove the meat from the bones, or carve it. Sprinkle the cinnamon over the meat and set aside. Soften the saffron in a bowl containing a little of the hot broth. Beat the eggs in the bowl with 1 tablespoon of lemon juice, another 3–4 tablespoons of broth (which must have cooled slightly), and then beat the eggs back into the main pot of soup. Do not let it boil.

Heat the olive oil in a separate pan, toss the pheasant in it to brown, and pour the rest of the lemon juice over it. Put chunks of the stale bread into soup bowls, pour the broth over them and divide the pheasant between each portion, or alternatively, put the whole lot in a terrine and ladle it onto the bowls. If you have no stale bread, fry some bread croûtons and add them to the soup.

pheasant with peanut butter, tomatoes, and flageolet beans

Thinking about how the Africans cook guinea fowl with peanuts, I came up with this way for pheasants. Trust me, it's very good.

2 pheasants, cut into quarters

1/4 cup (1/2 stick) butter

2 onions, chopped

1 pound tomatoes, skinned and coarsely chopped (about
  1 3/4 cups), or 14 1/2-ounce can of chopped tomatoes

1/2 cup game stock

2 tablespoons peanut butter

1/2 teaspoon chili powder

15-ounce can of flageolet beans, or 1 pound fresh
  cranberry beans

salt and pepper

Season the pheasant with salt and pepper. In a heavy flameproof casserole dish or other heavy pan for which you have a lid, heat the butter and brown the pheasant all over. Remove from the pan, and fry the onions until colored slightly. Return the pheasant pieces to the pan and add the tomatoes (if using canned include the juice), stock, and peanut butter. Bring to a boil, stirring well to mix in the peanut butter. Add salt, pepper, and chili powder, cover, and simmer for 15 minutes. If you are using fresh beans, bring them to a boil in lightly salted water and cook for 10 minutes; drain and add the beans to the pheasant pan, cover again, and cook for another 30 minutes, or until the pheasant is cooked. If you are using canned beans, just tip them in and cook for 30 minutes. Transfer to a serving dish and, if there is too much juice, return it to the pan and boil to reduce, then pour the sauce over the pheasant and serve with potatoes.

pheasant chitarnee

My grandmother's second husband, who had the wonderful name of Ezekial Manasseh, came from the Sephardic Community in Calcutta. When he came to Singapore his mother sent a cook with him who used to prepare this dish with chicken; as my father shot quite well, we had endless pheasants so my mother translated it to pheasant.

6 onions, finely chopped

3 tablespoons olive oil

3 cloves garlic, crushed

1 inch ginger, finely chopped

1 teaspoon turmeric

1 tablespoon fresh cilantro (coriander), chopped, or 1 teaspoon
   ground coriander

6 green cardamom pods, or 1 teaspoon ground cardamom

1–2 red chilies, finely chopped

2 pheasants

14^1/$_2$-ounce can of chopped tomatoes

2 tablespoons wine vinegar

salt and pepper

Cook the onions gently in the oil until they are golden. Add the garlic, ginger, tumeric, coriander, cardomom, and chilies, and cook a little longer.

Cut the pheasants into serving portions and add to the pan to sauté, turning occasionally, for about 20 minutes. Add the tomatoes and the vinegar and cook for 30 minutes until the pheasant is well coated with sauce, and the sauce is not too runny. If the dish is too sharp you may add a pinch of sugar. Serve with rice.

pheasant with Cremona mustard

Cremona mustard is that splendid Italian confection of glacée fruits in clear mustard liquid. Bizarre to us, if we receive it as presents from avant garde friends we recycle it as a present or open it, wonder at it, then throw it away. However it is very good to stuff a pheasant with, as the Futurist Fascist poet Marinetti tells us. I owe this translation to dear Robin Weir from his book *The Compleat Mustard*.

2 tablespoons Mostardo di Cremona *and a little extra syrup*

1 brace of pheasant with giblets

^{1}/$_2$ cup (1 stick) butter

4 slices back bacon (Canadian bacon)

^{2}/$_3$ cup sweetish white wine

1 tablespoon flour

2 shallots, finely chopped

3 strips lemon peel

1 sprig of thyme

lemon juice

salt and pepper

Chop the mostardo fruits and the pheasant livers and add them together. Mix with the butter and chill until firm. Preheat the oven to 425°F. Smear extra butter under the pheasant breasts and paint them with syrup. Halve the fruited butter and place in the cavity of each bird. Season with salt and pepper and lard with bacon. Put the pheasants in a roasting pan and pour the wine over them. Roast for 45–60 minutes, depending upon the birds. Baste frequently and add a little more wine if the bottom of the pan is getting dry. Ten minutes before they are done, remove the bacon and reserve; dust the pheasants with flour and return to the oven to brown. Whilst the birds are cooking, make the stock with the giblets, shallots, lemon peel, thyme and 1/4–1/2 pint water. Transfer the birds to a serving dish and keep warm. Strain the stock, add the pan juices to the stock, sharpen with lemon juice and serve.

claypot **pheasant**

I remember my mother's excitement when she bought a claypot which had just come onto the market. For some reason they never took off in Britain, but they are still around and can be easily picked up in thrift stores here. In fact, they are a simple way of cooking, and if the marketers had not tried to promote them as "healthy," they would probably have done rather well. They are very similar to the old French daube pots which are also made of terracotta clay. In any event, they are good for cooking pheasants. If you don't have one, use a heavy casserole dish. If you don't have or want anchovies, replace them with 1/2 teaspoon of salt and, for the capers, you can replace them with a squeeze of lemon juice.

6 potatoes

1 leek

4 ounces celeriac (about 1 cup, cut up)

2 parsnips

10 ounces Jerusalem artichokes (about 2 1/2 cups, cut up)

pepper

3 anchovies

1 tablespoon capers

1 pheasant

1 cup dry white wine

salt

Preheat the oven to 425°F.

Clean the vegetables and cut them into pieces. Place them in the pot and sprinkle with pepper and a layer of anchovy fillets and capers. Rub the pheasant well with salt and pepper and place on the vegetables. Pour in the wine and cook for 1 1/2 hours.

pheasant with sauerkraut

This Alsation recipe is a very good way of using up old birds. It is also useful for supper parties because you can do all the simmering early, and then just put it in the oven before dinner. I happily use 2 pheasants to this amount of sauerkraut.

2 tablespoons goose fat

1 pheasant, barded

1 large onion, finely chopped

2 pounds sauerkraut, rinsed and squeezed

1 cup white wine

1 cup Madeira wine

1 cup game or chicken stock

5 ounces bacon, cut into strips (about 3/4–1 cup)

salt and pepper

Melt half the goose fat in a pan and lightly brown the pheasant all over. Remove the pheasant to a plate. Add the onions to the pan and brown them lightly. Add the sauerkraut, both wines, stock, and a pinch of salt and pepper. Return the pheasant to the pan and simmer gently, covered, for 1 hour. Preheat the oven to 375°F. Transfer to a greased casserole dish, add the bacon, cover, and cook in the oven for 30–40 minutes. Season and serve.

circassian **pheasant**

The Circassians are from the Caucasus which is the birthplace of the pheasant. Although this dish is usually made with chicken, it struck me that they had pheasant before they had chicken, and it works very well. This is a good dish for using up old cock birds; as I have been heard to say there is a lot of good in an old cock. If you prefer you can poach the pheasant for less time, carve it, and pour the sauce over the slices.

2 pheasants
1 onion, roughly sliced
1 leek, chopped
6 allspice berries
10 black peppercorns
3 bay leaves

For the sauce:
4 ounces white bread, crusts off (about 3–4 slices)
1/2 cup milk
6 cloves garlic
6 ounces chopped walnuts (about 1 1/2 cups)
small bunch of parsley, chopped
1 tablespoon walnut oil (olive oil will do)
salt and pepper

Put the pheasants in a large pot along with the onion, leek, allspice, peppercorns, and bay leaves, and enough water to cover it all. Bring to a boil and simmer very gently for 1 hour or until the meat falls off the bones. Take the birds from the pot and remove the meat, discarding the skin and bones. Cut the meat into strips. Turn up the heat under the broth and boil for 15–20 minutes to reduce. Check the seasoning and strain.

Soak the bread in the milk for 30 minutes. Squeeze out well. In a mortar, pound the garlic and walnuts to a paste (alternatively you can do this in a food processor), add the parsley and the oil, and pound a bit more. Add the bread, season with salt and pepper and mix until it is all blended together. Transfer to a bowl and mix in spoonfuls of broth until the mixture is the consistency of mayonnaise. Put the pheasant on a serving dish and pour the sauce over it.

calabrian **pheasant** with macaroni

If you have pheasant, you often have it until it's coming out your ears, so this is an excellent way of using it up for a jolly supper.

3 tablespoons oil

1 large onion, chopped

1 pound uncooked pheasant meat, cut into bite-size pieces
(about 2 cups)

2 pounds tomatoes, peeled, seeded, and chopped (about 4 cups)

1 cup dry white wine

1 packet macaroni (enough for 4 people)

parmesan or hard cheese, for grating

salt and pepper

In a heavy pan, heat the oil and brown the onion and the pheasant meat for about 10 minutes. Season with salt and pepper, add the tomatoes and the wine, and simmer for 45 minutes. In a large pot, cook the pasta *al dente*, drain, then toss with the pheasant sauce and serve with the grated cheese.

pheasant with noodles and horseradish cream

This is a recipe invented by my friend Marianne More-Gordon, a most frugal but excellent cook whose collection of recipes, *Scraping from a Scottish Kitchen,* is eagerly awaited by the *cognoscenti*. Don't overcook the pheasant breasts—they should be slightly pink—they aren't chicken so you won't have any problems with food poisoning!

$^1/_3$ cup ($^3/_4$ stick) butter

4 pheasant breasts

4 shallots, chopped (if unavailable, use 4 tablespoons
chopped mild onions)

1 clove garlic

2 tablespoons bottled horseradish, or 1 tablespoon strong
fresh horseradish, grated

juice of $^1/_2$ lemon

$^2/_3$ cup heavy cream

1 packet black or green Italian noodles or make your own
chestnut noodles (enough for 4 people)

small bunch of parsley, chopped

salt and pepper

Heat the butter in a heavy frying pan for which you have a lid, and sauté the pheasant breasts until they are sealed. Remove them and sauté the shallots and the garlic until the shallots are pale gold; remove and discard the garlic clove.

Stir the horseradish into the shallots and add a tablespoon or so of water and the lemon juice. Season. Return the pheasant breasts to the pan, add the cream, and cover and cook gently for 15–20 minutes or until the breasts are just cooked. If the sauce is too wet, remove the breasts and zap up the heat to reduce; if it's too dry, add a little more cream or some dry white wine. Cook the noodles according to the package instructions and drain. Serve the noodles with the pheasant and sprinkle chopped parsley on top.

roast **pheasant** with truffled cheese

It is not that unusual to insert soft cheese beneath the skin and over the breast of a pheasant as a medium for containing herbs and flavorings and for keeping the bird moist. I love the combination of truffles and pheasants, but nowadays they are horribly expensive so I often buy those little Italian cheeses flavored with truffle scrapings (*ceasa di truffata*), and eventually realized that if I used one of these I would get less expensive truffled pheasant.

1 pheasant
1 large shallot or small mild onion
1 ceasa di truffata
1/2 cup (1 stick) butter, softened
flour
white wine
salt and pepper

Carefully insert your hand under the skin covering the breast of the bird and loosen it. Peel the shallot or onion and make a couple of deep incisions. Insert into the cavity of the pheasant. Carefully spread the cheese under the skin and over the breast of the pheasant. Season the pheasant, rub with softened butter, and wrap in tinfoil. Let stand for 1 hour to allow the truffles to spread their flavor.

Preheat the oven to 425°F. Roast the bird for 40 minutes in a flameproof baking pan. Fold back the tinfoil and let it brown for another 10 minutes. Remove the pheasant to a serving dish, place the baking pan on the stove, and thicken the juices with a little flour. Then add some white wine to make a gravy; if you have any champagne hanging about, that is even better.

issy's **pheasants**

My friend and colleague Isabel Rutherford is a splendid cook, and various of her recipes adorn my earlier works. This is her pheasant dish and, like all her recipes, it is deceptively easy and very delicious. She cooks every year for A. A. Gill—what higher recommendation do you need!

3/4 cup (1 1/2 sticks) butter
4 young pheasants
2 1/2 cups heavy cream
1 pound frozen peas
salt and pepper

In a large pan which has a closely fitting lid, melt the butter. Season the birds and place breast down in the butter and cook for 15 minutes. Turn onto the other side and cook for another 15 minutes. Pour the cream over them, cover tightly, and cook gently for 30 minutes.

Cook the peas, and arrange them on a carving dish. Remove the birds from the pan and whisk the liquid vigorously to mix the cream into the pan juices; let thicken slightly and check the seasoning. Carve the birds, arrange them on the peas, and pour the sauce over them.

quail

No other game bird has so many different species or such a wide range of distribution than these enchanting little creatures, which resemble pear-shaped, miniature partridges. There are over one hundred and thirty different types of quail worldwide, and they can be found in virtually every country below the Arctic. North America has six principal quail species: Gambel's (*Lophortyx Gambelli*) or desert quail, whose habitat is the arid parts of California, Colorado, Idaho, Nevada, New Mexico, and Utah. These little birds have silvery body plumage, black cheeks surmounted by a red cap, and forward-sloping black plume. They prefer to live in brush near to water, scratching for seeds at the edge of mesquite or hackberry thickets. California or valley quail (*Lorphortyx Californicus*), the state bird of California, has a black throat and face bordered by white bands, a white forehead, and backward-sloping plume. Their habitat is mixed woodland, chaparral, and valleys full of natural grasses, from California, Oregon, and Washington, spreading into several neighboring states and over the border into British Columbia. Montezuma's quail (*Cyrtonyz Montezumae*), otherwise known as Mearns or the Harlequin quail, has a distinctive black and white face, heavy white spotting on the flanks, and russet backward-sloping plume. These can be found among open woodland and grassy slopes in the Southwest, from southern Arizona to Texas and Mexico.

Mountain Quail (*Oreotyx Pictus*) are the largest—up to 11 inches, and perhaps the most distinguished looking quail of them all, with a tall, almost upright head plume, dark gray plumage, and distinctive russet throat. These are birds of high-altitude brush and scrub oak thickets in California, Colorado, Idaho, Nevada, New Mexico, Oregon, and into Washington.

Scaled quail (*Callipepla Squamata*) are often called "cotton tops" by hunters, due to their white head and crest. Stocky and rather plain looking in grayish black, scaled quail, of the Oklahoma panhandle, eastern Colorado, southwestern Texas, Arizona, and New Mexico are bad fliers, preferring to scuttle away from danger through their sparse grassland habitat. When finally forced into the air, they fly for short distances on frantically beating wings, before landing to continue their escape on foot. Masked quail, which is no longer a quarry species, and its near relative, the bobwhite (*Colinus Virginianus*), are America's most wide-ranging quail species. White-throated, russet-colored bobwhites inhabit the Midwest, eastern and southern states, as well as Oregon, Washington, Idaho, southern Arizona, the foothills of the Rockies, and parts of Canada. Bobwhites were chosen as the state bird of Georgia, often referred to as the "Quail Capital of the World." They prefer abandoned farmland and long grasses for their food source of seeds and insects, with plenty of brush cover on the edge of woodland to shelter in.

Quail were an extremely valuable natural food resource in seventeenth century Europe, with thousands of them caught in nets by imitating the call of both sexes using a quail pipe made from a cat's thigh bone. Those not eaten fresh were preserved in salt and sent in barrels to Russia, Syria, and the Lebanon. Early settlers in America netted huge numbers of quail by setting up a cylindrical net twenty feet long and one foot high, supported by willow wands. One end was closed and the other open, from which wings of netting extended for several yards. Quail do not fly unless they absolutely have to, preferring to scuttle ahead of danger on their short stumpy legs. Coveys of quail were herded gently by hunters on foot or horse back from adjacent grassland into the wings of the cylinder and then into the tunnel itself, where they were dispatched. Quail, like partridges and grouse, live in family coveys and when they fly, they explode out of cover in all directions at astonishing speed. They became America's principal sporting bird only when shotgun technology advanced sufficiently, in the second half of the nineteenth century, to enable sportsmen to shoot them walked-up over pointers and retrievers.

Since then, American sportsmen have cherished these little game birds. Netting became illegal at the end of the nineteenth century and by 1900 there were severe penalties for even owning a quail net. By 1912, all but three states in America had introduced strict bag limits, policed by state game wardens and adjusted each season depending upon specie numbers. A decline in all wildlife during the 1960s and 70s, due to habitat loss as a consequence of agricultural expansion and the widespread use of pesticides and herbicides, led to the formation of Quails Unlimited in 1981. This conservation body, dedicated to preserving quail and other wildlife habitat, raises millions of dollars annually toward education and conservation projects. This, coupled with ongoing government support through the Conservation Reserve Program established in 1985, which subsidizes farmers to establish long term conservation programs on environmentally sensitive land, has stabilized quail populations and assured their future.

To cook quail eggs

Bring to a boil in cold water and cook for 4 minutes. Plunge into cold water and peel. Eat with celery salt.

Aging

Quail in this country are mostly imported and aging isn't required.

Hanging

No need.

Plucking

The feathers are very small and it is a tiresome job but not difficult.

Drawing

As for pheasant (see pages 24–25).

Roasting

Quails are so small that they tend to dry out if roasted. Far better is to cook them over coals, when they take 15–20 minutes and are much juicier.

Allow 1–2 quails per person.

This recipe was given to me by a charming couple I met on an airplane. She is a professional cook so he does all the cooking at home—sounds okay to me! The recipe was actually for pheasant but it works awfully well with quail. If you want to be smart you can bone out your quail, but possibly life's too short for boned quail. For me it is a good way of using up all the fruit chutney I am given and it is equally nice with sweet chutney or green tomato or even lemon. Ring the changes and try it with other white game as well.

1 or possibly 2 quail per person
2 tablespoons butter per quail
1 tablespoon fruit chutney per quail
salt and pepper

Preheat the oven to 325°F.

Rub the quail all over with butter and salt and pepper and put a small piece of butter in each bird. Fill the cavity with half a tablespoon of chutney. Lay each quail on a piece of parchment paper or tinfoil and smear the remaining half tablespoon of chutney over the top. Wrap up the package and roast for 30 minutes. Either turn out of the paper or let people unwrap their own.

The lemons from this part of Greece are particularly highly scented and the dish becomes infused with their scent. We can't quite hope for that with supermarket lemons but this is still a delicious recipe. You can also cook wild duck in this fashion.

6 quails

juice of 1 lemon

4 tablespoons olive oil

2 bay leaves

1–2 sprigs of thyme

4 juniper berries, crushed

3 whole cloves

rind of $1/2$ orange, cut into julienne strips

2 ounces fresh bread crumbs (about 1 cup)

1 onion, chopped

3 tablespoons flat-leaf parsley

$1/2$ cup pine nuts, toasted

12 Greek olives

$1/2$ cup red wine

salt and pepper

Rub the birds inside and out with half the lemon juice, half the olive oil, and some salt and pepper. Crumble the bay leaves together with the thyme, juniper berries, cloves, and orange rind.

Preheat the oven to 375°F. Heat the remaining olive oil in a pan and gently fry the bread crumbs. Add the crumbled herbs and spices, and all the other ingredients except the olives and wine to the bread crumbs. Cook gently for a little longer and use to stuff the quails. There will be mixture left over; arrange this in an ovenproof dish and put the stuffed quails on top. Sprinkle the olives and the wine on top and cook in the oven until the quails are cooked—about 15–20 minutes.

quail stuffed with feta and fenugreek

Here is a Cypriot recipe which uses fenugreek; it grows wild on the Trodos mountains of Cyprus. The Indians use fenugreek extensively, calling it *methi*. Feta is made from local ewes' milk. Try and buy mature feta or another similar ewes' milk cheese.

bunch of fenugreek
8 ounces feta cheese (about 2 cups crumbled)
6 quails
oil from cheese or olive oil
salt and pepper

Chop the fenugreek and the cheese together and season. Rub the quails inside and out with salt and pepper. Heat some oil in a heavy ovenproof pan for which there is a lid, and brown the quails all over. Remove and let cool a little. When the birds are cool enough to handle, stuff with the feta mixture.

Preheat the oven to 350°F. Return the quails to the pan, which should still have some oil remaining, otherwise add a little more. Cover and cook in the oven for 30 minutes, or until the birds are cooked right through.

quail cooked in clay

This method of cooking, still found in the hills of Cyprus and remoter parts of Greece, is a perfect way of cooking quails and great fun to serve. You can buy clay in an art store or builder's yard. Each bird will need about 2 ounces of clay. Don't roll it, but flatten it out with the heel of your hand, and remember to keep it under a damp cloth or it will dry out. Alternatively you can use parchment paper instead of clay.

large bunch of mint, chopped
6 shallots, chopped
6 quails
olive oil
enough modeling clay to cover
salt and pepper

Preheat the oven to 425°F.

Mix the mint and shallots, season well, and stuff the quails with the mixture. Rub the outside of the quails with salt and pepper and olive oil, and wrap each quail carefully in a lump of clay. Seal each carefully.

Put the quails in the oven and bake until the clay is hard—about 20 minutes.

Serve with a little tack hammer to crack the clay open. When the mold is broken, out will come your perfectly cooked quail.

grouse

There are eighteen species of grouse worldwide, of which North America has more than half, split between those that live on the prairies (greater and lesser prairie chicken, sharp-tailed grouse, and the greater sage grouse with its rare cousin, the Gunnison's grouse), forest dwellers (which include blue, ruffed, and spruce grouse), and three species of ptarmigan (white-tailed, willow, and rock). All were historically important food sources to the native North American people, and the distinctive, aggressive territorial and mating displays which are common to all grouse species, became part of the culture of the native American tribes, particularly the displays of the five prairie species which have traditional mating territories, known as lekking, dancing, or booming grounds. The dominant cock birds establish and defend mating territories by performing a spectacular stamping dance, with

outstretched wings, tail held erect, and the purple air sacs at the side of their neck, inflated and exposed. This frenetic dancing, with its bowing and weaving, cackling, crowing, and moaning, became incorporated into the spring dancing ceremonies of the Plain's tribes. Grouse became symbolic of spring regrowth and often appear as decorations on primitive pottery.

In the seventeenth and eighteenth centuries, sharp-tailed grouse, with their white-flecked brown plumage, buff bellies, purple air sacs, and the extended two central tail feathers, had a distribution that extended throughout their preferred habitat of steppe, grassland, and mixed scrub, and early successional forestry across central and northern North America. At first, prairie grouse suffered more than forest- or tundra-dwelling grouse because of their initial

tameness towards humans and their open habitat that made it easier for them to be hunted. Habitat degradation, due to over-grazing, conversion of huge areas to cropland, conifer plantations, and urban expansion, has resulted in a dramatic drop in the US grouse population, with figures in Canada considered to be more stable. Sharp-tailed grouse now have a distribution from eastern Alaska to southwestern Yukon, across western and central Canada, western America, and east to the Great Plains. In the South, there are a number of scattered populations in Utah, Idaho, Montana, Wyoming, and Colorado. The government Countryside Restoration Program and other conservation initiatives, like the Grassland and Grouse Project, have done much to replace lost habitat and provide the food source favored by sharp-tails—berries, seeds, grasses, forbs, herbs, and insects in spring and summer; and fruits, insects, seeds, and most arable grains in fall and winter, with the buds and catkins of aspen, and birch in the snow. Although ground nesters, they will roost in trees or burrow into the snow. The shooting season falls between mid-September and the end of December, depending upon each state. Sharp-tails are generally walked-up over pointers, and explode into the air on frantically beating wings, becoming more difficult and wild as the cocks begin to pack later in the season. Some may be shot as they fly in to feed on stubble fields in rather the same way as doves, and require a similar amount of preparation as dove shooting.

The greater prairie chicken or pinnated grouse, from the long pinnae or tufts of feathers that stick up on either side of the cock's neck during their mating display, is a bird of the long grass prairies. About the size of a chicken, with strikingly barred dark brown and white plumage, they are particularly known for the booming sound they make when lekking, by inflating the orange air sacs on either side of their neck. Greater prairie chickens once occupied large sections of central northern US and Canada where there was a prevalence of prairie and sparse oak forests. The destruction of their grassland habitat now limits these birds to a patchwork of ranges within the ten US prairie states. It has virtually disappeared from Canada. Although greater prairie chickens are locally stable, their cousin, the heath hen, became extinct in the 1930s despite every effort to save it; the attwater prairie chicken is endangered and the lesser prairie chicken, an upland bird, is now found only in parts of Colorado, Oklahoma, Kansas, New Mexico, and Texas. Greater prairie chicken numbers are strictly monitored by state departments and some states have a season from September to January. They hold well to pointers if they are walked-up early in the season. Later on, when coveys start to build up, they become wilder. Identifying feeding grounds and lying up for them as they fly in to feed at dawn or dusk can be an exciting sport. Limited hunting for lesser prairie chickens is allowed in Kansas and Texas, mainly as a conservation exercise to weed out the old, dominant cocks whose continued

presence weakens brood numbers.

The sage grouse, North America's largest grouse, is an astonishing sight when displaying at a lekking or strutting ground. Normally an impressive bird with gray and white barred plumage and long, sharply pointed tail feathers, he transforms into a magnificent creature. His tail is open and erect like a fan, and air sacs in his neck inflate to create a white ruff which almost envelopes his head. Sage grouse have a range of distribution that extends from Alberta and Saskatchewan in Canada to California, Nevada, Colorado, and New Mexico, in areas restricted to the plains and valleys where its principal food source, the leaves of sagebrush, can still be found. During the winter they rely on sagebrush entirely, congregating in areas where it is tall enough to stand clear of snow. In the spring, sage grouse will expand their diet to include grasses and weeds but, lacking a muscular gizzard with grit in it like other birds,

they are unable to digest seeds or hard matter. The season for sage grouse is heavily restricted, usually between late August and early November and may only last for a few weeks. These birds will only be found where their food source exists. They hold well to a pointer and the best chance of a shot is near a water source, particularly in dry weather. Hens break cover ahead of cocks, which are deceptively agile in flight.

Of the three species of ptarmigan, which differ from other grouse by their feathered feet enabling them to walk on snow, willow ptarmigan are the ones that occupy sub-alpine tundra and boreal forest edges, moving down in winter to the cover of willow, birch, and aspen. Very similar to the Scottish red grouse, they are the largest of the ptarmigan, weighing two pounds. In the season—September to late November—they provide exciting, if hard-going, sport to good pointers, working willow thickens in the northern

valleys of Alaska and across sub-arctic Canada. Rock ptarmigan have the widest latitudinal distribution of all grouse species and can be found across arctic alpine tundra from North America to Eurasia including Japan. I once asked a Scottish game keeper what they ate and he replied, "rocks." An historically important food source to native communities living in the Arctic, they are still hunted by indigenous people and have become endangered near some settlements. They provide exciting sport to those that like rock climbing. The smallest species, the white-tailed ptarmigan, is a bird of western North America, primarily Alaska and the Yukon, with scattered alpine populations in the Rockies from Montana to New Mexico. These little creatures inhabit the highest peaks and are rarely shot except by the minority who wish to combine mountaineering with wing shooting.

Of the forest or timber grouse, spruce grouse are found throughout northern North America with a range extending from Alaska to Labrador and south into New England. They have no air sacs and during mating, they make a loud double clapping sound with their wings. Mixed spruce and birch forests are their favorite habitat but they are equally at home anywhere from sea-level muskegs to alpine spruce thickets. Their diet consists of any seeds, insects, and berries during the spring and summer, with buds and berries, like rose hips, cranberries, and blueberries, in the fall. In the winter they survive on spruce and pine needles, which gives them a resinous flavor. They depend on these trees throughout the year for cover and roosting sights. Spruce grouse have developed preservation techniques ideally suited to their habitat. Their gray, black, and brown plumage is perfect camouflage and they have a habit of sitting tight unless physically driven out of a tree, which earned them the soubriquet "fool hen." When finally flushed, they bolt into the safety of the next available tree, diving to gain air speed and weaving

with surprising speed to provide a very challenging shot. By and large, spruce grouse, which have a season from the end of September until December, are mainly hunted as a diversion by those after bigger game like elk or moose.

The largest of the forest grouse, the blue grouse, has a wider range of distribution, from southeast Alaska and Yukon, south along the Pacific coast to New Mexico and Arizona. They share many of the same characteristics and similar habitat, preferring tall spruce trees to roost in. During the spring, blue grouse make a hooting noise by expelling air through their air sacs. Sometimes a number will congregate in the same area to out-hoot each other. At one time hunters would imitate this noise to stalk and shoot them with .22 rifles. In the fall, blue grouse move down to muskeg and alpine areas to feed on berries, before moving back inside the timber line. Good sport may be had with pointers at this time of year although, like spruce grouse, they are rarely the specific quarry.

Finally we have the ruffed grouse, whom many regard as the king of game birds. They are the most widely distributed game bird in North America, found in parts of thirty-nine states—they are the state bird of Pennsylvania—and eleven provinces of Canada, with the highest population in the aspen forests of the Upper Great Lakes region. Ruffed grouse inhabit a wide range of forest types, their plumage differing from reddish to gray, depending upon whether they inhabit deciduous or mixed conifer and hardwood forests. Their preferred habitat is mixed species stands of hardwood shrubs and saplings, with damp areas interspersed with lush herbaceous growth to provide food, like rose hips, cranberries, and soapberries in the fall. In among this cover will be the cock bird's drumming post. Male ruffed grouse perform a territorial display on

an old stump or conveniently visible rock that involves raising their dark neck ruff, so that it surrounds their head, and creating a drumming sound by beating their wings. This hollow sound is created by air being forced into the vacuum created as the wings flap open and shut. Audubon hunted ruffed grouse in the spring, by tapping on an inflated pig bladder and stalking the bird that responded. Although ruffed grouse populations are stable overall, their numbers are linked to the cycle of the snowshoe hare and the effect of this animal's two principal predators, the horned owl and goshawk. As the snowshoe population peaks, and disease and predation dramatically reduce numbers, attention on ruffed grouse grows. Their numbers diminish, the predators move elsewhere, and the population builds back up. I suspect a similar situation to the red grouse in Scotland occurs as well, in that there are too many dominant cocks. Ruffed grouse are hunted from September until late December, walked-up over pointers with experienced hunters making for stands of young aspens, willows, alder, and berry-bearing shrubs. A pointer dog is essential, a good rough coated Brittany perhaps, for thick cover. Ruffed grouse and American woodcock are often hunted together and the same lightning quick reaction is needed to get off an accurate shot as they jinx and weave between trees.

There is something magic about grouse, they are such strange birds and resist any attempt at domestication thereby preserving the heather moorlands. My mother had a great tradition of eating grouse at the start of the season and, while her friends went to the Savoy, she would cart us all off to the Hilton where she said they cooked grouse beautifully. They did, but I suspect they only cooked them for her, and as she was known to double the bill by way of a tip if she couldn't work out 15 percent, they did so

with great care and attention. A lot of old grouse is discarded because people don't know what to do with it so I have tried to include a number of recipes for old and middle-aged grouse. The flavor of older birds is wonderful.

Aging
The Bursa Test to the rescue again, if the toothpick goes in a half-inch, it is a young bird and you should just roast it, in my opinion. Another test is to look at the primaries; if these are rounded and similar to the other feathers, it is an old bird. If it is a bird of the previous year, the primaries will still be pointed, but they will look tattered and faded. Adult grouse shed their toenails so if the nail is becoming detached, it is an old bird; also look for a transverse scar across the top of the nail where the shed nail was attached; if it is there, it is an old bird. Another test is to break the lower beak or crush the skull if the bird is young, but this is not always as reliable, as diet is a variant here.

Hanging
If the bird is young and the weather is warm, it will not need more than 2 days. Birds shot on the 12th are eaten right away and are perfectly good. No more than 4 days for young birds, and as long as you choose for older ones.

Plucking and Drawing
As for pheasant (see pages 24–25).

Roasting
Put a piece of seasoned butter in each bird and cover the breasts with fatty bacon or barding fat. Sauté the liver of the bird in butter, mash it, and spread the mixture onto a piece of white toast. Roast at 375°F for 30–40 minutes, depending on how rare you like it. Serve with bread sauce, gravy, game fries, and watercress salad. Allow 1 bird per person.

buttered grouse

This cold grouse dish is very good for a shooting picnic. It is a Yorkshire dish which always endears it to me. All grouse moors are beautiful (on a fine day) but it was in Yorkshire that a group of anti-hunt campaigners were trying to disrupt a grouse shoot and got lost when the mist came down. They rang the local constabulary for help on their cell phones to be told, "It's quite warm and we're very busy, ring us again in the morning." They spent a bedraggled, hungry night on the moors and straggled home at daybreak!

4 blades of mace
2 brace of grouse
4 ounces fatty pork or bacon (about 1/2 cup)
cayenne pepper
1 cup (2 sticks) butter
salt and pepper

Preheat the oven to 400°F.

Place a blade of mace on the breast of each bird and tie a piece of pork or bacon fat over it. Place the grouse in a greased roasting pan, season with salt and pepper, and roast them for 10 minutes. Reduce the heat to 350°F and roast for another 20–30 minutes, depending on the age of the birds.

When the grouse are cool enough to handle, cut them into portions (half a grouse) and place in a pie dish. Add the butter to the drippings in the roasting pan, season with salt, pepper, and cayenne, and pour it over the birds. Serve cold with crusty bread.

potted grouse

This is not only a way of using up old grouse, but provides a delicious appetizer and is equally effective with any other game bird. Serve it on hot buttered toast or thin oatcakes; it also makes an excellent sandwich filler. It should last for up to three weeks in a fridge or cold pantry.

4 grouse, with giblets
Seasoning: 1 tablespoon of salt, pepper, cayenne pepper
  mixed together
1 1/4 cups game stock
2/3 cup (1 1/4 sticks) softened butter
1/2 cup (1 stick) melted clarified butter
1 tablespoon port

Preheat the oven to 325°F.

Cut the birds in half and rub the fleshy side with the seasoning. Put the giblets in a heavy casserole dish and lay the birds on top. Add the stock, cover, and cook in the oven for 2 hours, or until the flesh falls from the bones.

When it's cool enough to handle, remove the meat. I shred it into small pieces but you can do the next step in a blender. Mix the softened butter, grouse meat, port, and some of the strained cooking liquid. Press into small custard cups or one large container.

Chill, then pour the clarified butter over it to close any air gaps, and let it set. Serve at room temperature.

casseroled **grouse** with marmalade

For this recipe you need a dark rich marmalade. If you are making your own, make sure you include black treacle or molasses or brown sugar. This is another method for using old grouse. I was aiming for a grouse and kumquat recipe, but it tasted of very little so I threw in the marmalade. Nowadays I omit the kumquats.

4 onions
2 old grouse
6 ounces smoked bacon, cut into cubes (about 1 cup)
sprig of thyme
1 1/4 cups stout or dark beer
3 tablespoons marmalade
1/3 cup dry sherry
1 tablespoon butter
small bunch of young turnips, well scrubbed
salt and pepper

Preheat the oven to 350ºF.

Chop the onions into quarters and put them into a heavy flameproof casserole dish, or other heavy pan for which there is a lid. Cut the grouse in half and add to the pan. Put in the bacon and thyme, and season with salt and pepper. Pour in the beer, bring to a boil on top of the stove, cover, and put into the oven for 1 hour.

Mix together the marmalade, sherry, and butter, and add to the pan. Then add the turnips—if they are truly young they will not need peeling; if not, peel them.

Return the pan to the oven and cook for another hour. If the dish is drying out, add a bit more beer.

grouse pie

This is a good pie for using up old grouse. The addition of steak to such pies stems from the Georgian age and enriches the gravy. It doesn't do much for the steak, which I tend to discard, but then I do like my steak so a good vet can bring it back to life!

brace of old grouse
1 pound rump or round
2 1/2 cups game stock
2 ounces bacon, finely chopped (about 1/4–1/3 cup)
2 hard-boiled eggs, cut in half
pinch of mace
pinch of nutmeg
6 juniper berries, crushed
1 tablespoon sherry
enough rough puff pastry or regular pie dough to cover the pie
beaten egg, for glazing
salt and pepper

Preheat the oven to 325ºF.

Divide the grouse into quarters, and cut the steak into 1-inch cubes. Arrange the grouse and the steak in a 2-quart deep pie dish, add the stock, and scatter the bacon and hard-boiled eggs on top. Add the spices, juniper berries, and season with salt and pepper.

Cover the dish with tinfoil and cook in the oven for 1 hour. Let the dish cool slightly and then add the sherry. Roll out the pastry or pie dough and cover the pie. Zap the oven up to 425ºF. Make a slit in the crust to allow the steam to escape, and brush with egg.

Cook for another 30 minutes or so until the crust is golden. Serve with greens and mashed potato.

carpaccio of grouse

I was shooting at Copstall in Wiltshire, England, the lovely estate that Paul van Gilsengen and his partner Caroline Tisdale have returned to wonderful organic conditions with wild bison, boar, and hens that see off the deer hounds. After a splendid day's shooting Max Hastings remarked that he loved raw grouse, so Michel Roux and I leapt at this and Andy the young chef prepared some carpaccio. It is truly excellent.

1 grouse breast per person
olive oil
lemon juice
bottled horseradish or freshly grated horseradish or wasabi
salt and ground pepper

Remove the breasts from the grouse, wrap in plastic wrap and freeze for 40 minutes to 1 hour.

Remove from the freezer, unwrap the grouse, and slice as thinly as possible with a very sharp knife. Arrange the slices on a dish and scatter with salt and ground pepper, pour some good olive oil over them, and some lemon juice, and let stand for 10 minutes. Dot with your chosen variant of horseradish.

Serve as an appetizer with a little arugula salad or on thin oatcakes as a canapé.

hazel hen in a russian style

This recipe comes from Elana Molokhovet's *A Gift for Young Housewives*, a sort of Mrs. Beeton for Russia, but the truffles and caviar have been omitted. You can now buy crayfish from China and whilst you may well ask what are they fed on, remember they, like all crustacea, are carrion eaters.

4 hazel hen
1/3 cup flour
1/4 cup (1 stick) butter
stock
1/3 cup Madeira or medium sherry
6 fresh field mushrooms, roughly chopped
1 egg, lightly beaten
bread crumbs made with stale bread, not bought!
oil, for frying
salt and pepper

For the ragoût:
12 field mushrooms
12 crayfish tails, cooked and cleaned
2 tablespoons butter
truffle oil
lemon juice

Remove the breasts from the birds as supremes—that is, including some of the wings by cutting them off at the first joint. Make a slit in the underside of the breasts for the stuffing. Mix a roux with the flour and butter, and add enough stock to make a thick sauce. Season with salt and pepper and cook a little longer. Add the Madeira and mushrooms; bring to a boil, and cook for 5 minutes. Stuff the breasts with this mixture and sew up. Dip them in egg and bread crumbs and fry them, or dip them in egg white and deep-fry them. Arrange on a platter and fill the center with crayfish tails and field mushrooms cooked in butter, season with truffle oil and lemon juice.

grouse pudding

The flavor of old grouse is fantastic but tough as old boots so here is a recipe to reap the benefits without the shoe leather. The original recipe cooks for 4–6 hours, adding more stock after 2 hours but unless your grouse died of arthritis or you have lost all your teeth and can't afford false ones, I think this is *de trop*.

For the suet pastry dough:
3¹/₃ cups all-purpose flour
pinch of salt
1 pound finely chopped suet (about 2 cups)
2¹/₂ cups water

2 old grouse
1 pound beef or venison skirt
3 tablespoons seasoned flour
2 pounds suet pastry dough
1 onion, chopped
2 field mushrooms, chopped
2 tablespoons port, Madeira, or medium sherry
1¹/₄ cups stock
salt and pepper

For the suet pastry rub the flour, salt, and suet together and add enough water to form a dough—this can also be done in a food processor. Strip the meat from the grouse and chop it, together with the skirt into cubes. Dust with the seasoned flour. Line a 2-cup pudding basin or ovenproof bowl with two-thirds of the pastry dough. Fill with the meats, the onion, and the mushrooms. Add the alcohol and enough stock to cover the meat. Season with salt and pepper and cover with the remaining pastry. Place the pudding basin in a square of cheesecloth, gather up the ends and tie. Steam for 4 hours, or 2 in a pressure cooker. Untie the cloth and flash the top under the broiler for a more attractive presentation.

grouse duntreath

If you buy birds later in the season, they are often not in the first flush of youth. This is a really excellent way of cooking such birds, and in fact I know very good shots who prefer this to any other method of roasting grouse. The water has the effect of partially steaming the grouse, and helps break down the fibers.

1 grouse per person
2–3 pieces of apple per person
2 slices bacon per person
salt and pepper

Preheat the oven to 300°F. Season the grouse inside and out with salt and pepper. Put a couple of pieces of apple in each bird and wrap the bird well in bacon. Stand the birds in ¹/₂ inch water and cover with a lid of tinfoil. Roast in the oven for 45 minutes.

Remove the tinfoil lid, pour off the liquid, zap up the oven to 450°F and roast for 10 minutes more to brown the birds. Serve with the usual trimmings.

grouse in a rye crust

This came about after I had cooked with Richard Blades at Simpsons for a program on Samuel Pepys. Richard had the idea of cooking a lamprey pie using a hot water crust made with rye flour, as this is more malleable than the wheat variety. My friend and butcher Colin Peat of Haddington found me a grouse so old I think it had died of arthritic shock. The end result has a most intense and extraordinary flavor, and is even good for those without teeth! The crust is not for eating but merely a cooking vessel. The word *coffyn*, despite its lugubrious modern connotations, simply means a box in Medieval English; in culinary terms it refers to a thick pastry dough box, with or without a lid, in which things were cooked and served direct to the table. In this recipe I suggest you bring the pie to the table and slice the top off and dish out the filling. This is a perfect dish for an Aga.

For the crust:

3¹/₂ cups rye flour

1 level teaspoon salt

¹/₂ cup lard

1 scant cup water

2 very old grouse

1 large strong onion

¹/₂ teaspoon nutmeg

¹/₂ teaspoon mace

¹/₂ teaspoon ground cloves

¹/₂ cup clarified butter

Sift the flour and salt into a bowl and make a well in the center. Put the lard and water in a saucepan, heat until the lard melts, and then bring to a boil. Pour the liquid into the flour and mix in quickly to form a pliable dough. Turn onto a floured board and knead until smooth, and use quickly as it hardens up. If you must keep it, do so in a bowl covered with a warm cloth. Shape the pastry dough by hand to make a large container (see page 141).

Preheat the oven to 400°F.

Cut the grouse into manageable pieces that will fit in your pie crust. Peel the onion and cut in half widthwise. Put one half of the onion, cut side down, in the pastry coffyn and place the other half on top of it. Arrange the pieces of grouse around the onion halves and add all the seasonings. Pour in the clarified butter and put the lid on the pie. Put into the oven for 30 minutes to set the crust, then reduce the oven temperature to 300°F and cook for 4 hours.

dove

There are several quarry species of dove in the United States—the white-winged dove and the band-tailed pigeon of the South and the West, and the Eurasian collared dove, an alien species that was introduced to the Bahamas from Holland in the 1970s and is gradually expanding westward. But the most abundant and widespread American game bird—a recent conservative figure put the population at 475 million—is the mourning dove (*Zenaida macroura*), so called because of their moaning, long-toned plaintive call. Mourning doves have a distribution across the continent from southern Canada to the Gulf of Mexico. They are migrants and huge flocks move south as winter encroaches, although some southern birds remain south all year.

Mourning doves are elegant, handsome birds with a slim 12-inch body, small head, slightly curved beak, and a long pointed tail, edged with a black and white stripe. Their crown, nape, and neck are slate gray, their wings flecked with dark spots, and the rest of the body is a pinkish buff. The only difference between sexes is the slightly larger size of the cock bird and a bluish sheen to his crown. Mourning doves are monogamous and both birds are deeply involved in the whole breeding process, sharing the incubation equally. Curiously, for such attentive parents, they are staggeringly incompetent nest builders. In March or April, the hen takes on the task of construction while the cock passes her the materials he collects by landing on her back. A process so distracting to both of them that the haphazard platform of twigs sometimes collapses at a later date, scattering eggs or fledglings on the ground below. Barring mishaps, or predation from squirrel, jays, and other birds of prey, the hen bird rears two squabs up to five or even six times a year,

particularly in the South. For the first three days of life the young are fed a cheesy smelling milky curd, known as pigeon milk, which is secreted by the crop lining of both parents. It is this initial high protein feeding, a characteristic of all pigeon species, and the resulting rapid growth rate of the young—they are fully fledged in about a month—that made pigeons such a valuable food source to the European medieval manor house culture of living larders.

Like the British and Continental wood pigeon, the increase in mourning dove numbers has more to do with a man-made environment than their natural prolificacy. The creation of a countryside made up of a patchwork of farmland, woods, and hedgerows has provided the ideal mix of feeding, roosting, and nesting habitat ideally suited to their needs. Even urban parkland, with its security and convenient proximity to the neighboring countryside, has become a popular roosting site, and most cities support considerable numbers. Their natural diet is weed seeds—grasses, pigweed, foxtails, wild sunflowers, and ragweed, to which modern agriculture has obligingly added vast acreages of wheat, corn, sorghum, and millet. Post-harvest waste grains are particularly attractive. Periodically, enormous flocks of up to 20,000 doves have been known to descend on arable areas, causing immense crop damage and, while the majority of states allow a shooting season, a few classify doves, controversially, as protected song birds.

The season for dove shooting, eagerly looked forward to by over 2.5 million aficionados, is usually from 1st September until 30th October, but can differ from state to state. As a migratory bird, they are monitored by the US Fish and Wildlife Service, which establishes a framework for individual states to set their own shooting

season. The same applies to the bag limit, which averages about fifteen birds. Dove shooting is a family tradition in many parts of the United States and it is considered to be a relaxed late-afternoon social event for family and friends, which generally ends in an evening barbecue. As dove shooting is one of the first game bird seasons to open and also because of their large quantities, doves, like wood pigeon in Britain, provide a wonderful opportunity for a live quarry refresher course for retrievers and for their owners to get the feel of it. And what practice it is. A mourning dove's phenomenal eyesight, instantaneous reaction to danger, aerial dexterity, and ability to change gear from a cruising speed of 45 mph to a scorching 60 mph in a fraction of a second, provide sporting challenges which, to prove successful, require immense concentration and lightning fast eye-and-hand coordination. Whether whistling in low over a harvested wheat field, skimming the tree tops towards their roosting grounds, or dropping in to decoys, mourning doves are extremely difficult to shoot. The principal US cartridge manufacturers cheerfully calculate a one in seven cartridge kill rate and state that 50 percent of their annual output is sold to dove hunters.

Passing on the sporting tradition is equally important on both sides of the Atlantic. The future of our countryside heritage lies in the hands of the next generation and there is no better way to introduce young shots to a lifetime of shooting and conservation than flighting doves in the United States or wood pigeons in Britain. Both are done from a concealed stationary position and this in itself leads to one of those rare bonding occasions that a parent has with their son or daughter. Dove numbers on an average afternoon flight will generally provide a young shot with the opportunity for a fair amount of shooting and they can be seen coming from quite a distance, enabling an adult to help with gun mounting and advice with mistakes. More importantly, setting up for an afternoon's flighting is a wonderful opportunity to teach the young country lore.

Success with any quarry species is knowing all about it—where and what it feeds on, where it goes to drink, where it sleeps, and so on. An advantage with doves is that they like to feed and drink together and will often come back to the same area year after year. Spending a few days watching dove movements through binoculars is essential to a successful flight, like the flight lines they take from feeding grounds—recently cut cereal fields or weedy areas with a high proportion of sunflowers or ragweed—back to their roosts in deciduous trees. In dry weather, doves congregate in the afternoons to drink from ponds, reservoirs, and rivers. As the migration period draws closer, large flocks tend to concentrate where they can obtain high protein food to build up reserves for the long journey ahead and can be found feeding on cereal aftermaths. Having made one's deductions, it is then a matter of erecting a camouflage hide in the right place and positioning decoys where they are clearly visible, and teaching the young the first principle of dove flighting—that doves can detect any movement from a long distance and you won't get a shot unless you sit absolutely still.

Doves are at their best between late spring and early autumn when they have been at the farmer's crops; this, of course, is the period when they are most often shot. I love dove; when I was a child my father used to have squabs flown in from Cairo, and when I look at the empty doocots all over Scotland I mourn for the passing of this part of the living larder. It is a tradition still found in Continental Europe and the Middle East and I have tried to select a variety of recipes to give this delicious bird its true range.

Aging

Young doves have softer, pinker legs and a round plump breast.

Hanging

Doves don't need hanging, and it is important to empty the crops as soon as possible.

Plucking

Doves are the easiest birds to pluck; the feathers simply float off them and float everywhere, so pluck them outside or in a barn.

Drawing

As for pheasant (see pages 24–25).

Roasting

Place a piece of seasoned butter in each bird and a piece of apple. Wrap the birds in bacon or barding fat. Roast at 400ºF for 20–25 minutes, basting as you go. Remove the bacon to brown the breast 10 minutes before the end. Allow 1 large dove per person.

andalucian **doves**

The Spanish eat a lot of pigeon, and I think this is a very good way of doing doves. I have cut the amount of oil in half, toasted the bread, and added capers which I always think add color and a bit of bite.

4 young doves
8 anchovy fillets
3/4 cup olive oil
8 small onions
1 1/4 cups dry white wine
2 cloves garlic
1 sprig of parsley
1 tablespoon capers
4 triangles of good sourdough bread
salt

Rub the doves with salt and stuff them each with 2 anchovies. Heat half the oil in a large pan. Add the birds and cook over a low heat for 15 minutes, turning them until they are lightly browned all over. Fry the onions separately in the rest of the oil for about 5 minutes until golden all over. Then add them to the birds together with the wine, garlic, and parsley. Simmer for 45 minutes until the sauce is reduced by half and the doves are tender.

Remove the parsley and garlic and skim off any surface fat. Arrange the doves on a serving dish, strain the sauce, and pour it over the birds. Surround them with the onions and sprinkle with capers. Serve with the toasted sourdough bread.

jellied **dove**

This is a very tasty dish for a cold table or a picnic. I tend to add a pig's foot whilst cooking for extra jelly. If you want to use one, cut it in two and add to the doves while they are cooking, remove it when the birds are cooked and eat it separately cold for your supper! When the doves are cooked, I take the meat off the bone and return it to the stock to set. The original is a bit messy to eat but probably more fun!

1/2 cup (1 stick) butter
3 young doves
6 sprigs of tarragon
2/3 cup dry sherry
game stock
salt and pepper

Preheat the oven to 325°F.

Mix the butter with some salt and pepper to season it, and put a pat in each bird along with 2 sprigs of tarragon. Put in an oven dish, pour in the sherry, and add enough stock to cover them.

Cover tightly and cook in the oven for about 2 hours, or until the birds are tender. If necessary add more stock as the doves must be covered during cooking.

Let the birds cool so that the butter rises and forms a solid seal before serving.

doves from emilia romana

This is a rather complicated party dish from Emilia Romana, but it really does repay the effort and will amaze your friends whilst using very cheap ingredients. Do try it. You can get it all ready to cook, keep it overnight, and bake it for the party on the day. The Italians add sweetbreads to the mold—if you have a supply, try it. Just cook them slightly in melted butter first, then slice and layer them into the mold.

a scant cup (1³/₄ sticks) butter

2 onions, chopped

2¹/₂ pounds doves, with giblets reserved

1 tablespoon tomato paste

1 cup white wine

2¹/₂ cups game stock

12 ounces arborio rice (about 1³/₄–2 cups)

8 ounces parmesan, grated (about 3–4 cups)

4 ounces cooked peas (about 1 cup)

2 tablespoons dried bread crumbs

salt and pepper

Heat ¹/₄ cup of the butter and cook 1 onion until translucent. Add the doves and brown well; brown the giblets at the same time. Add half the tomato paste and cook, turning until the birds and onion are coated. Pour in the wine, reduce the heat, and season with salt and pepper. Add the stock, a little at a time, to prevent from drying. Cook until the birds are tender—about 1–1¹/₂ hours. Remove the birds and set aside.

In a heavy pan melt another ¹/₄ cup of the butter and cook the second onion until translucent. Add the rice, stirring until coated with butter. Cook gently for about 3 minutes. Add water, a little at a time as necessary, and salt, and cook over low heat until the rice is *al dente*—about 12 minutes.

Transfer the rice to a large bowl and gently stir in 1¹/₄ cups of strained broth from the cooked birds. Fold in gently the parmesan and cooked peas.

Preheat the oven to 325°F.

Butter a large round pudding mold, and shake in the bread crumbs to coat. Alternate layers of the rice mixture with layers of the meat from the birds, thinly slicing the remaining butter and placing between the layers. Mix the remaining tomato paste with a little stock and pour in. Bake for 1 hour. Unmold and serve.

doves with raisins

A warming dish with a bit of gusto about it. The raisins and sweet sherry give it a Regency feel and bring out the richness of the meat.

1/4 cup (1/2 stick) butter
1 onion, chopped
4 doves
1/3 cup flour
1 1/4 cups game stock
2 tablespoons red wine vinegar
2 tablespoons honey
1/2 cup raisins
1/3 cup sweet sherry
salt and pepper

Preheat the oven to 350°F.

Melt the butter in a pan, and fry the onion until golden. Add the doves and brown all over, and then remove them. Stir the flour into the onions and cook until brown. Add the stock gradually, stirring as you go.

Put the birds into a casserole dish, and add the stock mixture and all the rest of the ingredients. Cook, covered, for 1 hour, or until the doves are tender.

dove in the hole

Originally "toad in the hole" was made with rump steak rolled up, and then Hannah Glasse in the eighteenth century made it with pigeons. It works very well.

For the batter:
1 2/3 cups all-purpose flour
3 eggs
2/3 cup milk
pinch of salt

4 doves
1/3 cup (3/4 stick) butter
1/3 cup drippings
6 well seasoned game or venison sausages
salt and pepper

Mix all the batter ingredients together in a blender and let it stand for 1 hour, then stir well.

Preheat the oven to 400°F.

Rub the birds with butter and season well. In a roasting pan, heat the drippings until smoking hot. Pour in a third of the batter and cook for 15 minutes, or until it's set.

Place the doves and sausages on the layer of cooked batter and pour the rest of the liquid batter around them (the batter should cover three-quarters of the birds). Return to the oven and bake for another 30 minutes until the batter is well risen and the doves are cooked.

dove with rice and eggplant

Individual portions can be made in large ramekins, in which case cut the cooking time to 45 minutes.

2 medium eggplants, sliced into 1/2-inch thick slices

5 tablespoons olive oil

1 large onion, chopped

4 doves, cut in half

1 teaspoon ground allspice

1 teaspoon ground nutmeg

1 teaspoon ground cinnamon

1 teaspoon black pepper

2 1/2 cups water

oil for deep frying

12 ounces long-grain rice (about 1 3/4 cups)

1 cup boiling water

salt

Sprinkle the eggplants with salt and let drain for 30 minutes; pat dry. Heat the olive oil in a pan. Fry the onion until golden, and brown the dove halves. Add the spices and salt and pepper. Add the water, cover, and simmer until the birds are tender—for about 1 hour. Remove the birds and onions from the liquid with a slotted spoon, and when they are cool enough to handle, strip the meat from the birds.

Deep-fry the eggplant slices in a frying pan. Grease a large heavy pan (for which there is a tight fitting lid) with a little olive oil. Arrange the eggplant slices in a double layer on the bottom. Sprinkle a handful of rice over these. Layer the meat and onions on top, then the rest of the eggplant slices. Add the rest of the rice, spread evenly, and press down well. Sprinkle a little salt on top and add the boiling water. Cover tightly and cook until the rice is tender and the liquid absorbed—about 1 hour over very low heat (add more water if it's drying out). Invert onto a plate and serve.

dove bistalia

You can see how this magnificent dish came out of the kitchens of the Ottoman Empire. It is a lot easier to make than it looks and will amaze your friends; you can even make mini ones. The trick is to use lots of oil on the pastry dough leaves. I have not attempted to tell you how to make leaves of *warka*, the traditional pastry used, which requires complicated things done on the back of a heated copper bowl with a flour and water paste. If you want to go there, I recommend Robert Carrier's *A Taste of Morocco* as the only reliable recipe for this. I tried it once—try everything once has always been my motto—and it was interesting and probably that bit better but not so you would notice with the effort required.

For the *chermola*:
1 large onion, grated
4 cloves garlic, chopped
1 teaspoon saffron
1 teaspoon ground ginger
4 sprigs of parsley, chopped
6 sprigs of cilantro (coriander), chopped
olive oil
salt and pepper

For the almond mixture:
1 pound ground almonds (about 5 cups)
6 tablespoons confectioners' sugar
1/4 cup orange flower water
2 teaspoons ground cumin

6 young doves, boned and quartered with their giblets
1 cup (2 sticks) butter
4 cups water
generous 1/2 teaspoon saffron
melted butter
6 hard-boiled eggs, shelled and chopped
pinch of cinnamon
23 sheets phyllo dough
2 egg yolks, mixed with a little water
salt and pepper

On the day before eating, mix all the *chermola* ingredients in a bowl. Add the dove quarters and giblets and rub in well. Leave overnight to absorb the flavors. Stir all the almond mixture ingredients together in another bowl, and set aside, covered.

The next day transfer the doves and *chermola* to a heavy pan for which there is a lid. Add the butter and water, season, cover, and simmer for 20 minutes. Add the saffron, and cook for another 20 minutes. Transfer the birds to a dish, removing any loose bones, and reduce the stock by two-thirds by boiling hard over a high flame.

Preheat the oven to 425°F. Brush the bottom and insides of a very large tart pan with melted butter. Place 1 phyllo sheet in the center of the pan, then place 5 more sheets overlapping the edges of the pan. Brush with butter and repeat with 5 more sheets. Sprinkle half the almond mixture in the center of the pan, cover with 2 more phyllo sheets, and melted butter.

Arrange the meat mixture in the center of the pan, leaving the dough around the edge clear. Put in the hard-boiled eggs, sprinkle the cinnamon on top, and sprinkle the remaining almond mixture over that. Turn up the overlapping phyllo sides, sealing with the beaten egg mixture. Add 2 more layers of 5 phyllo sheets and fold to the center, brushing with a final layer of butter. Bake for 20 minutes or until the crust is golden. Run a spatula under the pie and invert it onto an ovenproof dish. Return to the oven for 10–15 minutes to brown the underside. Dust with cinnamon and serve.

egyptian **dove** with green wheat

This was a favorite dish of my father's who had his pigeons imported from Cairo. In Egypt they raise fat squab especially for the table and stuff them with green wheat which remains preserved inside them after their deaths. Anyone who has had their vegetable garden scoured by doves will know what scavengers they are, so this dish is the Egyptian farmer's revenge! Green wheat or *farik* can be bought in Middle Eastern stores throughout the country, but if you live in wheat-growing country, I'm sure the farmer will spare you a dozen heads, especially if you ask him to dinner. In Egypt, the spinach that accompanies the doves is cooked to a slop, but at home we preferred it firm.

1/2 cup clarified butter

10 ounces fresh cilantro (coriander)

1 teaspoon coriander seeds, freshly ground

1 teaspoon cumin seeds

2 teaspoons mixed salt, pepper, and chili powder

1 pound farik or husked green wheat

6 doves or large squab

2 shallots, cut in half

2 tablespoons butter

8 cloves garlic, peeled and mashed

1 teaspoon fennel seeds

4 tomatoes, quartered

2 pounds spinach

salt

Heat half the clarified butter in a large frying pan. Add the cilantro, coriander seeds, cumin, the salt, pepper, and chili mixture, and the *farik* and cook for about 5 minutes until the *farik* is *al dente*. Stuff the doves with the *farik*, pushing it in tightly and truss well.

Boil a large pot of water, add 2 teaspoons of salt and the shallots. Add the birds and simmer (do not allow to boil) for about 35–40 minutes. Drain and pat dry; save the water.

Heat the rest of the clarfied butter in the frying pan and pan-fry the birds for about 10 minutes, turning as you go until they are golden brown; set aside to rest.

Heat the 2 tablespoons of butter in a large frying pan. Fry the garlic, fennel seeds, and tomatoes in the butter for 2–3 minutes; add the spinach and about 3 tablespoons of broth from the birds. Cover and cook until the spinach is just softened.

Put the spinach on a dish and arrange the doves on top. Eat with Arab flatbread.

american woodcock

Probably no other game bird commands such respect among sportsmen, or is so sought after on either side of the Atlantic as woodcock. In France, where the larger European species have been christened "golden queens of the woods," woodcock shooting is almost a religion. In Britain, until well into the eighteenth century, people believed the same bird, which migrates south from Scandinavia in winter, spent the summer on the moon (an argument put forward at the time by a body of academics who reasoned that, when most woodcock disappeared in March and April, they flew to the moon, spending three months enjoying the lunar landscape and four months travelling there and back). The American name for its smaller but almost identical cousin, the wood elf or timber doodle, charmingly encapsulates this mysterious little bird's elusive behavior.

American woodcock (*Scolopax minor*) are waders with a 6-inch body and 18-inch wing span, that have adapted to damp woodland, forest roads, and open clearings free of undercover with soft ground in which to feed. They are an odd looking bird (native Americans believed that when God created birds he made woodcock out of the leftovers), with a dumpy body, rounded wings, and big black eyes set high up on a large head, giving them virtually 360 degree vision while they probe for food with their disproportionately long beak. Woodcock inhabit the eastern half of North America, summering in the northern US states and in southeastern Canada, migrating south as far as the Gulf of Mexico whenever the first frosts of winter make the ground too hard for the soft, pliable tip at the end of their beak to penetrate it. Their principal diet is earthworms, to which they add insect larvae, sow bugs, slugs, spiders, and ants. They seek deciduous forests where loamy soil will provide them with a constant food source, as

they stand four square on short sturdy legs at the edge of a Minnesota alder swamp, or stamp their feet to provoke worm activity beside a Missouri sycamore thicket. Woodcock are crepuscular, feeding at dusk and just before dawn, slinking between trees to a favorite feeding site on slow, silent wing beats like a gigantic moth. They lie up by day on some dry, south-facing bank, where their camouflage plumage—a mix of dead leaf colors of cinnamon, blacks, yellows, and russets—blends into the undergrowth. Their spring courtship display is one of the great sights and sounds of nature, looked forward to with eager anticipation by ornithology societies.

Woodcock start their return migration during March, and in April the cock bird performs his mating ritual in a small woodland glade, establishing his territorial "singing ground" which he defends from other males. At dawn and dusk, the cock bird stands in the open, singing the first part of his love song, a protracted series of nasal "peents." This may last anything up to an hour when, suddenly, in mid peent, the little bird leaps into the air and spirals upward on rapidly beating wings to 300 feet, his extended primary feathers making a thrilling twittering sound. From here he glides down in a series of zig-zags like a falling leaf, vocalizing a soft liquid burbling sound, to land on the spot he took off from. Hen birds fly in to the singing grounds to mate, thereafter they are on their own, incubating their four buff-colored eggs in a well-hidden ground nest of dead leaves, and rearing the chicks with no help from the polygamous male. Chicks are born after three weeks and the young start probing the ground at three or four days, can fly short distances after two weeks, and are independent in little more than a month. They make their first migratory flight south in October and November.

Timber extraction by the early settlers created habitat that led to an increase in woodcock numbers and until lighter, more manageable shotguns made shooting on the wing feasible, most woodcock were trapped in nets, in much the same way as they were in the Old World. They generally follow the same route to their dawn and dusk feeding places and these were quickly identified. A fine net hung across a woodland road or the entrance to some airy clearing would guarantee a healthy catch. In fact, they were so easily caught there was a view prevalent in Europe for many centuries that woodcock had no brains and the name was commonly used to describe a fool. At the beginning of the nineteenth century, John James Audubon recorded incredible numbers of woodcock being taken nightly in the cotton and sugar plantations of lower Louisiana by men carrying lighted torches and armed with nothing more than sticks. By day, even with flintlock muzzle loaders, it was possible to shoot them in their hundreds. With the massive expansion in the population of the United States and agricultural improvements towards the end of the century, woodcock numbers stabilized.

The season for woodcock is between sunrise and sunset from September to mid-February, with the US Fish and Wildlife Service, which monitors woodcock numbers, being the final arbiters on bag limits and the actual number of shooting days. During the migratory period, quantities of woodcock "fall" into certain coverts each year and sportsmen concentrate along the traditional routes the birds take on their journey south. The behavior of woodcock when flushed by a good spaniel (the cocker was specifically bred for woodcock shooting) or marked by a pointer, could not be more different from its leisurely flight to and from a feeding ground. Generally sitting tight until the last moment, it breaks cover at deceptive speed, immediately jinxing from left to right, emptying its bowels and flying more erratically the faster it goes. Moving as tortuously in the open as it does in woodland, where they twist and turn between trees in an incredible display of aerial dexterity, woodcock are, next to snipe, the most difficult and challenging shot. This, coupled with their exquisite, gamey flavor, has made them one of America's most popular quarry species.

The most delicious of birds and honored wherever they are found by shots the world over. My godfather, Rudi Jurgens—one of the best shots in Europe—retired to the Neimeigen Marshes in the south of Holland as he thought snipe and woodcock the only birds worth shooting. Both should be cooked with the innards left in as both shit as they fly away and therefore empty their gut.

Aging
If you've got them, eat them.

Hanging
How ripe you like them is a matter for you, anything from 3–15 days depending upon the weather. Snipe should be hung for 3–4 days unless it is very cold.

Plucking
I pluck mine when the stomach feathers give way at the first pull. Be very careful when plucking snipe so as not to tear the skin.

Drawing
As for pheasant (see page 24–25).

Roasting
Rub the birds generously with softened butter and place a piece of barding fat over the breast. Place in a very hot oven at 425°F for 10–15 minutes—more if you must (for snipe, 6–15 minutes). You can extract the entrails, season them, and serve them on toast with the bird, but I just tend to serve sippets of toast with the birds. Alllow 1 per person.

woodcock with polenta

This is an Italian way of serving woodcock and it is very agreeable, especially if you have a lot of them. I never have that many and resented testing the recipe!

2 1/2 quarts salted water

1 pound cornmeal/polenta (about 3 cups)

3 woodcocks

3 thin slices pancetta or unsmoked bacon, chopped

1/4 cup (1/2 stick) butter

2 ounces raw ham, finely chopped (about 1/2 cup)

2 ounces pancetta or unsmoked bacon, finely chopped
   (about 1/2 cup)

1 tablespoon celery, finely chopped

1 tablespoon onion, finely chopped

2 sprigs of parsley, finely chopped

1 bay leaf

6 juniper berries, crushed

1/2 cup Marsala or medium dry sherry

1 tablespoon tomato paste

salt and pepper

Serves 3

Preheat the oven to 400°F.

Boil the water and pour in the cornmeal/polenta. Reduce the heat and stir constantly for 30 minutes until the polenta comes away from the sides of the pan. Tip it onto a clean counter and flatten to 1/2 inch, then let cool for 30 minutes. Divide into 12 portions and bake on a greased cookie sheet, in the oven, until lightly browned—about 15 minutes.

Season the woodcocks and tie the bacon strips around them. Melt the butter in a heavy pan for which you have a lid. Add the ham, bacon, celery, onion, parsley, bay leaf, and juniper berries, and cook until the onion is golden. Add the woodcocks and brown them all over, then lower the heat; mix the alcohol with the tomato paste and stir into the pan. Cover, and simmer for 20 minutes or until the woodcocks are tender.

Remove the woodcocks and put the remaining contents of the pan through a food mill or a blender. Untie the woodcocks and cut them in half through the backbone. Arrange on the toasted polenta and pour the sauce over them.

burnetts' **woodcock**

This is a dish I invented for my friends Jane and George Burnett. George is a keen shot and commented he couldn't find different ways to cook woodcock. He shoots more than most—I don't have that problem myself!

For the potato cakes:

1 pound waxy potatoes (about 3–4 medium)

2 egg whites

1 egg yolk

1 tablespoon capers, chopped

1 teaspoon French mustard

2/3 cup whipping cream

2 tablespoons (1/4 stick) butter

To make the potato cakes, boil the potatoes, drain until they have stopped steaming, and mash them. Beat the egg whites very stiffly. In a separate bowl mix the yolk, capers, mustard, and cream into the mash and fold in the egg whites. Form small cakes and fry them in butter until brown.

4 woodcock

1/2 cup (1 stick) butter

4 slices fatty bacon

For the sauce:

4 livers, (woodcock, pigeon, pheasant, or chicken)

1/4 cup (1/2 stick) butter

1/2 cup white wine

2 tablespoons game stock

6 juniper berries, crushed

squeeze of lemon

salt and pepper

Preheat the oven to 425°F.

Spread each woodcock with butter and cover with a slice of bacon. Roast for 10–15 minutes, depending upon how you like your birds.

To make the sauce, sauté the livers in the butter, then mash and press them through a mesh strainer. Put the puréed livers in a pan with the white wine and stock, and add the juniper berries, seasoning, and lemon juice, and simmer for a few minutes. Stir in any pan juices from the woodcock.

Put the woodcock on the potato cakes and serve with the sauce.

woodcock with truffles

This French dish, which can also be made with snipe, comes from a happier age when both truffles and woodcock were plentiful. If you have a truffle and are happy to use it, it is a delicious dish. Strangely, the garlic does not overpower the truffle. The original recipe calls for six truffles so be aware lottery winners everywhere!

4 woodcocks
2 tablespoons (1/4 stick) butter
2 cloves garlic, cut in half
as many truffles as you can afford, preferably black, thinly sliced
game stock
salt and pepper

Preheat the oven to 425°F.

Rub the birds with the butter, season with salt and pepper, and roast for 10 minutes, so they are still very rare.

Rub an oven dish, preferably earthenware, with the garlic cloves. Put the birds in the dish and surround with truffle slices. Season again and add the stock. Put the dish back in the oven and cook for another 12 minutes.

snipe

These shy, secretive little migrants have an astonishing breadth of distribution. Common snipe (*Gallinago gallinago*) can be found, at certain times of year, from Ireland to Japan, Siberia to the Horn of Africa and most of North and South America. In the United States, where in 2002 they were renamed Wilson's snipe (*Gallinago gallinago delicata*), they have a summer breeding range across the whole of North America, through Canada and up into Alaska, migrating to the West Coast, southeastern states, and to Central and South America as soon as the first hint of frost hardens the ground. During the season—15th September to 10th February—the southeastern states of America have some of the best snipe shooting anywhere in the world, whether in the coastal swamps of Louisiana or the rice fields of Carolina. Aficionados quickly become hooked and one of the greatest snipe shots of all time, the southern Louisiana plantation owner J.J. Pringle, abandoned a career in the navy to devote twenty years to pursuing snipe through the swamps bordering his land. Between 1867 and 1887, Pringle shot 78,602 with his own gun, before retiring to write what is still considered to be the definitive work on the subject, *Twenty Years Snipe Shooting*.

Very similar in shape and size (10½ inches) to American woodcock, snipe are shore birds, waders, creatures of swamps and damp empty places, of mists and reeds, the rumble of surf and screech of sea birds. The name for a quantity of them in flight—a wisp—could not be more descriptive. Seen briefly above a bed of rushes they soon melt away into the gray winter sky. A number of them on the ground are called a walk. They are artists of concealment, their striped plumage, the varying shades of yellow,

black, light and dark brown, and long, pale green legs are all the colors of marsh and estuary growth. Snipe feed at dawn, dusk, and moonlit nights on small mud and slime dwellers that share their habitat. Penetrating soft ground with their long beaks—a third of their body length—they rely on the highly sensitive, flexible tip to locate a variety of worms, invertebrates, crane fly, and other insect larvae. Although it usually probes for food, snipe will readily eat any surface or flying insect that comes within range, as well as small molluscs and baby frogs. Their eyes are positioned high on their heads, enabling them to see upwards and always be alert to aerial predators while they feed. Response to danger is so instantaneous that people believed snipe used their beaks to propel themselves airborne.

The first promise of spring, for many country people across the Northern Hemisphere, is an eerie, moaning sound that rises to a soft fluting crescendo. This beautiful wind music, which never fails to send a shiver down my spine, is a cock snipe drumming, performing his spectacular territorial and courtship display, climbing to a couple of hundred feet and diving with his tail primaries extended. This hauntingly beautiful sound is created by the snipe's feathers vibrating through the wind stream as it reaches a certain speed. When a hen is drawn to him, the cock snipe pursues her, diving with wings arched above his back, performing mid-air rolls and even flying upside-down in an effort to impress. The nest is a shallow scrape lined with grass, leaves, and moss near long grass or rushes which the hen pulls down to conceal her four khaki-colored, speckled eggs. The cock plays no part in the incubation, but performs his drumming, territorial flight to distract predators.

The young hatch after twenty days, are partially feathered, and can move about within hours of hatching.

Like all rare food, a snipe's delicious flavor is enhanced by the sheer difficulty in shooting them. Utterly unpredictable, they frequently fool even the best shot. Regardless of which continent they live in, most experienced sportsmen agree the only way to approach marshes or wet cultivated areas where you think they may be, is downwind. Snipe, when flushed, rise against the wind and hang in the air for a fraction of a second, before flickering away. Like woodcock, they zig-zag from side to side, straightening out after a couple of dozen yards before gaining altitude. They do this to conquer the wind and control their power of flight; from then on, they accelerate hard. This, and the fact that you can never tell what distance they may rise from you (in some weathers they lie so tight you can practically walk on them, in others, they consistently get up just out of range,) make hunting these elusive little people, both the most frustrating and occasionally, rewarding shooting.

Snipe are the most delicious eating, in my view, better even than woodcock. In Britain, we speak of a finger of snipe—the number held between the fingers of one hand, i.e. three—as being equivalent to our larger woodcock, in culinary terms. They are wonderful converters of food, appearing at the table like little balls of fat, and they used to be considered beneficial for invalids, as the flesh was believed to be easily digestible. This was possibly the reasoning behind Winston Churchill's reply, "a finger of cold snipe and a pint of port," when asked his favorite hangover cure.

snipe in a pie

I was served snipe pie in the Auvergne. It was an elaborate affair beautifully decorated with pastry dough cut outs of flying snipe, guns, and dogs. It was very large—this is a much smaller version for use at home.

1/2 cup golden raisins

cognac

a generous 3/4 cup (1 3/4 sticks) butter

4 pounds sharp apples, peeled, cored and chopped

1 shallot, finely chopped (if unavailable, use 1 tablespoon finely chopped mild onion)

6 juniper berries, crushed

6 snipe, drawn, trussed, and barded

1 1/2 pounds pastry dough

1 egg yolk, mixed with a little water

salt and pepper

Serves 6

Soak the raisins overnight in cognac, then drain and reserve.

Preheat the oven to 425°F. Melt half the butter and sauté the apples and shallot until golden. Stir in the raisins and juniper berries. Roast the birds for 10 minutes, then season them with salt and pepper. Roll out half the pastry dough and line a pie dish about 8 inches across and 6 inches deep.

Arrange the birds in the dish and then fill it with the apple mixture. Roll out the remaining pastry dough and cover the pie with it. Seal the edges and brush the top with the egg yolk, making a slit for the steam to escape. Turn down the oven to 400°F and bake for about 35 minutes or until the crust is golden. Melt the other half of the butter, stirring in the reserved cognac, and serve with the pie.

snipe curry

The Indian estuarine marshes team with wildfowl, and game books of the Raj show large drifts of snipe being shot. The curries recorded are rather fierce and fiery so, whilst giving a recipe for snipe curry in memory of my step-grandfather, who was a keen shot, I have used a rather delicate variant.

2 tablespoons oil

2 onions, chopped

1 tablespoon coriander seeds, freshly ground

1 teaspoon ground turmeric

1 teaspoon cumin seed

1 teaspoon fresh ginger, finely chopped, or 1/2 teaspoon ground

1 small chili, seeded and chopped

1/2 teaspoon ground fenugreek

4 snipe or woodcock

1 1/4 cups canned coconut milk

salt

Heat the oil in a heavy pan and cook the onions until golden. Add the spices and cook for another 5 minutes. Add the birds and cook them until they are well coated. Pour the coconut milk over them and add salt, cover, and simmer gently for 40 minutes or until the birds are cooked. Serve with rice and curry trimmings.

snipe pudding

Johnny had heard that Rosa Lewis, doyenne of the Cavendish Hotel, used to cook Edward VII his favorite breakfast of snipe pudding; Johnny tried making a conventional suet pudding à la steak and kidney using snipe with boneless steak wrapped around them—the steak was supposed to melt into the sauce! To our modern palates (not very, some would say) it was a waste of snipe. However, on reading Rosemary Wadey's excellent *The Pastry Book* I came across the statement that you could bake suet crust. Ah ha I thought, and here we are. Not what Edward might have liked but perhaps for his great-great grandson a modern (not very) snipe pudding.

1²/₃ cups self-rising flour
¹/₂ teaspoon salt
4 ounces chopped suet (about ¹/₂ cup)
²/₃ cup cold water
4 pieces sharp eating apple
4 snipe
4 spoonfuls white wine
¹/₂ cup (1 stick) butter, softened
salt and pepper

Sift the flour and salt and rub in the suet, then add enough cold water to make a dough. Using the heel of your hand, flatten out the pastry dough on a floured board. Preheat the oven to 400°F. Put a piece of apple in each snipe and pour in a spoonful of wine. Season the outside of the birds with salt and pepper, and rub each with a quarter of the softened butter. Place a bowl of hot water on the floor of the oven to stop the suet pastry dough drying out too quickly. Divide your dough into 4 and wrap each snipe in dough, securing the edges with cold water. Brush with a little beaten egg and bake on a greased baking sheet for 20 minutes. Reduce to 350°F and cook for another 30 minutes.

snipe with lettuce and capers

My Belgian great Aunt who was such a gourmet that the measurement around her waist when she married was the measurement around her neck when she died, used to cook snipe like this. You can use woodcock as well, but cook it for a little longer.

8 ounces unsmoked bacon, chopped (about 1 cup)
2 Boston lettuces, separated
4 snipe
6 shallots or 1 onion, finely chopped
1 tablespoon capers or caperberries, chopped
1¹/₂ cups white game stock
salt and pepper

Preheat the oven to 350°F.

Put the bacon in the bottom of a casserole dish and arrange the lettuce leaves on top. Put the snipe on top of the lettuce and add the shallots and capers. Pour the stock over it, season with salt and pepper, and bake uncovered for 35–40 minutes until the birds are cooked.

wildfowl

wildfowl

If I had to choose one category of shooting above all others, I would unhesitatingly pick wildfowling. It has all the components that I love about nature and the countryside. It takes place in weather that keeps the rest of the nation firmly indoors and in areas that have remained unspoiled, remote, isolated, and untainted by civilization. I love the stark mysterious estuaries where the wild migratory birds come to winter, the ozone smell of the sea, the wide horizons of forbidding gray skies, the bitter cold of pre-dawn mornings, and the music of sea birds—the call of the wild. Above all it is the challenge of pitting my knowledge of nature against those elements that influence where wildfowl may be at a certain dawn or dusk—the position of the moon, the tide, the temperature, and what available food source there is in certain areas. The success of all fieldsports depends upon careful planning, preparation, and understanding of the behavioral pattern of your quarry; wildfowl take this to another dimension with the vagaries of their movements, and part of the fascination is that one is so rarely right.

There is a romance and mystique unique to wildfowling that has much to do with the antiquity of the sport and the feeling of déjà vu that marshland evokes—a sense that these places, empty now except for a few marsh sheep and cattle, once supported busy communities. In huge areas of the northern world, the early survival of mankind depended upon wildfowl, particularly through the winter. Around 4000B.C., the earliest inhabitants of Britain, crossing over from mainland Europe, settled in the coastal marshes, building settlements of reeds and willow and surviving off the wildfowl and fish they caught in primitive nets and traps. Successive waves of invaders took over and enlarged these settlements, establishing primitive forms of agriculture and gradually pushing inland, but the basis of their survival continued to be nature's bounty from the vast flocks of sea and marsh birds. Salt was a vital element for winter survival and coastal communities were already producing salt when the Romans arrived. With typical efficiency they set about building sea walls, draining marshes and creating productive salt pans. Baskets of eels, pike, and perch, bundles of rushes and reeds for thatching and floor covering, and every species of wildfowl netted as they flew in to marsh pools would have gone up river to the Roman settlements of Londinium (London) and Camulodunum (Colchester).

The Anglo-Saxons built settlements around the edge of the marshes and reclaimed more land, creating valuable summer grazing for cattle and sheep, but there were still enormous areas where remote isolated communities lived on islands in the marshes, sharing their existence with great multitudes of marsh and sea bird. To upland farmers, the marshes and estuaries were dangerous places, populated by strange, uncivilized, fever-ridden, interbred people, worshipers of ancient gods, and possibly amphibian, who were as wild and unpredictable as the birds with whom they lived. The birds themselves gave rise to more marshland mythology, confirming that the marshes were supernatural. A rarely seen, strange bird called a bittern, made a hollow, spine-chilling booming noise. Bad enough by day, with its eerily ventril-oquial sound effect, but far worse by night. The weird bumping sound struck terror into the hearts of those that heard it and is supposed to be the origin of "things that go bump in the night." Furthermore, it was generally believed that bitterns boomed, by thrusting their long beak into the ground and blowing hard. Most ducks made identifying quacks, but widgeon whistled. Some, like tufted duck and scaup, disconcertingly swam under water like fish. Other birds like avocets, red-shanks, and godwits, yelped. Shell duck had an alarmingly human laugh. Snipe moaned, whimbrel whimpered, and water rail screamed and grunted. None of these sounds was remotely familiar to the comforting bird song of the uplands.

Another anxiety to inland people was the sinister way the marsh bird population fluctuated and changed between summer and winter. This was particularly noticeable among geese. Enough muddled mythology survived from pre-Roman times about the sexual symbolism of geese, but the fact that geese appeared in the skies in great honking skeins as the fall skies darkened, and left again in spring, required some explanation. For the North American tribes people the reason was simple: geese flying south were taking the spirit of growth away and would bring it back when it was time for plants to start growing again. For Europeans, geese seen flying by the light of the moon provided the answer. They flew to the moon, spending two months flying there, two months enjoying the lunar landscape, which was clearly a huge area of water, and two months flying back. However, barnacle geese evolved from a chrysalis, emerging from the white lace-like growths that a marine insect builds on driftwood, and disappearing back into the sea in the spring.

Whatever prejudices may have developed about the marshes, it didn't stop people eating their produce. As the population grew, fishermen trapped and speared the pike and eels, reed cutters harvested reeds for thatch, and wildfowlers trapped and netted, sending their catches by boat to the inland towns. Marsh reclamation continued under the Normans (after 1066), and through successive monarchies, without appearing to have any impact on the vast wildfowl population, or much impression on the total wetland acreage. In the early Middle Ages, some wildfowl, particularly mallard, herons, and cranes, became a popular hawking quarry among landowners and their guests along the marsh fringes.

The vast majority of wildfowl was caught in nets. Clap nets, which lay flat on the ground, were yanked upright on ropes as duck were spooked off pools. These were particularly effective on diving duck like pochard, scaup, and gold eye that leave water with a low trajectory. Other species like mallard, teal, and widgeon were trapped, as they dropped into pools, by nets of very fine mesh stretched between two poles. These "mist" nets were used to great effect on the shore and salt marshes, to catch great quantities of waders. Geese were caught as they landed on inland grazings. Greylag, the only goose to breed in Britain when all the others had migrated, were caught and domesticated, becoming the ancestors of the white farmyard goose. As the population and demand for wildfowl grew, clap-netting was gradually replaced by the more productive duck decoy—a series of netted pipes running 70 yards back from a pool along a curved connecting dyke, wide and high at the end protruding into the pool, and narrowing to a dead end as it rounded the corner of the connecting dyke. Ducks are naturally inquisitive and were lured down the pipes, either by decoy ducks or the surprisingly effective decoy dog.

The problem with netting, however, was its semi-permanency and, although wildfowlers saw new hunting methods developed which should increase their kill, these methods also had their drawbacks. Hail shot, small pieces of lead rattled around inside a metal box until they became roughly spherical, invented in 1520, provided them with the means they had been waiting for but this, too, had its limitations. Military matchlock guns using hail shot had been finding their way into civilian hands for some time, and both poachers and gentry, with their finer wheel-locks, had

achieved limited success on deer, and upland bird shooting was only possible as long as the birds were on the ground. Here you would find the upland gunner stumbling after partridge, leading his stalking horse, and weighed down with all the paraphernalia of powder horn and shot. Hail shot really came into its own with wildfowling, with the wildfowler settled deep in the rushes beside a carefully selected pool, matchlock balanced on its gun stand, and waiting for the dawn.

The limitation of the matchlock was its method of powder ignition. A spluttering slow match held in the jaws of a spring-loaded hammer, was thrust into a hole beside the breach when the trigger was pulled, igniting the main charge in the barrel. The whole art of wildfowling hinges on concealment and silence—neither criteria was really achieved by matchlocks. Lighting the slow match was a weather-dependant, noisy business and once lit, it spluttered away, giving off a plume of evil-smelling smoke, enough to frighten away any keen-sighted duck or goose. It is curious to think that over the next 250 years there were only two adopted revolutionary innovations in firearm design, both inventions of wildfowlers. The first was the snaphaunce, Dutch for "biting dog," an ignition system where a flint striking steel showered sparks into a small quantity of powder which ignited the main charge. This invention of a forgotten Dutch wildfowler was to become the flintlock, which remained the only ignition system until the early 1800s when the Rev. Alexander Forsyth developed the percussion cap.

One of the main wildfowling centers in England was the Wash in Lincolnshire, on the East Coast, a gigantic area of sea marsh and tidal creeks extending miles inland. The principal market town is Boston, home of John Winthrop, founder of the city of Boston, Massachussetts. When the

AVANT NOEL
Le marché des dindes et des oies en Normandie

"Winthrop" fleet of 11 ships left England in 1629, they had many people on board from the East Coast counties of Essex, Suffolk, Norfolk, and particularly Lincolnshire—all traditional wildfowling areas. These early settlers, who finally landed at the mouth of the Charles River, would have found a wildfowler's paradise, with great multitudes of waterfowl darkening the skies. There was every conceivable species of duck and goose: mallard, teal, widgeon, shoveler, pintail, redheads, canvas backs, black heads, eiders, scoters, long tails, Labradors, harlequins, and many others. Blue geese, snow geese, barnacles, brant, and great lumbering Canada geese, to name only a few, nested in the marshes and fed on the eel grass, wild celery, cord grass, and salt marsh sedges that grew on the estuary edges and tidal creeks, or migrated back and forth in the fall and spring.

The abundant waterfowl, fish, and shellfish would have provided the settlers with their first source of

fresh food. The fishermen and wildfowlers among the fleet would have been quick to employ their skills, setting their traps and bird nets. In time, they were to acquire new techniques from the coastal native tribes who had a long tradition in crafting duck decoys by attaching feathers to models made of mud and reeds. Later, once the settlers began to manufacture gunpowder, they employed firearms. Crafting beautifully carved and painted wooden duck decoys was to become part of North American folklore and is a tradition that persists today. As new waves of settlers arrived in North America and used the great rivers and massive lakes to carry them inland, wildfowl were a consistent and dependable source of food. Isolated northern outposts smoked and dried ducks and geese for

winter survival and fed off their eggs in the spring. The feathers could be used to stuff pillows, and the quills, from the wing feathers of geese, for writing. Goose grease, the softest of all fats, was a valuable commodity and had an infinite amount of uses other than for cooking. Wildfowlers in Britain traditionally coated themselves in goose grease to retain body heat in the bitter cold, a practice that saved many a Canadian voyageur from frostbite. Mixed with certain herbs, it was used to heal wounds and made into a warm poultice, to treat bronchitis. A layer of goose grease mixed with pounded bog myrtle was an effective protection against mosquitoes.

Despite the gradual increase in population and the urban demand for supplies of ducks and

geese, wildfowling methods remained little changed on either side of the Atlantic during the eighteenth century. The turn of the nineteenth century saw the beginning of a massive rise in the North American population that gathered momentum through the 1800s. It coincided with the invention of the percussion cap, a radical development in firearm technology that was to have a far reaching effect. The Rev. Alexander Forsyth, was, like many men of the cloth in those days, a keen shot. He was also part of a growing band of "gentlemen gunners" whose love of wildlife drew them to the ornithological paradise in which the professional wildfowlers made their living. On his goose shooting forays, Forsyth was frequently frustrated by the pan flash from his flintlock alerting geese, which were able to swerve aside before the main charge ignited. Experimenting firstly, with a hood to enclose the firing mechanism and conceal the flash but without success, he then devoted his energies to fulminate of mercury. Chemists had known for some time that fulminates of mercury or silver, when struck, produced an explosion. Forsyth experimented endlessly with fulminates, blowing the barrels on several guns before coming up with the idea of enclosing a tiny quantity of fulminate inside a container placed over a small tube threaded into the barrel and connected to the main powder charge. In the first two decades of the nineteenth century, Forsyth refined his new mechanism, but it was an American, Joshua Shaw, who eventually perfected the percussion cap, placing an explosive charge inside a thimble-shaped copper container which fitted over a hollow nipple protruding from the chamber. When struck by the gun's hammer this exploded, sending a flash down the nipple and igniting the main charge. It is strange to reflect that an invention of a Scottish minister of the church, refined by an American landscape painter, is still the ignition mechanism that fires every cartridge, bullet, and shell in every army in the world.

An expanding urban population in the 1800s put enormous pressure on wildfowlers on both sides of the Atlantic to provide more wildfowl. Percussion caps now enabled them to shoot in all weathers and at any angle for the first time, but they needed all their powers of inginuity to increase bags (amount of game killed in a single day). The necessity that led to the invention of punt gunning in Europe—a canoe-shaped boat, flat to the water, with what was virtually a cannon mountain in the prow, used to approach rafts of duck roosting at sea—also led to a variety of strange craft in America. Sneak boats, cat boats, and garveys were all designed to creep up on wildfowl and provide opportunities for maximum

bags, and sink boxes—or the highly dangerous battery boats—floated flat to the water with a tiny lip to stop the sea swamping them. In these boats, the gunner would lay, surrounded by decoys and ready to sit upright and blaze away when duck were drawn in. Everything was tried. They dug themselves in and shot geese on their shore roosts or followed them inland and shot them as they flew in to graze. This was the age of the market gunner, and wildfowlers risked their lives and their health in freezing, dangerous conditions to meet consumer demands, bagging hundreds of thousands, shooting all year round and taking advantage of both spring and winter migrations. The author, conservationist, and wildfowler, George B. Grinnell, estimated that 15,000 canvas backs alone were being taken by a variety of means daily, in the Chesapeake Bay area. Other sources give incredible figures of wild ducks in their hundreds of thousands being sold annually in markets throughout America.

Since the beginning of the nineteenth century, when wildfowling was still essential to the survival of many small communities, an increasing number of sporting naturalists have become attracted to the harsh environment of the salt marshes and estuaries, and their wild beauty and openness. Wildfowling has since inspired hundreds of authors and artists. It was some of these and in particular, George B. Grinnell, editor of Forest and Stream, Founder of the Audubon Society, and advisor to Theodore Roosevelt, appalled at the indiscriminate slaughter and habitat loss through land reclamation, who began to agitate for laws to regularize shooting. Efforts to protect dwindling wildfowl had begun with protected areas in California in 1870 and a ban on market hunting in Arkansas five years later, but these legislations were largely ignored and it was not until 1913 that momentum in wildfowl conservation began to gather pace. In that year,

President Howard Taft passed an act placing migratory birds under federal protection. This was followed in 1918 by the Migratory Bird Treaty Act, signed by the United States and Britain, on behalf of Canada, which established bag limits for waterfowl, protected threatened species, banned market hunting and the use of shotguns larger than 10 bore. Overnight, wildfowl disappeared from restaurant menus.

Controls on harvesting wildfowl did much to preserve endangered species but a greater threat came from habitat loss through land reclamation, particularly draining wetland areas. In 1934, President Roosevelt pushed the Migratory Bird Hunting and Conservation Act through Congress and initiated the federal Duck Stamp Program to raise money for the purchase of national wildlife areas. To date, the sale of duck stamps has raised nearly $700 million and purchased more than five million acres of land. Probably the most important breakthrough in wildfowl conservation took place in Canada, where most of North America's wildfowl breed. In 1937, a keen wildfowler and printing magnate, Joseph A. Knapp, founded Ducks Unlimited to raise funds from American wildfowlers to help restore the wetlands in breeding areas of the Canadian prairies that had been lost in the great drought. Through the generosity of several million wildfowlers, nearly $2 billion has been raised over the last 68 years which has contributed to the conservation of 11 million acres of prime wildlife habitat—a conservation triumph which has since been followed by responsible countries worldwide. Nearly two million wildfowlers in North America are actively involved in preserving their traditional hunting sport. Wildlife and habitat conservation, through shooting interests, has safeguarded a significant part of North America's heritage over the last 100 years. It is the responsibility of today's young sportsmen to ensure that this legacy continues to be protected.

duck

The ducks most usually eaten are mallard, widgeon, and teal. Widgeon are held superior as they are grass feeders, but less common, so unless your lover is a wildfowler, you will find they are not usually available. Teal are quite small and make a single portion so I tend to allow a duck per person unless they are very large. Wild duck adapts also to stewing and other similar dishes. The North Kent Wildfowlers in the UK complained that you never find recipes for pochard so I have included two, but all the duck recipes are pretty much interchangeable, allowing for the size of teal and adapting accordingly. The last meal I ate at the Connaught while it was the last great Belle Epoque French Restaurant left, and before the management turned it into yet another part of the Gordon Ramsey Machine, was teal cooked beautifully in a little chaffing dish and ignited with armagnac—the taste was sensational.

Aging

The webbing of a young duck can be torn easily, and the feet and bills are brighter on a young bird.

Hanging

2–3 days are all that is needed. In warm weather ducks are better hung without their innards; the guts can be removed with a button hook without tearing the vent. If a duck has been feeding on the foreshore it may smell fishy, in which case insert a potato and a teaspoon of salt in the cavity and place the bird in a pan with a half-inch of boiling water, and bake at 350ºF for 10 minutes. Drain the bird, remove the potato, and proceed with the chosen recipe, remembering to deduct 10 minutes from the cooking time.

Roasting

Mallard—place a piece of butter seasoned with herbs or crushed juniper berries or even an onion into the cavity. Smear the breast with butter and roast in a very hot oven (450ºF), basting with the butter and some red wine or port or orange juice for 20 minutes. This gives a fairly rare bird, but don't cook for more than 30 minutes in any event or they will sole shoes!

Pochard and *Widgeon*—as above.

Teal—as above but only cook for 12 minutes and no more than 20 minutes.

Carving

Carve exactly as for goose (see page 92). Being smaller, the thigh and drumsticks may also be served unless the bird is very rare.

orange and herb **duck**

Although this recipe is designed for mallard, it works perfectly well with any wild duck, even pochard! If using the small duck, you may need more than one breast per person. This recipe serves two.

breasts from 2 wild duck
salt and pepper

For the stuffing:
1/4 cup (1/2 stick) butter
1 teaspoon brown sugar
1/2 teaspoon each salt and pepper
4 ounces fresh thyme, sage and parsley, chopped
6 ounces fresh bread crumbs (about 3 1/2 cups)
1 shallot, chopped (or 1 tablespoon chopped mild onion)
rind and juice of 2 oranges

Preheat the oven to 350°F.

Carefully slice the duck breasts so that you can open them flat and place them on a piece of tinfoil and lightly season them.

Melt the butter in a frying pan and sauté all the stuffing ingredients, except the orange juice. When the stuffing looks done, add the juice and check the seasoning. Place the stuffing on one half of each duck breast and fold the other half over.

Wrap each one in tinfoil and bake for 40 minutes in the oven. Open each package carefully onto a hot plate so as not to lose the juices.

duck casserole

There are many ways of casseroling ducks and really the ingredients are a matter of choice and can vary to your taste. This is one I really like as the anise taste of the fennel goes very well with the duck. There are usually fava beans knocking around in my freezer and, unless they are small, I usually peel them.

3 tablespoons olive oil
1 onion, chopped
3 mallard, cut in half
salt and pepper
1/2 pound fava beans (if unavailable, use lima beans), blanched and drained (about 1 1/2 cups)
juice of 1/2 orange
juice of 1/2 lemon
12 black olives, cut in half and pitted
2 heads of fennel, sliced
1 1/4 cups red wine
1 pound new potatoes (about 3–4 medium), brought to the boil in cold water, cooked for 20 minutes, and drained
salt and pepper

Preheat the oven to 350°F.

Heat the oil in a heavy pan for which you have a lid and fry the onion. Add the duck halves and brown well. Season them with salt and pepper, add all the ingredients, except the potatoes, and bring to a boil.

Cover and cook in the oven for about 1 hour, or until the ducks are tender. Serve with the new potatoes.

duck allan jarrett

This is an adaptation of a Roman dish, and I have dedicated it to Allan Jarrett, Chairman of BASC and President of the Kent Wildfowlers. The Kentish marshes were frequented by the Romans and they gathered a wild harvest from the land the Wildfowlers cherish so carefully today. Allan challenged me to find a recipe for pochard and this one works very well. However it is advisable to immerse the pochard in warm water, bring to a boil, and simmer for 5 minutes, then take it out, dry it, and then proceed as below. This is to remove possible fishiness as it is a shore feeder.

For the stuffing:
2 spicy sausages, (Polish, Spanish, or Italian)
4 dates or preserved damsons
2 ounces ground almonds (about 2/3 cup)

salt and pepper
1/4 teaspoon anise seeds
2 tablespoons butter
2 1/2 cups duck stock
1 teaspoon oregano
1 teaspoon thyme

2 mallard or other wild duck
1/2 cup red wine

For the sauce:
1 teaspoon celery or cumin seeds
1 teaspoon fennel seeds
1/2 teaspoon rosemary
dash of wine vinegar

Preheat the oven to 375°F.

Remove and discard the skin from the sausages, and mix all the stuffing ingredients together, and insert it into the cavity of the ducks.

Roast the duck for 45 minutes, basting from time to time. After 30 minutes, bring the wine to a boil and pour it over the ducks.

Pound together the celery or cumin seeds, fennel seeds, and rosemary; add the vinegar and transfer it all to a saucepan. Remove the cooked ducks to a warm platter, and add the pan juices and wine to the spices. Bring to a boil and reduce slightly. Serve with the duck.

mallard with sausage and chestnut stew

This is an adaptation of a Roman dish from Apicius's cookery book from the first century A.D. I am a fan of the author, for when he was down to his last million sesterces (which he considered the price of a good party) he killed himself so that the money would pay for his wake! Now that's what I call a real hedonist.

1/4 cup (1/2 stick) butter
4 ounces salt pork, finely chopped (about 1/2 cup)
3 mallard, cut in pieces
1 onion, coarsely chopped
1 large carrot, sliced
2 cloves garlic, crushed
1 1/2 cups (1/2 bottle) red wine
1 1/4 cups stock
1 bouquet garni of parsley, thyme, and a bay leaf
1 large spicy sausage, sliced
20 chestnuts, shelled
salt and pepper

In a large heavy pan for which there is a lid, melt the butter and brown the salt pork for 5 minutes. Remove the pork and brown the duck pieces in the fat. Remove the duck and sauté the onion and carrot until soft, and add the garlic. Pour off the remaining fat. Add the wine to the pan and boil for 15 minutes until it has reduced by a third.

Return the duck and pork to the pan, add the stock and the bouquet garni and simmer for 1 hour. Remove the duck pieces to a dish and discard the pork pieces. Purée the stock and skim the fat from the top.

Return the duck and stock to the pan, and add the sausage and chestnuts. Season with salt and pepper. Cover and simmer until it is heated through—about 25 minutes. Serve with mashed potatoes.

duck with gin-soaked sloes

In all the years of my drinking I sadly threw away the sloes from yet another finished bottle of sloe gin. I had to be sober to read Prue Coats' lovely *Poacher's Cookbook* and discover finally what to do with them. I no longer make sloe gin so I have to go around begging them off my friends!

2 slices bacon, chopped
1 onion, chopped
1 stalk celery, chopped
2 tablespoons gin-soaked sloes
2 wild duck
2 tablespoons sloe gin
salt and pepper

Preheat the oven to 350ºF.

Put the bacon, onion, and celery into a heavy pan for which there is a lid. Stuff the sloes into the cavities of the ducks and place the birds on top of the vegetables, breast side down. Season with salt and pepper. Cover and cook for 1 hour. Remove the lid, turn the ducks, breast side up, and cook for another 15 minutes to brown.

Remove to a warm dish and put the vegetables through a food mill or in a blender. Add the gin to the pan juices and ignite with a match to deglaze. Stir in the puréed vegetables and serve with the ducks. Add water or more gin if the sauce is too thick.

mallard with port

Duck and port and oranges are a combination made in heaven—I hope you enjoy this dish.

2 wild ducks
1/4 cup (1/2 stick) butter
8 ounces bacon
juice of 1 lemon
4 ounces orange marmalade (about 1/2 cup)
11/4 cups game stock
1/2 cup port
1 teaspoon tomato ketchup
salt, pepper, and cayenne pepper

Preheat the oven to 325°F.

Brush the duck breasts with melted butter and cover with strips of bacon. Roast the ducks for 45 minutes, then zap the oven to 400°F. Remove the bacon, score the breasts, and sprinkle with salt, pepper, and cayenne. Pour the lemon juice over them and return to the oven for 10 minutes. Carve the birds and arrange on a serving dish, and keep warm.

Add the marmalade, stock, port, and ketchup to the pan juices and boil to reduce to a thickish sauce. Finish the sauce by adding a little butter and cooking for a few minutes longer to give a lovely glaze to the sauce, then serve with the duck.

pochard with parsley and blackberries

This is actually a Swedish dish designed for eider—as much of a challenge as pochard. The Swedes eat all types of wild duck including eiders, which are a huge nuisance to mussel farmers in the Scottish lochs where they can strip a mussel rope in minutes. Eiders are protected in Britain.

4 ounces fresh parsley, chopped (about 2 cups)
1 tablespoon fresh cream cheese
1 large shallot, chopped (or 1 tablespoon chopped mild onion)
4 pochard breasts
salt and pepper

Preheat the oven to 350°F.

Blend the parsley and cream cheese together in a blender or food processor until it's totally green. With a spoon, mix in the shallot and season well.

Split the breasts without cutting through them. Spread a layer of the mixture on each breast and fold over again. Bake in the oven for 15 minutes. Rest in a warm place.

For the sauce:
1 tablespoon oil
1 small onion, chopped
1 small carrot, chopped
scant cup beef stock
4 ounces blackberries (about 3/4–1 cup)
salt and pepper

Heat the oil and sauté the onion and carrot until soft. Add the stock and blackberries and simmer. Strain, season with salt and pepper and serve with the pochard.

duck pizzas with caramelized pineapple

This dish was inspired by a delicious appetizer I had at Bonnars Restaurant in Haddington in East Lothian, Scotland; the chef whipped it up for me as I am allergic to mushrooms. It is quite delicious, and you can make your pizzas bigger or smaller at will. *Concasse* of tomato is merely homemade tomato paste, made by peeling and seeding tomatoes and cooking them very slowly with a little oil and seasoning until the juice is first expelled, then evaporated.

For the dough:

1 package active dry yeast

1/2 teaspoon sugar

1 cup warm water

1 pound white bread flour (about 31/3 cups)

pinch salt

oil

Mix the yeast and sugar in a bowl. Add half the water and let it become frothy—about 10–15 minutes. Add the flour, salt, and 3 tablespoons of oil and mix well together. Add enough water to make a firm dough and knead well. Rub all over with some oil and leave covered for 2 hours to rise.

For the filling:

1/2 cup sugar

1/2 fresh pineapple or 1 can pineapple chunks

4 tablespoons (1/4 cup) concasse of tomato or tomato paste

the meat from 1 roast mallard

Put the sugar in a heavy pan and just cover with water. Without stirring, cook over low heat until a caramel is formed; let it reduce until it is treacly and a good color.

Cut the pineapple into small pieces and put in a bowl. Pour the caramel over it and toss until all the pineapple pieces are well coated. Put the pieces on a wire rack and let them cool, making sure they are all separated, or they will stick.

Preheat the oven to 475°F.

Break the dough into 20 small balls and flatten each ball to 1/2-inch thick. Spread with the concasse or tomato paste and place strips of duck on each pizza and then bits of pineapple on top. Cook for 10 minutes in the oven on an oiled baking sheet.

Other suggested pizza toppings

Pheasant lightly coated with devil sauce (a mixture of soya sauce, worcestershire sauce, dry mustard, and whipped cream) with red onion and capers

Partridge with celery strips and finely chopped walnuts

Strips of venison with thinly pared celeriac (just blanched)

Carpaccio of venison with thyme, oil, and balsamic vinegar and slivers of shallot

White-tail liver cut in very thin strips, tossed in butter with pine nuts

Salmon flakes with blue cheese and sliced gherkins

salmis of wild **duck**

This is a good dish to make if you have a mixed bag of different duck.

4 young ducks, including the livers

3 ounces unsmoked bacon, chopped (about 1/2 cup)

1 onion, chopped

1 clove, crushed

5 juniper berries, crushed

1 stalk celery, chopped

1 bay leaf

1 1/2 cups red wine

2 tablespoons butter

3 slices toast soaked in stock and squeezed dry

salt and pepper

Season the ducks and roast in a preheated oven at 425°F for 30–40 minutes, until they are browned and tender. When they are cool enough to handle, quater the ducks, and cut away the rib cages.

Transfer all the roasting juices into a pan, and add the bacon, onion, clove, juniper berries, and celery. Season with salt and pepper, then add a bay leaf and the wine. Bring to a boil and cook for about 30 minutes, or until the sauce has reduced by half.

Melt the butter and sauté the livers quickly, then put them and the toast through a food mill or into a food processor.

Strain the sauce and simmer a little longer, skimming as you go. Stir in the liver mixture and, without boiling, heat the sauce, stirring until it has a creamy consistency. Arrange the quartered ducks on a dish and pour the sauce over them.

roast **mallard** with quinces

In my village there lives an erudite Professor who despite the Scottish climate grows very good quinces. Two years ago his tree produced two hundred or so and I was the grateful recipient of a box. The fruit filled the house with their wonderful smell and I bottled some and baked some, and, as it was a year I received quite a lot of duck, I did this:

2 mallard

6 quinces (3–4 ounces each)

1/4 cup (1/2 stick) melted butter

1/2 cup white wine

salt and pepper

Preheat the oven to 350°F.

Wipe the duck with a damp cloth and season inside and out. Peel, core, and quarter the quinces and stuff them into the cavity of the ducks.

Put the ducks in a roasting pan, melt the butter, and pour it over the birds. Roast them for 10 minutes. Pour the wine over the ducks and return them to the oven to cook for 40 minutes, basting as you go.

Zap up the temperature as high as it will go. Return the ducks for a few minutes to crisp the skin.

teal with oranges

A nice little dish for a splendid little bird, not quite the Connaught but in memory of its splendid food...

2 Seville oranges

2 strips barding fat

2 teal

4 shallots, finely chopped (or 1/4 cup finely chopped mild onion)

1 tablespoon Grand Marnier or cognac

salt and pepper

Preheat the oven to 450°F.

Peel the rind from the oranges and cut the rind into thin strips. Squeeze the oranges and keep the juice.

Bard the birds and roast for about 12 minutes in an ovenproof and flameproof pan. Remove the barding fat, making several long slits along the breasts to allow the juices to flow. Season with salt and pepper, and add the shallots, the rind and the orange juice. Return to the oven for another 5–10 minutes, depending upon the size of the birds and how rare you like them.

Transfer the birds to a dish. Over the stove, heat the contents of the roasting pan and pour in a little Grand Marnier or cognac, and then ignite with a match to deglaze. Pour it over the birds.

cold duck salad with lucy's dressing

`This is a great way of using up leftover duck and is delicious as an appetizer or lunch dish. The dressing is named after my young friend Lucy Tibbitts who helped me invent it at one of her mother's lunch parties. If you can't find fava beans use peas instead.

5 ounces cooked duck meat (about 1 cup)

2 red peppers

8 ounces cooked fava beans (unless they are very young, remove the skins—the bright green is attractive with the peppers)

1/2 tablespoon French mustard

1 clove garlic, crushed

juice of 1/2 lemon

1/2 tablespoon ginger syrup

olive oil

salt and pepper

Cut the duck into enticing pieces; broil your peppers, remove and discard the skins, and slice into strips.

Make a dressing by mixing the mustard, garlic, lemon juice, salt and pepper, and ginger syrup together, trickling in the olive oil to form a smooth dressing—use a lot of muscle!

Mix the pepper strips and the fava beans together and dress with two thirds of the dressing. Arrange the duck strips on the top and pour the rest of the dressing over them. Serve with good bread.

goose

Carving

Assuming you are, like me, right handed, position the bird so that the thigh bones are facing towards you. Place the prongs of the carving fork on either side of the breast bone and, using the flat of the blade, prise open the right hand thigh. With the curved point of the carving knife, separate the thigh where it attaches the body at the hip socket. This will almost certainly be very stiff and will require a certain amount of manual twisting. The thigh and drumstick of a wild bird are sure to be tough and should either be put back in the oven and served as a second helping or set aside for deviling, or converting into confit, at a later stage. Do the same with the wing and repeat on the opposite side. Once the thighs and wings are removed, the bird is ready for carving.

Begin by making an incision down the length of one side of the dividing breast bone. Make a second incision exactly parallel to the first and $1/8$ and $1/6$ inch from it, turning the blade of the knife in towards the breast bone as it nears the bone and cutting inwards to free the slice. Lift it out and lay it on a plate. Continue taking long strips of meat in this manner until the breast bone drops down towards the thigh and wing

joints. Then turn the carcass on its side with your fork and remove the last few slices by carving towards you from the wing joint to the thigh joint. Turn the bird and repeat on the other side.

I had never eaten a pink-foot until the first programme in the *Clarissa and the Countryman* series, and I must tell you it is one of the most delicious things I have eaten; I now drive through the park in Edinburgh looking longingly at the pink-feet on the loch. Previously I had only eaten Canada goose, the young of this species is good if it has been feeding on grass, but if it has been feeding on the foreshore you need the potato trick I used for duck (see page 80), or plunge the bird into boiling water and then dry carefully. If you are lucky enough to have a pink-foot the best thing is to roast it, otherwise here follow some recipes.. If you have more than you can usefully use, cut the breasts off them.

Aging

At the beginning of the season a useful clue to age is the notch in the tail feathers where the downy juvenile plumage has fallen out and not yet been replaced. This is a V-shaped notch about a half-inch deep and wide. In a young pink-foot, the bill is a blotchy flesh color, the legs pale pink, and the head pale and brownish; the plumage on the breast and belly is speckled and looks immature. In the adult, the beak is banded pink on black, the head is dark—almost black, the breast and belly plumage is clear, and the legs are the pink that gives the bird its name. With greylags, the bill of the juvenile is pale orange, the breast and belly slightly speckled, and the legs a grayish pink. The beak of the

adult is a clear orange, the plumage is spotted on the breast, but the belly is not speckled and the legs are a darker pink. With Canadas, the cheek patches of the juveniles are grayer, turning to white in the adult bird. Size is the main indication with Canadas.

Hanging

3 weeks for Canadas and greylags, 2 weeks for pink-feet.

Plucking

Geese are difficult to pluck as the feathers are very stiff, and so you will have sore thumbs. Find a friendly butcher or bribe a nice young man. You will need to singe after plucking as the carcass is unlikely to be clean unless you are very proficient.

Roasting

Wild goose being dry, benefits from stuffing. There are many variants for stuffing, from foie gras to potatoes, but the important thing is to make sure it contains plenty of butter to keep it moist. I like to fry an onion in butter, and mix in apple, lemon rind, lemon juice, bread crumbs, salt and pepper, herbs, anchovies, pickled walnuts, and about a half-cup of butter in all, but use your imagination.

Stuff the goose, rub with butter, and roast, breast down or on a trivet. Put in at 450°F for about 10 minutes, then reduce to 325°F. Baste frequently, adding wine, orange juice, or stock if the pan juices dry out. In total it will take 1–1$1/2$ hours depending on size. Test with a skewer. Give 3–4 slices to each person. A wild goose will serve 4 people.

goose with red cabbage and treacle

The front cover of our book *Sunday Roast* shows Johnny and me looking like something from a Norman Rockwell picture but on the table in front of us is a pink-footed goose with red cabbage; it is a lovely combination.

1 goose (pink-foot or young Canada)
sugar
1 tablespoon olive oil
1 onion, chopped
3 sharp eating apples
1 good-sized red cabbage
2 tablespoons black treacle (or molasses)
1/2 cup sharp alcoholic cider
salt and pepper

Preheat the oven to 350°F.

Rub the goose fiercely with salt, pepper, and sugar.

In a heavy pan for which you have a lid, heat the oil and fry the onion until golden.

Core and roughly slice the apples, shred the cabbage, and add these to the onion. Add the treacle and cider, stir well and let it cook for 10 minutes. Place the goose on top of this, cover, and put in the oven for 45 minutes. Remove the lid and cook, uncovered, for another 25 minutes, or until the goose is cooked.

canada goose stuffed with olives and prunes

Old Canada geese are pretty horrible and not much use for anything, but young Canadas can be quite good eating. This is a dish I invented when working for Rebeka Hardy at Danehill; her husband had shot it on the Solway Firth and we were determined to eat it.

6 ounces pitted prunes (about 1 1/2 cups)
armagnac or cognac
1 young Canada goose
8 ounces pitted green olives (about 2–2 1/2 cups)
barding fat
1 onion, chopped
3 stalks celery, chopped
rind of 1 orange, cut into strips
salt and pepper

Marinate the prunes overnight in armagnac or cognac. Drain them (but keep the marinade), and stuff the olives with slices of prune, reserving some of the prunes. Stuff the cavity of the goose with the stuffed olives and leftover prunes. Season the goose and bard the breast.

Preheat the oven to 350°F.

Arrange the onion, celery, and orange peel in the bottom of a roasting dish. Put the goose on top and cook for 1 hour in the oven. Remove the fat. Take a ladle full of armagnac or cognac, add the prune brandy, set fire to it, and pour it over the goose. When it has finished burning, return the goose to the oven and roast for another 15 minutes. Strain the pan juices, reduce them a little and serve with the goose, as well as the stuffing.

roast **goose** with dumplings

This is a Hungarian recipe. I used to go every year to the Gay Hussar in Soho, London, to eat pike, wild cherry soup and roast goose, indeed it was the last meal I shared with my mother before her death. Lake Balikon is black with wildfowl during the autumn migration and much goose is consumed.

4 ounces bacon, finely chopped (about 2/3 cup)

4 ounces lard or goose fat (about 1/2 cup)

1 onion, chopped

1 parsnip, chopped

1 heel celery, chopped

1 carrot, peeled and sliced

1 clove garlic, crushed

1 goose

2 tablespoons flour

2 1/2 cups white game stock

1 teaspoon paprika

1 bay leaf

1 teaspoon marjoram

10 peppercorns

1/4 cup Hock or fruity white wine

1 teaspoon French mustard

1/2 teaspoon sugar

juice of 1 lemon

salt

For the dumplings:

1 egg

3 tablespoons lard, chicken fat, or butter

2–3 tablespoons water

12 ounces flour (about 2 1/2 cups)

salt

Preheat the oven to 500°F, or as high as it will go.

In a large flameproof roasting pan, cook the bacon gently, then add the lard and melt. Add the vegetables and garlic and cook gently for a few minutes. Put the goose on top of the vegetables and roast in the oven for 20 minutes.

Remove the goose and place the roasting pan on the stove. Sprinkle flour on the vegetables, and then add the stock and paprika. Bring to a boil and simmer for a few minutes. Carve the goose and place the pieces on top of the vegetables, and then add the herbs, peppercorns, and the wine. Cover and cook over low heat on top of the stove until the goose is cooked—about 1 hour.

Remove the goose pieces and keep warm; then push everything else through a strainer or food mill. To the purée add the mustard, sugar, lemon juice, and salt.

To make the dumplings, mix together the egg, 1 tablespoon of your chosen fat, the water, and salt. Mix in the flour. Do not work the mixture too much and let it rest for 10 minutes covered with a damp cloth. Shape into dumplings. Boil a large pan of water and add salt. When the dumplings have all risen to the surface, remove them with a slotted spoon, rinse in cold water, and drain.

Before serving, fry the dumplings in the remaining 1 tablespoon of fat and serve with the goose.

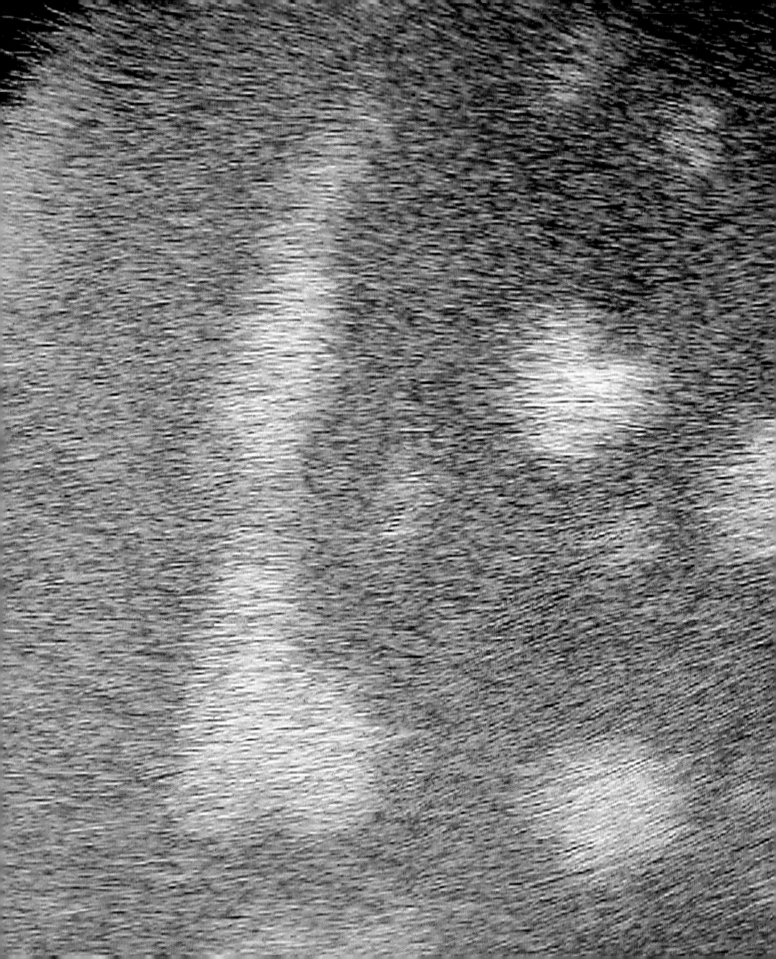

cloven hoof

cloven hoof

Since the end of the Ice Age, deer, which includes any member of the *cervidae* family, from European roe deer to Indian sambar, were the early hunter's principal quarry. Size made them an obvious target and the best return relative to effort expended. There were and still are today, an enormous number of different deer living in the wild worldwide, and more venison, the meat of any of the *cervidae*, is eaten today than all the other game species put together. To meet consumer demand, an increasing volume of venison is farmed in Europe, Scandinavia, Australia, New Zealand, Britain, and North America. The rest comes from the management of wild deer in their natural environment as part of animal welfare practices connected to acceptable stocking rates and to protect forestry and farming; it also brings wild venison into the food chain and provides an essential input to rural economies from sporting tourism.

The seventeenth century settlers would have been delighted at the variety and number of deer species they found from one end of the continent to the other. Great, lumbering prehistoric moose. Another animal, bigger than the Scottish red deer, was assumed, incorrectly, to be an elk. Elegant mule and white-tailed deer and the little, antelope-like pronghorns—all valuable sources of meat and hides. Deer were an important part of the culture of many native American tribes and the early settlers found that the Indians used similar hunting methods to those practiced in Europe at that time. Firearms were still immensely cumbersome and impractical for shooting game. A few might be wounded with a bow and hunted-up with a dog, but when meat was needed in any quantity, the only way was to employ skills that had remained unchanged for centuries across Europe, Asia, and America—getting as many people together as possible and driving whole herds of deer

towards a dead-end valley or area of boggy ground where the fleeing deer could be ambushed and slaughtered.

As rifles improved during the eighteenth and nineteenth centuries, deer were an important element of the hunting, trapping, fur, and skin economy of the period, providing valuable meat, hide, antlers, and, in the case of elk, teeth. Pressure on the deer population increased as settlers sprawled westward and numbers of deer began to drop dramatically through commercial market hunting, habitat disturbance, and being destroyed as agricultural pests. Bison are always used as an example of the terrifying ease with which a species can go from immense numbers to virtual extinction in decades, but in the late 1800s, elk, pronghorn, mule deer, and white-tails were all in danger of becoming extinct. A similar situation was occurring in Great Britain. Most of the natural forests had been cut down and the red deer, deprived of their habitat, had gradually moved into the highlands of Scotland where in the late eighteenth and early nineteenth centuries, they were systematically culled to make room for sheep. Roe deer were considered vermin and, except for a few in private parks, had been completely eliminated by the 1850s.

Since the 1900s, deer populations have risen again. This is thanks to pioneering sportsmen conservationists like Teddy Roosevelt, who could see all too clearly the depressing downward trend in wildlife species, and initiated hunting regulations and early conservation projects that have been built on by successive generations. The boreal forests of Canada provide the longest range of habitat to North America's biggest game species, moose, which can now be found from Alaska, east to Newfoundland, and south into the Rocky Mountains in the US.

Elk or more correctly, wapiti, from the Sawnee word describing their pale winter coat, were virtually wiped out by 1900. Among the first conservation projects was the introduction of 83 cows and half a dozen bulls in Cabin Draw, near Cherelon Creek in Arizona, in 1913. From this original stock, the Arizona elk population has grown to 35,000. Thanks to the continued efforts of the Elk Foundation, whose aim it is to promote the sound management of wild elk by restoring, conserving, and enhancing their natural habitats, the bellowing bugle of bull elk can be heard today in huge private ranches or on national forestry land, from coastal forests to alpine meadows, from dry desert valleys to mountain snow lines, from sub-arctic Canada to most southern states of the US, except Florida.

Elk like to lie up in cover during the day, emerging at dusk to drink and feed. They are both grazers and browsers, with a highly varied diet consisting of grass, leaves, and the shoots of young trees. The breeding season is September to late October, with the bulls bellowing and fighting to gather their harems of up to 40 cows. Fatalities sometimes occur with 900-pound bulls charging each other with their massive antlers lowered. Cows calve in May or June and calves stay with their mother until they reach sexual maturity at about 18 months. After the rut, cows and bulls separate and, during the winter, cows, calves, and yearlings herd together in numbers that may reach several hundreds, followed by their principal predators—wolves, bears, and coyotes. Wolves and bears will attack juveniles and adults. Coyotes working in packs will attack sick adults and distract a cow to take her calf.

The season for elk is staggered: in September, when elk are less wild, it begins for archery enthusiasts; in October, it starts for black-powder muzzle loaders, and in November, rifle hunting begins. Elk are usually still hunted or stalked in thin forestry or on open ground below the tree line. Licenses, issued by ballot, are generally restricted to one bull per season and special licenses for cows may be issued where localized elk numbers are becoming unmanageable.

The lovely little white-tailed deer are North America's most abundant deer species, with a distribution covering most of southern Canada, the whole of mainland US, and the northern part of South America. Before European settlement, the North American population was estimated at around 40 million and the meat was a welcome source of protein, with the hides used for bedding, clothing, and shelter for both the native tribes and early settlers. For the native American tribes, white-tails also provided sinews for bow strings, fish lines, and stitching, and their horns

and bones were used for awls, needles, hide scrapers, and ornaments. Habitat destruction through forest clearance for agricultural expansion and unrestricted hunting had reduced numbers by 1900 so much that by the late 1920s, some states banned shooting them. Game licensing and conservation benefiting all wildlife species, artificially-protected habitats in state and national parks, an increase in food source from farming, and a decrease in predators, have enabled the white-tailed deer population to build up to in excess of 20 million, about half the estimated figure for the pre-European settler numbers. Their preferred habitat is open woodland with desert species inhabiting most areas within 10 miles of water. They move with breathtaking gracefulness through trees or mesquite bushes at speeds of 40 mph. White-tails, like roe deer in Britain, are now pests in

some areas, predating into farmland, forestry, and urban gardens, even overturning trash cans to eat the contents, often dying as a result of ingesting garbage and, in particular, plastic.

Their rut occurs between October and December. Unlike elk, white-tailed stags do not defend rutting territories but will protect the immediate area around a doe until mating has been completed, before moving on to look for another. Does give birth to spotted fawns in May or June—generally to twins but occasionally to singles if she was in poor condition during the rut, and sometimes to triplets. The offspring remain hidden in dense vegetation, with their head and neck extended flat to the ground, waiting for the doe to visit them for their thrice-daily feed, until they are big enough to run with her. Fawns are independent at seven months,

with does sexually active at a year and the bucks at two. Young bucks may live in groups of two or three, becoming solitary as they get older. White-tails normally stay together in small family groups of a doe and her fawns. Occasionally they will join others in herds of several hundred and, during a heavy fall of snow, create "deer yards" by trampling a large area flat, in a communal effort to get at the herbage buried below.

The season for hunting white-tails starts in early September for archery enthusiasts, moving to black-powder muzzle loaders in October, and rifles later in the month, depending upon state game laws. In some states, with a high density of human population, rifle shooting is illegal and deer may only be taken with shotguns, firing solid slug cartridges or buckshot. White-tails are usually shot from a high seat or hide, positioned beside well-used deer paths, the edges of woodland, or arable land that they are known to frequent in the early morning or at dusk as they emerge from cover to feed or drink. Sometimes they are stalked through woodland or driven from it to waiting guns, if the state allows it. Young bucks can be drawn to a deer call or two antlers rattled together, but older bucks, being more wary and suspicious, will rarely respond.

Their close relation, the slightly larger and considerably less elegant mule deer—called after its large sensitive ears which move continuously to pick up the sound of approaching danger— have a range that covers southwestern Canada, the western half of the US, including the four desert regions, and into parts of Mexico. A sub-species, the black-tail, inhabits the extreme west of this range beside the Pacific seaboard. Mule deer have a wide variety of habitat depending upon their geographical location, ranging from alpine regions below the snow line, through prairies to deserts, preferring open arid areas to

woodland. They do not run like other deer when disturbed but take off in a series of bounding leaps when their acute sense of hearing alerts them to danger. Covering the ground at an astonishing 45 mph for short distances, their leaping enables them to see over the deep bush cover and to change direction in mid flight to outmaneuver pursuers. Mule deer have adapted to arid conditions by feeding in the cool of the day at dusk and daybreak, lying up in a shady secluded place and conserving body fluids by day. Rutting takes place between October and December, with swollen-necked bucks fighting for the does. The victor of these encounters then engages in a high speed chase with the doe before copulation takes place, staying with her for a few days before leaving to find another. Does give birth to a single fawn in their year of mating, and multiples thereafter depending upon condition. Fawns normally remain with their mother until the following rutting season.

Like all North American deer species, mule deer suffered from over-hunting and habitat destruction through agricultural over-grazing up to 1900. Continuing conservation sensitivity has ensured that the population has returned to sufficient numbers, monitored annually by game departments, to allow two million of them to be shot by licensed hunters each season. As with other deer, bow hunting starts in the fall followed by muzzle loaders. Rifle shooting or heavy-load shotgun hunting, depending upon state restriction starts in November, with the season ending in late December. Mule deer are generally shot from ground hides situated near a well-used deer path or stalked in the "open hill manner" in much the same way that red deer are in Scotland. Bag limits by quota are usually restricted to two bucks, and a special license may be obtained in some states for does.

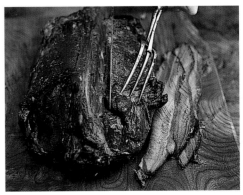

Finally, in the deer species, North America has the enchanting little pronghorn, the surviving member of an ancient family dating back over 20 million years and unique to that continent. Their range extends from mid-western Canada, south through western America, particularly the four desert regions, to Mexico, living in grassland, brush, bunch-grass, and sage brush areas of open plains and semi-deserts. Their diet includes grasses, forbs, shrubs, cacti, chamiso, and crops. They have phenomenal long distance eyesight—they are able to spot movement four miles away—and are capable of speeds of up to 60 mph if disturbed. They are able to warn other pronghorns by contracting their rump muscles so the white hair stands on end, which is visible to other pronghorns two miles away, and they exude a scent from their musk glands which can be smelled a mile away.

Pronghorn were once as numerous as bison but hunting and over-grazing the prairies so reduced numbers that by 1920, only an estimated 20,000 remained. Part of the reason for their demise was their natural curiosity. They will approach anything unusual and early hunters found that they could be drawn within rifle range simply by waving a handkerchief on a stick. Conservation and strictly controlled shooting restrictions have brought numbers back to around one million. The season opens in late August for bow hunters, later for muzzle loaders and then rifles, with the season ending earlier than for other deer. Pronghorn are stalked across open country using the folds in the ground as cover.

Carving

The method of carving venison is determined by the size of the carcass, but is basically the same as for lamb or mutton.

Saddle

Here the carver has a chance to show off. Allow yourself plenty of room as you will be carving slices from the rump, saddle, and fillet for each plate. The venison will require turning to get at the fillet and you will be working at speed. Insert the fork in the meat to the left of the backbone and run the point of the knife down the length of the backbone until it meets the hip bone. Remove the knife and cut straight down over the ribs beside the hip bone. This leaves a clear right-angled incision separating the saddle meat from the rump. Make another incision $1/6$-inch thick, parallel with the first, angling your knife towards the chine when it meets the ribs to free the meat. Lift out the slice and place it on the plate. Move the fork to the left side of the rump and insert. Carve horizontally across the rump towards the hip bone, adding the slice of rump to the plate. Now, ensuring your knife is firmly fixed beside the backbone, lever the venison over, cut a slice of fillet towards the chine, and serve.

Leg

Carve as for a large leg of lamb. Take the knuckle end wrapped in a cloth in the left hand, cut right across the joint at the meatiest part, down to the bone leveling the knife when the edge of the meat is reached on either side. Make a second incision, $1/6$-inch thick, parallel with the first making sure that the knife is angled so that the first slice is a thin wedge. Continue taking slices on either side of the original, maintaining the wedge shape until this side is completed. Turn the meat over and proceed as before.

With the little legs of antelope, position the leg so that the thickest area at the hip end is uppermost and insert fork. Cut a small wedge at the point where the meat at the knuckle end begins to widen. Angle your knife at 35° and carve slices $1/6$-inch thick until you reach the pelvic bone. Then turn the meat and carve the remainder in slices parallel to the bone.

Saddle of mule-deer or white-tail are carved depending upon their size, does are smaller than bucks. Smaller roasts are carved as lamb, larger ones like a loin of pork. Make an incision along the backbone but instead of carving parallel strips, carve slices across the saddle and over the ribs $1/6$-inch thick, angling the knife as you touch bone to free each slice. Be sure to keep the knife at an angle of 35°.

A saddle from the red deer, wapeti, or moose would be carved like a sirloin of beef, across the ribs from the chine. In this instance, keep your slices to $1/8$-inch thick, there will be no shortage of flavor. A haunch will be carved like a leg of mutton, either as a whole, or divided into a shank half leg or rump. To carve these, start at the point where the meat has been divided and carve back towards the knuckle with a shank end, and towards the pelvis for the rump, remembering always to keep a slight angle to the meat.

The first thing you must do with a deer, and quickly, is to paunch it—meat goes off very quickly or at best is tainted if the entrails are not removed. You will need a very sharp knife as deer hide is tough. Make a slit from the vent up to the thorax and handle the deer so that the paunch comes out, it is then easy to cut it free. Keep the liver and kidneys as they are delicious but, unless you are intending to make haggis or humble pie with the lights and lungs, leave the rest out on the hill, carefully buried. Your deer will need hanging in a cool larder, and if it's not fly-proof, wrap the carcass in cheesecloth and put some bog myrtle around the anus. Remove the head before hanging. Flay the deer which really only needs a sharp knife and attention to detail, and butcher it as for a sheep. I suggest you may need professional help at this stage or at least a butchery book.

west country **venison** with cider

In Britain our equivalent to moose and elk is the red deer and in the West Country (Devon and Cornwall) we hunt this beast on horseback behind hounds. At the time of writing, existing legislation maintains that the stag hunting south of the Bristol Channel is the most effective and humane way of keeping the population under control in the heavily wooded coombs and open moors of the region. Alcoholic cider is also a great product of the region so it is an obvious meld.

2–3 pounds venison
2¹/₂ cups alcoholic cider
¹/₃ cup flour
¹/₄ cup (¹/₂ stick) melted butter
¹/₂ teaspoon ground allspice
a bunch of mixed herbs
2 onions, finely chopped
4 ounces carrots, finely chopped (about ³/₄–1 cup)
¹/₃ cup venison stock
salt and pepper

Marinate the venison for 8 hours in the cider, turning it from time to time. Remove, dry, and sprinkle with flour, salt, and pepper. Reserve the cider.

Preheat the oven to 350°F.

On the stove, brown the venison in the butter, sprinkle with allspice, and add the herbs and vegetables. Pour the cider and the stock over it. Cover tightly and cook in the oven for 2 hours.

Traditionally this dish is served with watercress, I wilt mine in a little melted butter, and season it with salt and pepper, and serve as a vegetable.

texas **hash**

Again hash is a good way of using up ground venison, of which there always seems to be a lot of from the forequarter. You can, if you prefer, chop it very finely rather than grind it which I feel gives a nicer texture, but hey, what the hell! Life's too short.

1 pound ground venison (about 2 cups)
3 tablespoons oil or bacon fat
3 large onions, chopped
1 pound cooked tomatoes—canned will do (about 2 cups)
2 jalepeño chiles, chopped
1 teaspoon chili powder
2 medium potatoes, thinly sliced
6 ounces Monterrey or cheddar cheese, grated (about 1¹/₂ cups)
salt and pepper

Preheat the oven to 350°F.

Brown the meat in the oil or fat. Add the onions and cook until they are soft. Stir in the tomatoes, chiles, chili powder, and the salt and pepper and cook for about 5 minutes longer. Spread into a flat oven dish, layer the sliced potatoes on top and sprinkle with the grated cheese.

Cover with a lid or foil and bake for 45 minutes. Remove the cover and cook for another 15 minutes or until nicely browned.

venison with wild mushroom stew

This is a central European recipe; I can't remember whether it came from a Polish or a Hungarian friend, but it is jolly good. Use a mixture of wild mushrooms—whatever is growing. If you have none, use field mushrooms but the colour may suffer!

1 pound venison
14 ounces leanish pork
olive oil
5 ounces Polish boiling sausage, roughly sliced (about 1 cup)
2 large onions
2 cloves garlic
3/4 teaspoon paprika
14 ounces sauerkraut (about 1 3/4 cups)
8 ounces dried mushrooms (about 5–5 1/2 cups)
20 ounces fresh mushrooms (about 6–7 cups)
1 cup game stock
1 cup white wine
3/4 teaspoon caraway seeds
bouquet garni of marjoram and thyme
2 1/2 cups light cream
salt and pepper

Cube the meats and brown them in olive oil. Transfer with the sausage to a large heavy pan for which you have a lid.

In another pan, chop the onions and garlic and sauté until golden. Mix in the paprika and add it all to the meat. Add all the remaining ingredients, except the cream. Bring to a boil, stir in the cream, cover, and simmer for 1 hour. Check the seasoning (add more salt and pepper if necessary) and serve with flat noodles or mashed potatoes and greens.

venison with beets

The brilliant food writer Claire Macdonald (the wife of Godfrey, the Lord of the Isles) discovered there is an enzyme in beets that breaks down the fibers in venison. When I was staying at Kinloch Lodge, the blissful hotel on Skye in Scotland, she told me it would tenderize even the toughest old stag.

2 pounds venison, cut in cubes
seasoned flour
oil
2 strong onions, chopped
10 juniper berries, crushed
3 medium beets, chopped
1 tablespoon red currant jelly
1 1/4 cups burgundy or other strong red wine
2/3 cup game stock
3 sprigs of thyme (dried will do)

Preheat the oven to 325ºF.

Toss the venison chunks in the seasoned flour, heat some oil, and brown the meat in the oil. Transfer it to a heavy flameproof pan for which you have a lid. Fry the onions in the first pan and then add to the venison.

Add all the other ingredients to the venison. Bring to a boil, cover, and put in a slow oven for 2 hours, or until the venison is tender. Serve with mashed potatoes or colcannon (mashed potatoes mixed with buttered greens).

red wine **venison** burgers

Burgers are a good way of using up surplus rare venison; here the red wine in the burger gives a nice rich flavor. You can make a lot at once and freeze them for barbecues.

1 pound venison
6 ounces bacon
1/3 cup dry red wine
2 tablespoons finely chopped shallot (or mild onion)
olive oil
2 tablespoons parsley, finely chopped
1 tablespoon red currant jelly
salt and pepper

Put the meat and bacon through the grinder together, or chop in a food processor. Add half the red wine and the shallot to the meats, mix well, and season with salt and pepper.

Form into 4 burgers, pressing hard so they are tightly formed, and rest in a cool place for at least 30 minutes. Heat a little oil in a frying pan and fry the burgers—don't turn until they are browned on the first side. Cook for about 5 minutes each side, more if you like them well done. Remove the burgers and keep them warm. Pour off any surplus fat.

Pour the rest of the wine into the pan, raise the heat, and stir in the red currant jelly. Cook until the sauce is hot and the jelly melted. Add the parsley, pour the sauce over the burgers, and serve.

venison liver with puréed peas

This is a very simple way of serving venison liver, but slightly different. I think it works rather well.

1 pound, 10 ounces peas, fresh, frozen, or canned
3 tablespoons light cream
1 1/2 pounds liver
1/2 cup seasoned flour: salt, pepper, dried mustard,
  and a little cayenne pepper
butter
salt and pepper

Cook the peas and purée them until they are almost smooth. Add the cream and season with salt and pepper.

Slice the liver finely, and toss in seasoned flour. Heat a little butter in a heavy pan and quickly sauté the liver so that it is still pink.

Put the peas on a dish, lay the liver slices on top, and pour the pan juices over them.

venison pastie

This is what Robin Hood took on his picnics! I love pasties and indeed, when I am making mine, I usually don't cook the venison first. However I am the first to admit that this is chewy and, in the interests of harmony, I am offering you the more conventional method. Add anything to your pasties that amuses you but do use lard in the pastry dough—I can't understand people who will happily eat bacon but gasp in horror at the thought of lard.

For the pastry dough:

8 ounces all-purpose flour (about 1²/₃ cups)
¹/₄ cup (¹/₂ stick) butter
¹/₄ cup lard
4 teaspoons cold water
pinch of salt

Sift the flour and salt into a bowl. Cut the butter and lard into small pieces and rub them into the flour using your hands until the mixture resembles bread crumbs. Add enough water to make pliable dough. Knead lightly, form into a ball, and wrap in a damp cloth; chill for 30 minutes.

For the filling:

1 pound venison, cut from haunch or saddle
2 medium onions, chopped
¹/₂ cup red wine
²/₃ cup stock
bouquet garni of thyme, parsley, and a bay leaf
2 tablespoons red currant jelly
cornstarch
a sliver of apple or a few red currants
1 egg yolk, mixed with a little milk
salt and pepper

Cut the venison in small pieces, and put in a saucepan with the onion, wine, stock, salt and pepper, bouquet garni, and jelly. Bring to a boil and simmer until the meat is tender—about 40 minutes. Strain the liquid, then boil it hard to reduce to about 1 cup. Thicken with a little cornstarch mixed in cold water and reserve.

Roll out the dough and cut into 4 circles, about 4 to 7 inches each. Put the meat mixture onto one half of the dough circles, and add a sliver of apple or a few red currants to each one. Dampen the pastry dough edges, fold over, and crimp firmly together.

Preheat the oven to 400°F. Place on a greased baking sheet and brush with a little egg. Make a slit in the top of each pastie, and bake for about 30 minutes.

Reheat the sauce, and pour a little into each pastie through a funnel. Serve hot or cold.

norwegian **venison** with sour cream

I was served this dish by a Norwegian friend I had at the time called Ninni; it struck me as quite delicious. Since then I have seen a similar Russian recipe for hare done in much the same way which I expect would be rather good. In Norway the dish would be made with elk or moose but I make it with venison. The Scandinavians use a white malt vinegar, but I use wine vinegar. I have to confess that I stir the cream in at the beginning—it doesn't look so appealing—but you have to reduce the sauce at the end in any event. I leave it to you, gentle reader.

For the marinade:

1 cup wine vinegar

2 cups water

4 pounds venison, chopped into 2-inch cubes

seasoned flour

2 carrots, sliced

2 Hamburg parsley root, sliced (or use celery)

2 onions, sliced

3 tablespoons butter

2 1/2 cups strong ale

2 cups sour cream

1 tablespoon fresh dill, chopped

Marinate the meat for at least 2 hours. Drain the meat, dry it, and dust it with seasoned flour.

Preheat the oven to 350ºF. Put the meat in a casserole dish with all the vegetables. Melt the butter and pour it over the meat and vegetables. Then pour in the ale. Cook, covered, for about 1 hour. Strain the roasting juices into a clean pan and reduce by half over a high heat. Mix in the sour cream, pour it over the meat, and cook for another 1 hour. Sprinkle with dill and serve.

venison hotpot

Hotpot was designed for the long bones of the Lancastrian sheep which acted as a frame to hold in the other ingredients. Sheep breeds have changed so much that you can't really often find that effect with mutton, but venison chops do very well instead. As far as I know, no one nowadays makes black pudding (blood sausage) with deer's blood but in Orkney and the Isle of Harris (Scotland) they make theirs with sheep's blood. It is quite delicious and really suited to this venison dish but any good black pudding will do. Stewart Higginson at Grange-over-Sands makes a wonderful one which I stock up with when I am visiting lovely Holker Hall.

8 venison chops, with bone shortened

4 venison kidneys (use lamb's if none available)

2 pounds potatoes, sliced

4 slices black pudding (blood sausage)

2 onions, sliced

1 1/4 cups stock

2 tablespoons oil or butter

salt and pepper

Preheat the oven to 350ºF. Trim any fat from the chops. Heat a little oil in a pan and brown the chops and the kidneys over a high heat for 3–4 minutes.

Put a layer of potatoes in a deep ovenproof dish, lay some of the chops over the top, then a layer of kidneys and then a layer of onions. Continue with a layer of potatoes, then black pudding, and so on, seasoning each layer with salt and pepper. Add the stock. Finish with a layer of potatoes, and brush the top with oil or dot with butter. Cover and cook for 2 hours. Remove the lid, increase the heat, and cook for another 30 minutes to brown.

white-tail **deer** with red onion

White-tailed deer fillet (tenderloin), like all deer meat, should be eaten on the rare side unless it is stewed. Like squid it should be cooked a little or a lot but medium cooking doesn't suit. Do not cook your fillet to anything beyond medium rare or it will be like boot leather.

For the marmalade:

3 red onions

1/4 cup (1/2 stick) butter

5 tablespoons treacle (or molasses)

2 tablespoons red wine vinegar

Slice the onions and lightly sauté them in melted butter. Add the treacle and the vinegar and simmer for 40 minutes. Adjust the sweet and sour balance to your personal taste.

1 medium leek

1 white-tailed deer fillet (tenderloin)

salt and pepper

caul fat or fatty bacon

Preheat the oven to 350°F.

Cut the leek in half lengthwise, rinse, and simmer in a little boiling salted water until flexible.

Seal the fillet on a hot pan, and season with salt and pepper. Wrap in leek leaves and bind with caul fat or fatty bacon.

Roast the fillet for 15–20 minutes. Let it rest for 10 minutes and serve with marmalade.

white-tail **deer** with fresh pear chutney

I was recently a witness at the wedding of my friends Michael and Neillia Graham-Stewart and I pointed out to Michael that, now that he was a married man, he should give up his vegetarian ways. He admitted he couldn't even remember why he had become a "veggie" and so I offered to cook him anything his heart desired. He chose fillet of roe deer (like white-tailed deer) and had three helpings so they should now live happily ever after!

For the chutney:

2 pears

1 small chile

1 clove garlic

1 small piece ginger

1 cinnamon stick

pinch of ground cloves

1/4 cup sugar

2 tablespoons apple cider vinegar

Peel, core, and chop the pears roughly. Put all the ingredients together in a small pan and cook gently, stirring until the sugar has dissolved: simmer until the pears are soft. This takes about 15 minutes.

1 teaspoon thyme

1 bay leaf

2 pounds white-tailed deer fillet (tenderloin) or boned leg

salt and pepper

Preheat the oven to 350°F. Roll and tie the meat, if needed. Mix the herbs and pepper together and rub them into the meat. Heat the oil and brown the meat to seal on all sides. Season with salt and roast for 15–20 minutes. Serve with the chutney, and potato and white bean cakes (see page 115).

white-tail **deer** fillet benedict

This is a very handy supper dish or for the more robust breakfast. The Benedict who invented this was Benedict Astor who, descending to the dining room of the Waldorf Astoria in New York with a crushing hangover, invented his breakfast. It does adapt very well to roe deer.

For the Hollandaise sauce:

3 egg yolks

1 tablespoon cold water

1 cup (2 sticks) unsalted butter, cut in small cubes

1 tablespoon lemon juice

salt and pepper

1 poached egg per muffin

1 thin slice white-tailed deer fillet (tenderloin) per muffin

1 English muffin or 2 crumpets per person

1 or 2 scallions per muffin

salt and pepper

In the top pan of a double boiler over boiling water, put the yolks, water, salt and pepper, and beat until the yolks are smooth. Whisk a handful of butter cubes into the yolks, beat until the butter is absorbed, and keep going until all the butter is used and the sauce begins to thicken. Stir in the lemon juice.

You can also do it in a microwave: melt the butter and keep in a measuring cup. Put the egg yolks in a bowl with the water and beat until smooth. Pour in the butter, beating as you go. Put the bowl in the microwave at power 5 (medium) and run for 3 seconds, remove, and stir vigorously. Return for another 5 seconds and repeat. Once the required thickness is reached, add a few drops of cold water to stop it cooking.

Poach the eggs and drain them well.

Heat a little butter in a frying pan and flash-fry the deer slices, seasoning with salt and pepper as you turn.

Toast the muffins or crumpets and lay some slices of scallions on the muffins, and lay one slice of meat on top of each. Put a poached egg on top, and pour the Hollandaise sauce over them.

german roast **venison** with brussels sprouts and walnuts

For the marinade:

1 cup robust red wine

2 onions, sliced thickly

2 carrots, sliced

4 sprigs of thyme

2 bay leaves

10 peppercorns

4 whole cloves

2 tablespoons flour

1 haunch white-tailed deer

7 strips of salt pork or fatty bacon

2 tablespoons olive oil

1 pound Brussels sprouts (about 3^1/$_2$–4 cups)

3 ounces chopped walnuts (about ^{3}/$_4$ cup)

^{3}/$_4$ cup (1^1/$_2$ sticks) butter

Mix the marinade ingredients together, put in the haunch, and marinate for 24 hours, turning from time to time. Remove the venison and pat dry; strain and reserve the marinade liquor.

Preheat the oven to 450°F. Place the venison in a roasting pan and cover it with strips of pork or bacon and the oil. Roast for 25 minutes, reduce the temperature to 325°F and roast, allowing 15 minutes per pound in total. Remove to a dish and keep warm.

In a clean pan, combine the roasting juices and the remainder of the marinade, bring to a boil, and reduce by one third.

Cook the Brussels sprouts and the chopped walnuts together in butter until the sprouts are tender, and then blend them together in a blender. Carve the meat, arrange slices on a plate alongside some of the puréed sprouts, and ladle the sauce over them.

bollocks to **blair**

In America you think kindly of **Mr Blair** because he brought Britain to your aid in the war in Iraq. In Britain he is the enemy that the hunting, shooting, and fishing communities have fought relentlessly to defeat his efforts to ban and proscribe our sport. Johnny and I have traveled many miles and signed thousands of books at Game Fairs, Hunt Supporters' Suppers, Wildfowling Dinners, *et al*. Ninety-nine times in a hundred Johnny has inscribed below his name the phrase "bollocks to Blair," a sentiment heartily echoed by the sporting and farming types at these events, and indeed by very many city-dwellers as well. I feel my dear friend deserves a delicious recipe for giving such a morale boost to so many, so here is a recipe for him. I have turned down several invitations to cook at Downing Street for Mr. Blair; I hope one day I may cook this in their kitchens to celebrate his departure. Sweetbreads are also good cooked this way.

^{1}/$_3$ cup (^{3}/$_4$ stick) butter

6 roe deer testicles, split in half

1 cup game stock

^{1}/$_3$ cup heavy cream

2 tablespoons green peppercorns

1 teaspoon cayenne pepper

salt

Heat the butter in a sauté pan and fry the testicles, turning them as you go, until they are lightly colored. Remove from the heat and salt lightly. In a separate pan, heat the stock and bring to a boil. Add the cream and green peppercorns, and cook over a good flame for 10 minutes, stirring as you go. Pour the sauce over the testicles, and return to the sauté pan and simmer for 7–8 minutes. Add the cayenne and check the seasoning. Serve with rice or with toast made from good country bread.

flank of **moose** stuffed and rolled

The Swedes eat a large quantity of game, and they cull 100,000 elk (moose) each year, all of which are consumed within the country. Flank steaks are a neglected cut from most beasts and they taste very good; it is a cut I tend to use for Stroganoff recipes. Here is a simple but yummy way of preparing flank. Serve with whatever roast vegetables you wish, I have used parsnips and baby turnips.

2-pound flank in a piece
4 ounces fresh oyster mushrooms
2 tablespoons butter
3 tablespoons tapenade (black olive paste)
6 anchovy fillets
butter

Preheat the oven to 400°F.

Start slicing the elk through the center, and two thirds of the way through, open out and flatten to 1½ inches thick.

Cut the mushrooms into strips and sauté them in the butter until they are just soft. Spread the meat with tapenade and arrange strips of mushroom and anchovy on one half. Fold the meat closed and tie tightly with string. Rub the venison well with butter and roast for 40 minutes.

Remove from the oven and rest for 10 minutes.

potato and white bean cakes

This dish came about because I tried a Croatian recipe for bean and potato mash, which, to put it politely, wasn't very nice; not wanting to throw away the result I decided to make cakes of it and was pleased with the result. Once the cakes are made, you can freeze them and take them out to fry. They do best in lard or pork fat but if you eschew this, use oil. Let them be well done before you turn them.

4 ounces dried white beans (about ½ cup)
8 sprigs of sage
2 pounds potatoes (about 6–8 medium)
2 tablespoons olive oil
1 medium onion, finely chopped
½ cup pork fat or lard
1 teaspoon salt
black pepper

Put the beans and sage into cold, salted water and simmer for 1–1½ hours or until the beans are tender, and then drain.

Put the potatoes, unpeeled, into cold, salted water and cook until they are done—about 20 minutes; drain and peel. Mash the beans and potatoes together and mix in the onion; add salt and pepper to taste.

Form into small flat cakes. Heat the lard and fry the cakes on both sides until golden.

wapeti ciste

The word *ciste* is the Welsh for coffyn, the original term for meat cooked in a pastry case or, as we call it, a pie.

8 venison chops

1/4 cup (1/2 stick) butter

4 deer kidneys (use lamb kidneys if unavailable), sliced

1 onion, sliced

4 ounces carrots, sliced (about 1 cup)

1 teaspoon parsley, chopped

1/2 teaspoon fresh thyme, chopped

1 bay leaf

3 cups game stock

8 ounces pie dough

salt and pepper

Trim the chops, stripping the end bones free of fat and gristle. Heat the butter and brown the chops and the sliced kidneys. Add the onion and carrots.

In a medium saucepan, arrange the chops vertically, going around the inside of the pan with the bone ends sticking up. Place the kidneys and vegetables in the center, season with the parsley, thyme, bay leaf, salt, and pepper, and add enough stock to just cover the vegetables.

Cook, covered, for 30 minutes, then taste and add more salt and pepper if necessary. Roll out the pastry dough to fit the saucepan, press down over the top of the stew so that the bones protrude though the pastry dough. Cover tightly, leaving space for the ciste to rise, and simmer for 1 hour.

venison chili with lemon, beans, and a tomato sauce

There was a time in my life, whilst I was cooking at Wildes club, when I made chili 5 days a week for several years. I made a lot of changes and found venison makes a good substitute for beef. The lemon juice adds a certain *je ne sais quoi*, as does the beer.

juice of 1 lemon

2 pounds ground minced venison (about 4 cups)

olive oil

2 onions, chopped

2 cloves garlic, finely chopped

1/2 teaspoon thyme

2 x 14 1/2-ounce cans of chopped tomatoes

15-ounce can of kidney beans

1 bottle of beer (ale—not lager) or stout

2 tablespoons chili powder

1 tablespoon sweet chili sauce (or use ordinary chili sauce or Tabasco sauce with a little added sugar)

salt and pepper

Pour the lemon juice over the ground meat, mix in and let it stand for 30 minutes. Heat the oil and fry the onions and garlic; add the marinated venison and brown well. Season. Add all the other ingredients, stir well, cover and cook slowly for 4 hours. Add more beer if it becomes too dry.

wapeti loin with spiced blood oranges

This is a dish I invented at Natwich Food Festival where I came across spiced blood oranges made by a farmer's wife whose company is called Cahoon. They are such a wonderful invention and go very well with duck and all types of deer, as well as making a delicious pudding with meringues.

For spiced oranges:

10 oranges

2¹/2 cups white wine vinegar

2¹/2 pounds sugar (about 5³/4–6 cups)

1¹/2 cinnamon sticks

2 ounces whole cloves (about ²/3 cup)

Slice the oranges and put them in a pan, barely cover with water, and simmer, partly covered, until the peel is tender.

Slowly cook the vinegar, sugar, cinnamon sticks, and cloves together in a pan until the sugar has dissolved and then boil for 5 minutes to create a syrup.

Drain the oranges and reserve the cooking liquor. In a pan, lay half the oranges in enough syrup to cover them and simmer for 30–40 minutes until the oranges look clear. Add the remaining oranges, and if they are not covered, add some of the reserved liquor. Cook as before, cover with syrup, and let stand overnight. If there is not enough syrup, boil up some more. If the syrup is too thin, pour it into a pan, reboil, and then return it to the oranges.

Put in jars and leave for eight weeks before using.

2 tablespoons butter

1 pound wapeti loin

1 shallot, chopped (if unavailable, use 1 tablespoon chopped mild onion)

2 tablespoons spiced oranges, with their juice

¹/2 cup red wine

salt and pepper

Melt the butter in a heavy sauté pan or frying pan and seal the loin properly all the way around. Season with salt and pepper and set aside. Fry the shallot in the butter until soft, then stir in the oranges. Return the meat to the pan and pour the wine over it. Keep the heat fairly high and cook, turning the meat frequently, for 10 minutes. Add more wine if necessary.

Remove the pan from the heat and the meat from the pan; slice the meat and if it is too rare, return the slices to the pan to cook a little more—the meat should be rare. Arrange on a dish and pour the oranges and pan juices over it. Serve with potatoes and strong-tasting greens.

saddle of **wapeti** with anchovies

Saddle of wapeti is a splendid cut for a dinner party as it looks most impressive. Meat larded with anchovies as a form of adding salt also brings a depth of flavor and has no fishy taste.

1 saddle venison
2 x 2-ounce cans of anchovy fillets
2 ounces lard or pork fat for barding (about $^1/_4$ cup)
lard or olive oil for frying
3 onions, sliced
$1^1/_4$ cups red wine
salt and pepper

Preheat the oven to 425°F.

With a very sharp pointed knife, make insertions all over the meat, and into each, put an anchovy fillet. Season with pepper. Cover the meat with barding fat and secure it well.

In a heavy flameproof and ovenproof pan, melt the lard, and fry the onions until colored. Place the meat on top of the onions, add salt to taste and pour the wine over it.

Roast for 15 minutes to seal the meat, and then reduce the heat to 325°F, allowing 15 minutes per pound.

Serves 6–8.

wapeti glazed and stuffed from cremona

1 pound strips of venison flank

For the marinade:
$^1/_2$ cup olive oil
$^1/_2$ cup red wine
ground black pepper

For the stuffing:
2 tablespoons butter
2 shallots, finely chopped (if unavailable, use 2 tablespoons
    chopped mild onion)
2 ounces black olives, pitted and chopped (about $^1/_2$ cup)
1 tablespoon chopped fruit from the cremona mustard
2 tablespoons bread crumbs
1 egg

For the glaze:
2 tablespoons syrup from Cremona mustard mixed with
    1 teaspoon dried mustard powder or flour

Mix the marinade ingredients and marinate the venison for 2–3 hours, turning occasionally. Remove from the marinade and pat dry. Reserve the marinade.

Preheat the oven to 350°F. Melt the butter and fry the stuffing ingredients together, breaking in the egg to bind, and mix well. Flatten out your venison making a slit in the meat if necessary to flatten it. Spread the stuffing on the meat and roll up like a jelly roll. Tie with string at various points to secure.

Place in a covered casserole dish, pour in the marinade, and roast in the oven for 45 minutes. Remove and transfer to a roasting pan and paint the meat with the glaze, return to the oven for another 10–15 minutes continuing to baste with the syrup.

moose carpaccio with cheese and lingonberry compôte

antelope stewed with black currants

This is a Swedish recipe designed for moose. You can buy lingonberries in IKEA if you are lucky enough to have one, or use cranberries or red currants. The cheese in this recipe was originally hard cheese spiked with aquavit, but in its absence, use Romano. If you like, soak the cheese in a little brandy, then let it dry before slicing it with a potato peeler.

10-ounce strip of loin or tenderloin of moose
olive oil
1/2 red onion, shredded
1/4 cup lingonberries
1 tablespoon honey
sprig of fresh thyme
4 ounces Romano, slivered
fleur de sel (or sea salt)—if unavailable, use kosher salt
ground pepper

Freeze the meat. Defrost slightly and slice as thinly as possible. Let it thaw, arrange it on plates and brush with olive oil, and sprinkle with the salt and ground pepper.

Gently simmer the onions with the berries and the honey for 5 minutes. Season to taste with salt and pepper and freshly chopped thyme. Cool, divide between each plate, and add the slivered cheese.

The antelope, the most beautiful and graceful of the deer family, is quite small in size and does not yield the larger cuts of other deer species. It is, however, a sweet and delicious meat, and I offer this, and the following recipes, for your delectation.

2 pounds boneless antelope
flour seasoned with salt and pepper
olive oil
1 3/4 cups game stock
1/2 pound black currants, destalked (about 2 1/2 cups)
12 shallots, peeled
1 teaspoon thyme
1 bay leaf
salt and pepper

Cut the meat into chunks and roll it in the seasoned flour. Heat a little oil and brown the meat.

In a heavy pan, bring the stock to a boil and add the black currants. Return to a boil and add the meat, a few pieces at a time so the liquid stays at a boil. Add salt and pepper, the whole shallots, thyme, and bay leaf, and simmer for 45 minutes.

antelope meatloaf

Meatloaf is a great invention; you can serve it hot with potatoes or mashed rutabagas or carrots, or cold with a salad.

1 1/2 pounds ground antelope (about 3 cups)
12 ounces crackers, crushed (about 2–2 1/2 cups)
1 onion, chopped
4 ounces olives, pitted and sliced (about 1 cup)
2 eggs, lightly beaten
2 tablespoons horseradish
2/3 cup tomato juice
1 tablespoon dry sherry
salt and pepper

Preheat the oven to 375°F.

Mix all the ingredients well in a bowl. Grease a 9 x 5-inch loaf pan and press the mixture well into it. Bake for I hour.

Turn out onto a warm dish and serve.

sage cobbler

A cobbler is a dish I am very fond of. It is mostly found in America where it has survived modernization.

2 pounds boned antelope
3 1/2 tablespoons self-rising flour seasoned with salt and pepper
  (or use all-purpose flour with a pinch of baking powder)
2 tablespoons oil
3 onions, thinly sliced
2 ounces dried peas, soaked overnight and drained (about 1/3 cup)
2 1/2 cups game stock
salt and pepper

For the scone topping:
1 2/3 cups all-purpose flour
1 1/2 teaspoons baking powder
1/2 teaspoon dried sage (or 1 teaspoon fresh, chopped)
1/4 cup (1/2 stick) butter
1 egg, lightly beaten
2 tablespoons milk

Preheat the oven to 225°F. Cut the meat into 1-inch cubes and dust with seasoned flour. Heat the oil and fry the onions until golden, and then add the soaked peas. Add the meat, brown it and then transfer everything to a 1 1/2–2-quart casserole dish. Season to taste with salt and pepper, and add the stock. Cover and cook for 2 hours.

To make the scone topping, sift the flour into a bowl, add the baking powder, a pinch of salt, and the sage. Rub in the butter. Mix to a soft dough by adding egg and as much milk as necessary. Knead and roll out to 1/2-inch thick. Cut into 8 circles. Arrange these on top of the casserole and brush with milk. Zap the oven up to 425°F and bake for 20–30 minutes until the scone dough is risen and golden brown.

persian **meatballs**

venison sausages

I used to have a cigarette case exquisitely enameled with Persian riders pursuing a deer across an open plain. I have long since drunk it away but the image remains. If you don't have access to sumac or white mulberries, use dried cherries, or at a pinch, raisins soaked in a little lemon juice. For antelope, use leg meat and roast the saddle, but for other deer meat, use whatever you have. I have used beef fat in deference to Persia's Muslim state, but bacon fat will do.

1¼ teaspoons cumin seeds (roasted in a hot pan until they pop)

1½ pounds antelope

¼ cup beef fat

2 onions, finely chopped

2 teaspoons dried mulberries or sumac berries, chopped

2½ cups game stock

dash of red wine vinegar

1 tablespoon olive oil

2 cloves garlic

1¼ pounds cooked chickpeas (about 4 cups)

3 pounds spinach

salt and pepper

In a food processor, mix the meat, fat, onion, salt and pepper, cumin seeds, and half the berries together. Grind until they are all blended, but not too smooth, then make into small balls. Sprinkle a teaspoon of salt into a heavy pan, put in the meatballs, and cook for 5 minutes until they are brown all over. Add the stock and a dash of red wine vinegar and cook for another 15 minutes at a gentle simmer. In another pan, heat a little oil and cook the garlic cloves until they start to brown, then discard them. Stir the chickpeas into the oil along with the remaining berries, and put the spinach on top. Season well with salt and pepper, and add a little stock. Cover and cook for about 5 minutes or until the spinach has wilted. Drain the spinach and chickpeas, lay them on a dish, and place the meatballs on top.

Natural sausage casings are the best. You will need to soak your casings in warm water (about 90°F) for an hour or two to remove excess salt and soften them. This has the added benefit of stopping them bursting when cooking or smoking them, and also allows them to stretch better to take more filling. A 4-foot length of sheep casing makes 1½ pounds sausages, the same amount of pork casing, which is wider and more elastic, makes 2½ pounds sausages. Venison is a very dry meat so it is necessary to add fat, pork fat or beef suet being the most favored.

Machines: if you have a Kenwood food mixer or some such, you can buy a sausage filling attachment. I have a hand pump rather like an outsize syringe which Johnny gave me, or you can simply stuff by hand using the handle of a wooden spoon. When I was a child, we used to kill our own pigs and spent forever making sausages. One useful tip is if you are butchering your own beast, freeze the meat you have earmarked for sausages and make them at a more serene time. If you wish, you can sort out the intestine and wash them through for sausage casings, but having done this for years when young, I tend to buy my casings nowadays.

You can make sausages with any game and make changes to your heart's content—rabbit and pear goes well—adding fruit allows you to reduce the fat input, as does mushrooms; add half the quantity of fruit or mushrooms to that of meat. Flavorings or spices are yours to choose. You can even make fish ballotines. Grind the meat and the fat together to save mixing it later. However, remember that uncooked sausages don't have a long shelf life so open-freeze them on a tray at once so they're not touching, and then put in a bag, or you won't be able to take out just a few as needed.

Have fun and let me know your successes if and when we meet!

Basic Recipe:

2 pounds ground venison (about 4 cups)

1 pound ground pork fat or beef suet (about 2 cups)

*2 teaspoons of the herb or spice of your choice, finely ground
(try half thyme-half bay leaf for starters)*

2 teaspoons salt

1 teaspoon black pepper

Chill the venison and fat and then grind together; mix in your herbs or spices and seasonings. Fry a small piece of the mixture and taste it—if necessary adjust the flavorings. Stuff it into the casings and cook or freeze them.

4 pounds caribou from the shoulder, haunch, or brisket

*1/3 cup seasoned flour, made with English mustard powder,
cayenne pepper, salt, and pepper*

1/4 cup beef drippings

3 carrots, chopped

2 onions, chopped

1/2 small jar red currant jelly

4 whole cloves

1 stick cinnamon

2 1/2 cups milk

2 1/2 cups game stock

Rub the meat with the seasoned flour. Melt the drippings in a heavy ovenproof pan for which there is a lid, add the meat, and brown it slowly. Remove the meat, and fry the onions and carrots in the fat.

Add about 2 tablespoons of water, along with the browned meat, red currant jelly, cloves, and cinnamon. Cover, and simmer very slowly, either in a slow oven (325°F) or on top, turning from time to time and adding a little water. It will take about 3 hours. Remove the meat to a warmed serving dish in a very low oven to rest.

Make the pan gravy with half milk, half stock and serve with dumplings (see page 126) and boiled vegetables.

caribou as sauerbraten

The thought of caribou always sets me off reciting the poems of Robert Service. It is a delicious meat. Recently someone tried raising it in Scotland but, in a land with so much venison, I think the venture failed. You must be careful when cooking it as it can go stringy quite easily but it lends itself beautifully to braising and pot roasting.

3 pounds caribou, round or rump

1¹/₄ cups strong game stock

6 peppercorns, crushed

6 juniper berries, crushed

dry English mustard powder

¹/₂ tablespoon dried thyme

1 bay leaf

¹/₂ cup red wine vinegar

3 tablespoons butter

1 onion, sliced

3 tablespoons flour

175g (6oz) tomato paste

1 tablespoon Madeira or medium dry sherry

Put the meat in an enamel, earthenware or other heavy casserole dish with a tight fitting lid. Mix the stock, seasonings, and vinegar and pour them over the meat. Leave in a cool place for 3 days, turning daily. On the fourth day, remove the meat and reserve the liquor.

In a heavy pan, melt the butter and fry the onion, then add the meat and brown it all over. Remove the meat and stir in the flour. Add the marinade liquor and stir until it has thickened. Put the meat in the gravy and season with salt. Simmer, covered, for 3 hours, or until tender. Remove the meat and carve. Mix the Madeira and tomato purée into the pan juices and serve with the potato dumplings.

For the dumplings:

¹/₂ pound mashed potatoes (about 1 cup)

1²/₃ cups flour

1 teaspoon baking powder

1 teaspoon salt

1 onion, finely chopped

1 tablespoon hard cheese, grated

1 tablespoon melted butter

3 egg yolks, beaten

Mix all the ingredients together well. Shape into 16 balls. Drop into boiling salted water, cover, and cook for 12 minutes.

wild boar

The gamey, close-grained meat of these notoriously savage and unpredictable creatures has been prized for centuries across the whole of Europe, Scandanavia, and southern Russia. Domestic pigs turn feral very quickly and the bush country of Australia and New Zealand have large populations of those that escaped from the early settlers. Introduced in 1893 to North America, and again to several estates in the South during the 1920s, wild boar escaped and cross-bred with wild domestic pigs. There is now an abundance of this sort of feral beast which provides excellent pork and a testing hunting experience across many southern states. Pig hunting in Alabama is so popular that it has become practically a religion.

A roast of wild boar will be much smaller than domestic pork and should be carved like wapeti venison, the leg in the same way as mutton, and the saddle or loin from the chine over the ribs.

My friend Peter Gott raises 120 wild boar at a time in his woods in Cumbria so I have had access to quite a lot of this meat. When buying boar, make sure it is purebred as some of the crosses have a very coarse flavor. Boar is not counted as game in Britain as it had died out by the time the Victorian game laws were drawn up and therefore has to be taken to the slaughter house! In Continental Europe, it is both hunted and shot. It is a very dangerous beast indeed and its death is treated with respect and pageantry. I remember being in a friend's garden in Tuscany and seeing the damage a pair of boars had done. The beast is excellent eating and has a surprisingly subtle flavor, not strong at all. When I was a child, my father kept pigs and we used to kill them and have a swinefest. If you shoot one, bring in the experts as it is quite fussy work. To debristle the beast requires much time, effort, and boiling of water. The blood should be saved for black pudding and blood sausage and the intestines, which make excellent sausage skins, are very extensive.

wild boar with red beans and sour plums

There is a variety of sour plum which grows in southern Russia and Iran which you can occasionally buy in Middle Eastern shops. However ripe plums with a little lemon juice will do, and I tend to supplement these with the Japanese Umeboshi plums which you can find quite widely. I often bottle just ripe plums in wine vinegar which works very well for cooking. If you are using canned beans, put them together with the boar after you have browned it.

1 pound dried red kidney beans (about 2 1/3 cups)
olive oil
2-pound shoulder or leg of boar, cut into cubes
flour seasoned with salt and pepper
2 onions, chopped
1 clove garlic, crushed
1 pound plums
6 Umeboshi plums
1/2 teaspoon cayenne pepper
1 12-ounce bottle of beer (ale—not lager)
salt and pepper

Soak the beans overnight in cold, unsalted water. Drain and put them into a large pot of water, bring to a boil and cook hard for 10–15 minutes, then lower the heat and cook for 1 hour.

In a frying pan, heat the oil, dust the meat with the seasoned flour, and brown it in the oil. Add the onions and garlic to the pan and cook until colored. Cut the plums into pieces and add them along with the cayenne pepper.

Drain the beans and put them in a heavy flameproof pan for which you have a lid, and add the boar and plum concoction. Season with salt and pepper, add the beer, and cook covered, at a very low heat in the oven at 325°F or on top of the stove for another hour.

wild boar from the haute savoie

For the marinade:

2 carrots, chopped

3 onions, chopped

3 cloves garlic, crushed

1/4 cup olive oil

thyme

1 bay leaf

6 black peppercorns, crushed

1/2 cup Marc or some form of aquavit

2 1/2 cups red wine

1/2 cup red wine vinegar

Cook the carrots, onion, and garlic in the olive oil gently for 5 minutes. Add all the rest of the ingredients and simmer for 20 minutes. Allow the marinade to cool and pour it over the boar. Keep in a cool pantry or garage, covered, for 6 days turning as you go, or in a fridge for two weeks.

Serves 6–8.

1 haunch boar

40 whole cloves

1/4 cup lard

flour

juice of 1/2 lemon

cayenne pepper

salt and pepper

Preheat the oven to 475°F.

Remove the boar from the marinade and stick the cloves all over it. Season with salt and pepper and smear with the lard. Put the boar in the oven in a flameproof roasting pan and turn the joint after 15 minutes. After 30 minutes, reduce the heat to 425°F and cook for about 2 hours, turning every 30 minutes. Remove the boar, strain the marinade, and add flour to the pan scrapings. Cook for 2 minutes and then stir the strained liquor into the sauce and lift it with lemon juice and a little cayenne to taste.

boar with red wine and coriander seeds

This is another Cypriot recipe used to cook the half wild pigs that run loose in the hills. I really like the combination. Don't be put off by the amount of coriander seeds and remember, only pulvrize it as you need it.

3-pound piece boar loin
6 teaspoons coriander seeds, pounded in a mortar
1¼ cups strong red wine
2 tablespoons olive oil
salt and pepper

Cut the rind from the meat, score the fat on the boar, and cut the removed rind into small pieces and keep. Rub the boar vigorously with half the ground coriander and a generous sprinkling of pepper. Cover, and leave for 3 hours, then pour the wine over it, cover again, and leave overnight. Remove from the marinade and dry well.

Preheat the oven to 350°F.

Heat the olive oil in an ovenproof dish and brown the boar well all round. Pour the marinade over it and sprinkle in the rest of the coriander and add some salt. Put the skin pieces around the meat. Cook in the oven for 2 hours, basting as you go.

cumberland boar pie

This is my adaption of the original Cumberland pie, the forerunner of mincemeat pies, which was originally made with mutton. I have adapted it to boar for my friend Peter Gott who raises wild boar in Cumbria and does such wonderful things with them. His partner Christine also makes wonderful pies, so this is for them. These pies were designed to be made in bulk and stored for several months, the sugar being a preservative. I have given a recipe for 2 large Christmas-size pies but you can make them any size you want. It is a typical medieval pie but don't knock it until you've tried it. This recipe serves 8–10.

1½ pounds pie boar meat
2 pounds seedless raisins (about 4 cups)
2 pounds currants (about 4 cups)
4 ounces candied peel (about ¾ cup)
pinch of nutmeg
pinch of apple pie spice
2 pounds soft brown sugar (about 4½ cups)
½ cup rum
4 pounds hot water crust pastry dough (see page 141)
1 egg
salt and pepper

Put the meat, raisins, currants, and mixed peel through the meat grinder, and then mix with the nutmeg, apple pie spice, sugar, salt and pepper, and the rum.

Make the pastry dough and line 2 raised pie molds, setting enough dough aside for lids. Fill the pies with the mixture and cover with the dough lids. Crimp the edges and make a hole in the top. Brush with beaten egg and bake for 30 minutes at 425°F, then reduce to 325°F and bake for another 2 hours. Remove the pies from the molds and serve hot or cold. You can store them in a cool pantry.

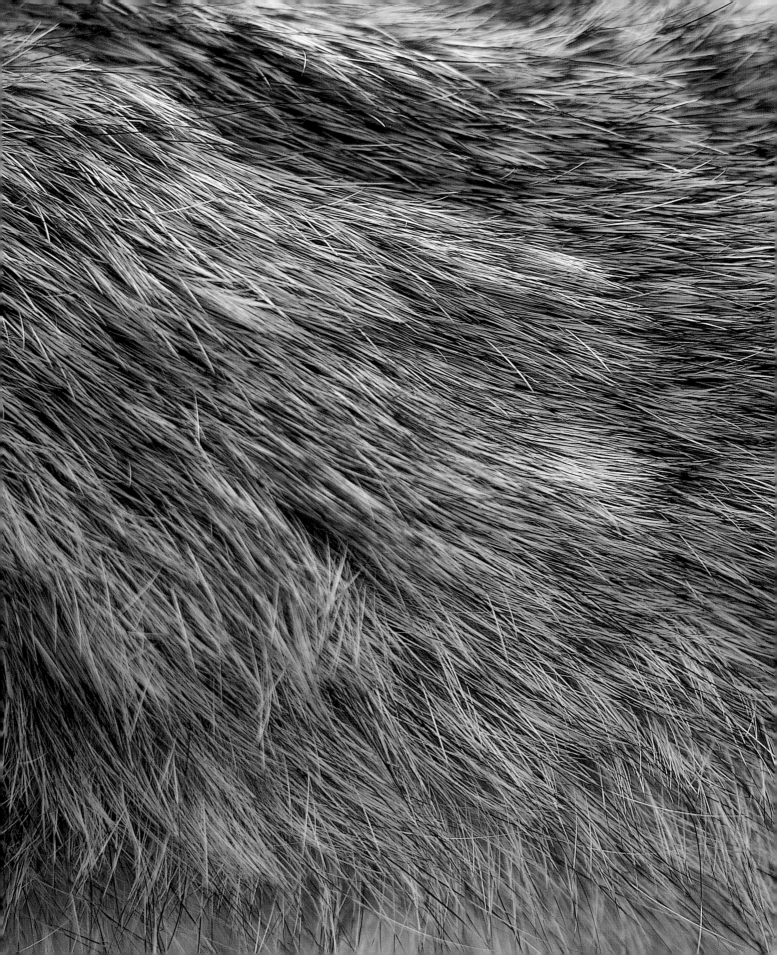

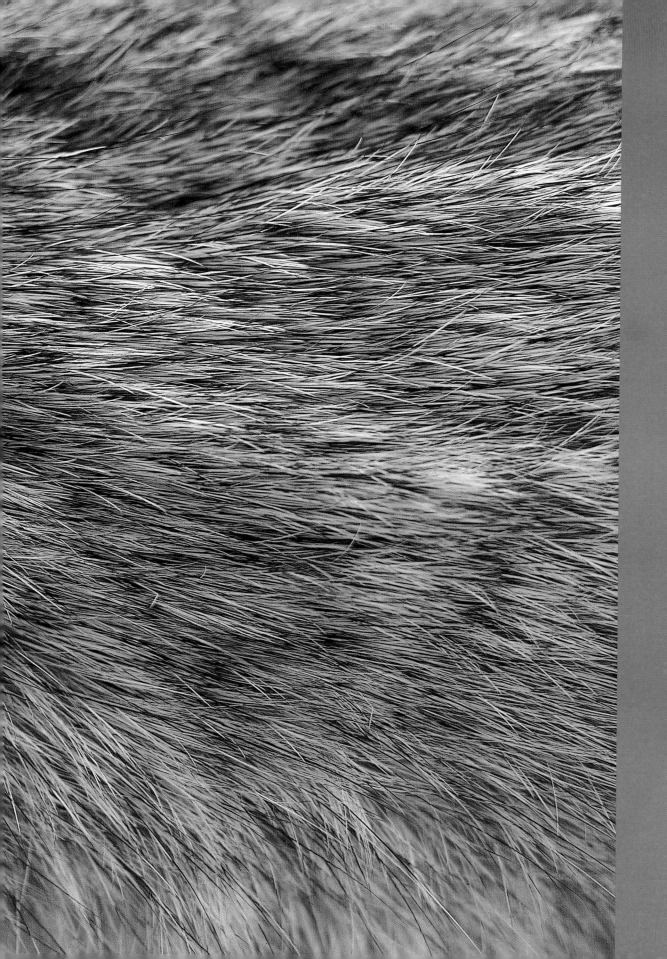

hares and rabbits

hare (jackrabbit)

North America has three principal hare species—the black and white jackrabbit, and the snowshoe hare. These have a variety of almost indistinguishable relations, like the tundra or arctic hares of the remote, far northwestern coastal regions, and the antelope hare of the Sonoran and Chihuahan deserts. There are also a number of European brown hares in northeastern US, southern Ontario, around the Great Lakes, and south of the Canadian Shield.

There are some thirty different species of hare worldwide, across the whole of Eurasia, from Britain to the east coast of China, through parts of Africa, and in North America, from Alaska to extreme southern Mexico. No other animal has featured so prominently in the myths, legends, and pagan religions or in as many cultures than the hare. The European Celts worshipped hares and regarded them as sacred. It was forbidden to kill them, except for occasional sacrificial purposes, at a time when all wild animals were the principal food source and of vital importance to survival. The hare was the favorite animal, light bearer, and primary spirit of Oestre, the immensely powerful Celtic Goddess of dawn, fertility, and rebirth, whose festival was at the start of the vestal equinox in Europe (the start of spring fecundity). The early Christian monks, who cunningly placed their religious festivals around dates already recognized as traditional times of worship by the people they wished to convert, transformed one of the hottest parties in the pagan calendar into the anniversary of Christ's crucifixion, but they kept the name, Easter, and its symbols of fecundity: the egg and the "bunny" which was originally the hare.

All cultures made the association between the position of the full moon and its influence on the seasons, and attached great significance to the pattern on the lunar surface, which resembles a hare. Hares were a god to the North American Indians, particularly the Algonquin, and were worshipped in their moon dances. The Great Hare of the tribes people was the savior, hero of the dawn, guardian, creator and transformer of seasons and regrowth; the great Manabozho, who formed the earth and lived on the moon with his mother, was a provider of all waters, master of the winds, and brother of the snow. He was a trickster and magician, symbolizing the agility of the mind, which can outwit physical force. Unlike the European Celts, this glowing accolade did not stop the North American Indians eating them and making good use of their soft, luxurious pelts.

All the hare species display similar characteristics, which are unusual by any standards. They can travel at speeds of 45 mph and turn on a dime in full flight. This in itself commanded considerable respect from early people, but their behavior, which seems almost humanly irrational, and a scream when caught or injured, hideously childlike, convinced them that hares were more than simply animals. As surface dwellers, hares have developed elaborate defensive tactics to disguise their scent from predators and protect their young. Hares are crepuscular, feeding at dawn and dusk, lying up by day in "forms" or "seats"—shallow hollows they scrape out of the ground in a position that gives them a clear view of the surrounding countryside. They are capable of slowing their heart rate while crouched, with ears flat against their back in the form, to reduce body temperature and minimize their scent. If disturbed, their heart rate immediately increases to three times its normal rate, pumping oxygen through their system and enabling them to burst into high speed. When a hare leaves or approaches its form, it doubles back and forth, making sudden leaps and 90-degree turns to break up the scent line. Does breed pretty well all year round, depending upon temperature and availability of food, and their exuberant, chaotic mating display of gamboling, leaping and shadow boxing, is one of the phenomena of the countryside, whichever continent they live in.

Hares are vegetarian, eating whatever grasses, cereals, and legumes that are available, resorting to twigs, leaves, bark lichen and the shoot of young trees, bushes, or shrubs in the winter. They digest their food twice, ingesting the soft feces from the previous evening's feed as they lie up during the day. A doe can have up to four litters a year of between two and four leverets. For years people believed that hares were hermaphrodite and that both sexes were capable of breeding. This was disproved during the nineteenth century, but the doe's capability to be pregnant and conceive at the same time is almost unique in the animal kingdom. Unlike most wild creatures, which are born blind, bald, and defenceless, leverets have fur and can see almost immediately. Once the birthing process is over, the doe scrupulously cleans each one and then moves them to separate hiding places where each little animal waits, silent and immobile, for their daily feed. About an hour after sunset, she visits each leveret in turn and suckles them. Once fed, she stimulates the urinary area with her tongue, swallowing any discharge to ensure that the leveret remains scent-free for the next 24 hours. She then moves them to a different location.

Snowshoe hares, which have a distribution across the boreal forests of Alaska, Canada, and the northern and mountainous areas of the forty-eight contiguous states, including parts of California, are one of the smallest and shyest hare species and, unlike other hares, inhabit forests. They shed their coats twice a year, replacing the light brown summer coat with a thick white winter one as the hours of sunlight recede in the late fall, which is when they acquire hairy pads on their feet to enable them to run on the snow. Snowshoes share a similar range of distribution and habitat as ruffed grouse, and cyclic fluctuations in population play an influential role in the ecosystem of the areas in which they live. Northern snowshoes are the principal food source of lynx, coyote, foxes, horned owls, and other raptors. As snowshoe numbers build up over a period, in areas where there is a plentiful summer food source—grasses and weed plants on the edges of woodland and forest clearings—there is a natural increase in predators feeding off them. Inevitably the population reaches a point where the available food source is insufficient, particularly through the winter when their diet is reduced to bark, twigs of aspen, alder, willow, lichen, and those buds that they are able to reach by standing on their hind legs. Snowshoes have been known to eat carrion in desperation and even to become a nuisance to trappers, by stealing bait. With the inevitable collapse in numbers, predators then concentrate on ruffed grouse. The population of these birds then drops, the predators move elsewhere, and gradually, the snowshoe population starts to build up again. Seasons and bag limits vary from state to state, in some there is no closed season at all. Snowshoe and other hare aficionados favor a beagle as a hunting dog. A good beagle will work a hare back towards his master, providing him with an opportunity for a shot.

European brown hares were introduced to Great Britain by the Romans, for coursing with greyhounds, and became one of the five Noble Beasts of Venery under Norman forest laws, for hunting with hound packs. Sentimental colonists imported European hares to Australia, New Zealand, parts of South America, and to the East Coast of Canada and northeastern US, for both coursing and hunting with packs of beagles. There are European hares in New Jersey, New York State (where a wealthy resident of Dutchess County imported several ship loads of hares, 500 at a time, from Hungary), Connecticut, and in Ontario, Canada, extending round the great Lakes. The season tends to be mid-December to the end of February, with a bag limit of one, depending on the state.

White-tail and black-tail jackrabbits are by far the most populous rabbit species in the US. Called "Jacks," after the donkey-like large ears which assist their phenomenal eyesight, they are present in most states. White-tails favor scrubby higher ground, from British Columbia and east central California to Manitoba and northern Missouri; their numbers expanded during the 1800s due to deforestation. Black-tails prefer more arid semi-desert conditions in central and western US, and in Baja California and northern Mexico. All hares perform spectacular leaps when disturbed or pursued, but Jacks are capable of clearing over 20 feet. When Lewis and Clark were exploring South Dakota in 1804 and first saw white-tails in what is today, Lymans County, Lewis recorded breathlessly in his journal, "I measured the leap of one and found it to be 21 feet. They appear to run with more ease and to bound with greater agility than any animal I ever saw." The more agile black-tails in their open prairie environment are coursed with greyhounds and by members of Saluki and Borzoi coursing clubs, keeping an ancient sporting tradition, which started over 4,000 years ago, intact. White-tails are generally shot, hunted-up by beagles, with seasons and bag limits state-dependent, but generally from late autumn to the end of January, and bag limits of around four hares.

Carving

A roast hare or jackrabbit is presented with the legs drawn up into the body and secured with a wooden skewer. The best meat on a hare is along the backbone and to ensure an even distribution of meat, I like to carve a hare onto a serving dish, and have it taken to the table. Remove the meat from the saddle by carving slices not less than 1/8-inch thick, parallel with the backbone. Detach the hind legs and slice off meat parallel with the thigh bone. Forelegs and shoulders have so little on them that they are served in one piece. Finally, turn the carcass over and remove the delicate little fillets. Because of their size, rabbit and blue hare are served cut up. Turn the carcass and sever the fore end just below the shoulder blade. Now, divide the saddle by cutting down the center of the backbone.

When I was young there were hare shoots where a thousand hares would be killed in a day—a grown hare consumes 40 pounds of vegetation in a week, thereby proving my point that there's not a lot of good in lettuce! When I first moved to Scotland I found a hare hanging on my door as a present from Johnny and it was the first beast in my game larder here.

Aging

A young hare or jackrabbit has ears that tear easily, a smooth coat, and small white teeth. Hares are best between autumn and early spring although, as vermin, can be taken any time; the medieval monastics used to eat them in Lent, using a curious argument that they didn't qualify as meat.

Hanging and Skinning

A hare should be hung, head down, with a bowl below the head or its head in a plastic bag to catch the blood. Once the blood is drained, mix it with vinegar and keep it in the fridge to add to the dish. Hang it for 1–2 weeks depending on the weather. I paunch (gut) it after it is skinned. I do this over the bath wearing a swimming costume but that is perhaps *de trop*... it is what my mother did so heredity takes over. (I once lost an admirer when I opened the door thus attired with blood to the elbows; he was a rather wimpy sort of chap.) Sever all 4 legs at the first joint, then cut through the skin of the hind legs halfway between the leg joint and the tail. Peel the skin from the hind legs. Tie them together and hang over a bowl with a little vinegar beneath to catch the blood. Pull the skin over the body and forelegs. I remove the head but you can skin it and keep it on. Cut the hare up the middle, but don't cut into the gall bladder. Tip the blood from the rib cage into the bowl. Discard the guts, keeping the liver. Rinse in cold water and dry with paper towels. Remove the blue membrane. A hare serves 4–6.

My favorite pub is the Cholmondley Arms at the village of the same name on the A49 in Cheshire, England, where Guy and Carolyn Ross-Lowe win award after award for their pub and its food. They manage to keep a great pub atmosphere and wonderful food—not easily done. This is Carolyn's excellent hare terrine recipe.

For the marinade:

1 1/4 cups red wine

1 tablespoon olive oil

6 juniper berries, crushed

1 hare, flesh removed and cut into longish strips

1 pound fat pork, ground

1 pound lean pork, ground

1 onion, finely sliced

2 tablespoons butter

1 clove garlic, crushed

2 teaspoons fresh thyme and parsley, chopped and mixed

1 pound bacon

salt and pepper

Mix the marinade ingredients together, add the hare strips, and leave for 2 days. Mix the ground fat pork and lean pork together. Sweat the onion and the garlic in the butter for 5 minutes and then discard the garlic. Mix the onion with the pork, herbs, and salt and pepper. Preheat the oven to 325°F. Line a 2-pound terrine with bacon and put in half the ground pork mixture. Press down, then put some hare strips on top, and continue this until the mixture and the hare are used up—about 4 layers. Cover with bacon. Cover the terrine and wrap in two layers of tinfoil. Cook in a *bain marie* (water bath) or roasting pan of water for 45 minutes. Allow to cool. Press in the terrine under weights, place in the fridge until cold, leave for 24 hours, and serve.

hare swet

Swet is the Swedish for stew and this is a seventeenth century recipe I found when visiting Lekeslotte, a fantastic twelfth century castle on an inland sea 100 miles across. The summer exhibition at the castle was on hunting which in Sweden is mostly shooting or tracking moose or bear with hounds. There was even a room of different pelts for the children to feel, imagine trying such an exhibition in anti-hunt Britain. The Swedes are the nation that invented political correctness but they recognize the normality of hunting, shooting, and fishing and, when they have eaten their own moose, elk, and roe, they buy a vast amount of our venison.

1 hare

1 bottle red wine

olive oil

5 ounces speck (fatty bacon), cut into 2-inch squares

12 onions, chopped

1 piece ginger the size of your thumb

4 cloves

4 teaspoons nutmeg, freshly grated

1 cup water

salt and pepper

Cut the hare into pieces and marinate it in the red wine for 8 hours. Then remove the hare from the wine, reserving the wine, and pat dry with paper towels.

Brown the hare in a little oil on both sides. Add everything to the hare, including 1¹/4 cups of the wine from the marinade. Bring to a boil, cover, and cook until tender—about 1¹/2–2 hours, depending on the size and age of the hare.

baron of hare

This is an Austrian recipe and I'm not sure where the name comes from, although I suppose it's some Hapsburg pretension to compare it to Baron of Beef. It is quite delicious and somewhat different.

1 saddle of hare

strips of fat pork for larding

1 teaspoon salt

1/2 teaspoon paprika

flour

1/2 cup (1 stick) butter

1 cup sour cream, perhaps a little more

1/2 cup strong beef or game stock

1/4 cup vinegar

1 bay leaf

4 juniper berries, crushed

1/2 teaspoon thyme

juice of 1/2 lemon

2 tablespoons capers

pinch of sugar

1 tablespoon butter kneaded with 2 teaspoons flour

Preheat the oven to 375°F. Lard the hare with the pork fat and rub it with the salt and the paprika and sprinkle well with flour. Brown the hare on all sides in melted butter. Add 3/4 cup of the sour cream, and the stock and vinegar, and add the bay leaf, juniper berries, and thyme. Roast for 1 hour or until tender—the meat should be pink and juicy—and baste from time to time, adding more sour cream if necessary. Transfer the meat to a dish and keep warm. Strain the pan juices, and measure them; add the lemon juice, capers, sugar, and enough heated sour cream to make 2¹/2 cups of sauce. Whisk in the butter and flour and bring it to a boil, stirring until it thickens. Adjust the seasoning and serve the sauce separately.

jugged hare

lagas stifado

This is the traditional way of cooking hare and a very good and rich dish. I remember the German restaurant Schmidts in Charlotte Street, Soho, London, used to serve it for lunch every Wednesday and it was hard to get a table on that day.

1 well-hung hare

1 teaspoon vinegar

olive oil

flour seasoned with salt and pepper

game stock

1 onion, studded with cloves

bunch of thyme, marjoram, and parsley

1 bay leaf

pinch of nutmeg

pinch of mace

2 tablespoons red currant jelly

2/3 cup port or claret

salt and pepper

Cut up the hare, saving the blood and liver. Mix the blood with the vinegar to prevent it congealing. Preheat the oven to 350°F. Heat some oil in a pan, dust the hare pieces with seasoned flour, and brown them in the oil. Transfer to an oven-proof dish and pour the stock over it to cover. Add the onion, herbs, and spices. Cover tightly and place in the oven for about 3 hours.

Strain the liquid into a pan and return it to a boil. Add the red currant jelly. Pour a little liquid into the blood and stir until smooth. Add the blood to the gravy and cook to thicken, but do not boil. Add the wine and season with salt and pepper to taste. Arrange the meat on a dish and pour the sauce over it. Garnish with a forcemeat ball (see page 149) and heart-shaped sippets of toast.

In Ancient Greece, if a man wanted to please his lover he went out hunting with greyhounds and brought her (or more probably him) back a hare. This event is recorded in Homer and other poets and is engraved and embossed on the sides of vases and drinking vessels. No-one sees fit to say how it was cooked, but this is most probably how:

1 hare, cut into 12 serving pieces

1 1/2 cups red wine vinegar

6 cloves garlic

6 juniper berries, crushed

6 myrtle berries

4 bay leaves

4 tablespoons olive oil

1 tablespoon honey

1 tablespoon dried crushed red bell peppers, or paprika

2 tablespoons ground coriander

1 pound shallots, peeled

1 1/4 cups strong red wine

1 tablespoon capers

1 sprig of thyme

salt to taste

Put the meat in a large bowl and add the vinegar, garlic, juniper and myrtle berries, and the bay leaves. Cover and marinate for 24 hours, turning the meat in the marinade several times.

Preheat the oven to 350°F. Remove the meat to a casserole dish. Bring the marinade to a boil in a small saucepan and strain it over the meat. Add everything else, except the thyme, and keep back half the olive oil, and cook in the oven for 20 minutes. Reduce the heat to 300°F, and cook for 2 1/2 hours. Add the thyme, salt, and the remaining olive oil, and cook for another 15 minutes.

raised **hare** pie

A good raised hare pie was usually eaten to celebrate the feast of the pagan goddess of spring whose name was Oestre and her symbols of fertility were the egg and the hare. Ring any bells? Christianity steals most things and the hare has now become the Easter bunny. There are still parts of the country where the tradition continues so here is a recipe for you to honor her, too.

Many people are daunted by the thought of raising a hot water crust, it is like so many things in life, until you do it you will always fear it. The things to remember are that as soon as your pastry dough is cool enough to handle comfortably, you must work it—you cannot leave hot water pastry dough until later. Choose the mold to work with—a glass or a piece of wood—and raise the pie around it. It is rather like pottery, you can raise it freehand without a mold but until you are used to the process it may look a bit wonky, like your first attempts with clay. Try not to make it too thick, you will improve as you get less scared of it—my first efforts would break a mammoth's tooth! And remember, when you are filling it, to leave room to pour in the stock to form jelly. Once you have got the hang of this, you will be so proud.

I make my game stock with a pig's foot and/or a veal knuckle when making pies, but using gelatin is more usual.

For the hot water pastry dough:
3 1/3 cups all-purpose flour
1 1/2 teaspoons salt
1 cup milk and water mixed, or plain water
1/2 cup lard

1/2 pound pie veal
1/2 pound cooked ham
1 onion
mace
nutmeg
4 dried apricots
handful dried cherries or cranberries (soaked in cold tea to swell)
12 ounces hare, cut into small pieces (about 2 1/2 cups)
beaten egg to glaze
1 pig's foot or 2 level teaspoons gelatin
1 1/4 cups game stock
salt and pepper

To make the pastry dough, sift the flour and salt into a bowl. Heat the water and lard together and bring to a boil, pour into the flour, mix together quickly to form a stiff paste, and raise a pie and lid from it—use a mold around which to shape the dough (see left).

Preheat the oven to 400°F.

Chop the veal and ham together with the onion and add plenty of salt and pepper, mace, and nutmeg. Put half the meat mixture in the bottom of the pie. Chop the fruit and mix it with the hare meat, and put on top of the veal mixture. Add the rest of the veal mixture, put the pastry dough lid on top and make a hole in the center. Decorate and brush with beaten egg and cook for 30 minutes.

Glaze again and reduce the heat to 350°F and continue to cook for 1 1/2 hours, covering with parchment paper when it has sufficiently browned. If you haven't cooked a pig's foot in your game stock, then dissolve the gelatin in the stock, and as the pie cools pour in through the hole in the top. Chill until firm, preferably overnight, before serving.

rabbit

In 1624, so the story goes, a party of Dutch emigrants to America, struggling ashore after months of eating rancid corned beef, were so delighted to find the inhospitable peninsular of land south of today's Brooklyn inhabited by rabbits, that they promptly christened it Konijn Eiland. The conies that provided them with their first fresh food looked almost exactly the same as the grizzle-gray rabbits found in Holland, but were very different. These were indigenous Cottontail rabbits (*Sylvilganus Floridanus*), found throughout the United States to parts of southern Canada, and are today North America's most abundant ground game species.

Cottontails have adapted to the immensely diverse climactic and topographical conditions within the continent of North America to create several different species: Pygmy cottontails of sage-bush dominated areas of the Great Basin and Colombia plateau; Nuttalls or Mountain cottontails, of high altitudes of the West and North; desert cottontails, found from Texas up to north Dakota, feeding off creosote bushes, cactus, and mesquite; and marsh cottontails, of the moist forest edges, damp thickets, and marshes from Virginia to Alabama and Florida, where a sub-species, restricted to the Lower Keys area of Florida, bears the distinctive scientific name of *sylvilagus palustris hefneris*, in honor of the founder of *Playboy* magazine.

The extraordinary swamp rabbit of the coastal Deep South, which is amphibious and will submerge to escape predators, has a staple diet of any aquatic vegetation but is equally partial to cane and young corn. The New England cottontail of open fields and meadows are found from the Hudson River Valley to the foothills fo the Appalachian Mountains. The most numerous of all is the Eastern cottontail, with a distribution extending from southern Canada down the eastern United States to Mexico and parts of Central America, with another population in Texas, New Mexico, and Arizona.

The species differ in size and coloration, from the tiny Pygmy cottontails which are no bigger than 10 inches and weigh about a half-pound, to their enormous swamp cousins, which can grow to 26 inches and are reputed to reach weights of up to 11 pounds, but their characteristics are basically the same. The one main difference that early settlers would have noticed is that, unlike European rabbits which are communal and live in burrows, cottontails are generally, solitary surface dwellers who rarely venture far from cover. Cottontails live in shallow depressions known as "forms" which they scrape out of the soil, relying on their sense of smell, acute eyesight, and hearing to warn them of danger. If disturbed, they are capable of bursts of speed exceeding 20 mph and run in a zig-zag fashion, making leaps of up to 15 feet to break their scent line. If pressed, they will take refuge in a woodchuck burrow, rock crevice, or hollow log. Except for those species that have adapted to it, like the marsh and swamp cottontail, they avoid water but will swim to avoid danger. After a heavy fall of snow, a dirty trail can be seen leading to the temporary burrows they create in drifts or to a safe haven under snow laden branches forced to the ground.

Cottontails start to mate as early as January depending upon weather, altitude, and food supply. Their mating display is an exuberant exhibition of shadow boxing and gymnastics. Male and female squat, nose to nose, facing each other like sumo wrestlers. They suddenly spring upright and box with their forepaws, sometimes with considerable violence if the doe is not receptive. The buck now leaps over the doe turning 180 degrees in mid air, while she spins to face him as he lands. High speed chases and a repeat of the leaping and boxing will be performed several times before mating is allowed.

Gestation is roughly a month depending on locality, and the doe makes a nest in a sheltered site, lined with grass and fur plucked from her belly, well concealed from aerial predators in which to have her "kittens." A doe may have seven or eight young up to six times a year, which are born blind, bald, and defenseless, from spring to late fall. Cottontails are crepuscular, feeding at dawn and dusk or moonlit nights, lying up by day and eating the soft feces from the previous night's feed. After birthing, the doe leaves her young hidden in their nest, only visiting them under cover of darkness for their nightly feed, the kittens instinctively remaining silent while she is away. They are independent of their mothers after two weeks and unless born late in the season, will breed in the first year. This prolificacy among cottontails is nature's defense against very high losses due to avian and mammalian predation. As surface dwellers, they are vulnerable to a wide range of predators—hawks, owls, crows, stoats, weasels, lynx, and foxes as well as coyotes, badgers, possums, raccoons, dogs, cats, and a variety of snakes. In the humid south, alligators are a constant threat to swamp cottontails. The young of all species are particularly susceptible to heavy rain and many drown in the nest bowl in the first few days of life.

Cottontails are herbivores and will eat virtually any green vegetable matter that grows in their particular topographical habitat. As the source of green matter reduces with the onset of cold weather, cottontails switch to twigs, bark, and the terminal shoots of young trees and shrubs. Cottontails had long been part of the diet of the native Americans and their presence was a welcome addition to the food source of early settlers when bigger game was unavailable. Rabbit meat is excellent and the skins were highly prized for a whole range of uses, from caps to bed covers.

Cottontails make distinctive runs from their forms on the edge of cover to their feeding grounds and were caught by snares made of horsehair or twisted plant fibers. As in Europe, their population increased in proportion with civilization. Every agricultural advance seemed, from the cottontail's point of view, to have been done specifically for their benefit and inevitably they became a pest species, predating into urban gardens and districts where grain production coincides with woodland and brush cover. The population of all species fluctuates from year to year with high densities building up in areas of good habitat and plentiful food. In these instances, nature's system of checks and balances comes into play. Stress caused by over-grazing leads to fetal re-absorption. In large numbers, rabbits become prey to a debilitating range of ecto and endo parasites—fleas, ticks, lice, and chiggers, and lung, liver, and stomach worms. These in turn lead to the spread of diseases associated with over-grazing like coccidias and pneumonias.

Rabbit shooting, whether in Britain or America, is a great sport for old and young, beginner or expert. It is a wonderful way to introduce children to shooting or break in a young dog. In Britain, rabbits are very often bolted from their underground homes by a ferret, with the gun standing above the burrows waiting for them to pop out. In America, where the season runs from November 5th to February 28th with a bag

limit of five, the popular equivalent is hunting them up with an exuberant and hard working little beagle—no child could possibly be bored when there's a beagle about. Contrary to popular opinion, rabbits don't run in a circle when hunted, but tend to run to the limit of their grazing territory before turning back to the safety of known ground. If a dog puts up a rabbit, the young shot has plenty of time to load his gun and think about where the rabbit might re-appear from and most importantly, where the dog is in relation. This is such a perfect opportunity to teach young people that for all the thrill and excitement, any shooting is about calm, collected, well thought out actions in which rushed decisions, haste, and confusion must never play a part.

As a farmer in southern Scotland, I have shot, ferreted, and hawked hundreds of rabbits for the pot, to protect crops, and to teach my children to shoot, and had thought that rabbit shooting held no more surprises for me. But the idea of sploshing through swamps and bayous, competing against alligators, copperheads, and cottonmouths for an 11-pound rabbit that swims under water, fills me with a longing to come out to Louisiana and see how it's done.

It is always a mystery to me why we don't eat more rabbit in Britain. Various excuses abound such as people ate too much during the war. Well the wartime population is not the dominant purchasing force now! I was born in 1945, the year the war ended and am four years off the pension the government won't give me. The other great excuse is myxamatosis; well I remember the horror of mixi rabbits dying in the hedgerows in the 1960s but, in the same way that foot and mouth or BSC haven't diminished

the demand for beef, or swine fever that for pork, mixi hasn't put me off rabbit. We import much of our rabbit from France, domestic and less tasty than wild, or much much worse from China, where the feed is polluted with human excrement which they use as manure for their vegetables; meanwhile we bury tonne upon tonne of our own rabbit. No Australian feels sentimental about rabbit and I am half Australian, but I hate waste and I cannot understand why what was once a massive country industry is no more and perfectly good food is thrown away. A friend of mine when he was a boy used to sell a thousand wild rabbits a week into Smithfield and Leadenhall Markets. So please give rabbit a go, and I mean wild rabbit.

When you kill a rabbit paunch (gut) it at once as it goes off quite quickly. Skin it in the same way as hare but do not hang it. Young rabbits have soft ears that will tear and sharp white teeth. A small rabbit feeds 2–3 people.

W. Kemble
1884

This is a Spanish rabbit stew, but it may be a bit oily for your palate, in which case reduce the amount of oil slightly. The anchovies are there in place of salt to add a deeper texture, but you can add salt instead.

4 tablespoons olive oil

1 large rabbit or 2 smaller ones, cut into pieces

1 large sprig of thyme

5 teaspoons black peppercorns, crushed in a mortar

3 cloves garlic, chopped

2 1/2 cups game stock

3 anchovy fillets

pinch of cinnamon

1 tablespoon capers and/or lemon juice

Heat half the oil in a big, heavy-bottomed pan and brown the rabbit pieces. Transfer them to a flameproof casserole dish or other heavy pan and add the rest of the oil, the thyme, pepper, and garlic. Cook over a low heat for 10 minutes. Add the stock, anchovy fillets (or salt), cinnamon, capers and/or lemon juice. Bring to a boil, reduce the heat, and simmer for 1–1 1/2 hours, or alternatively transfer to a slow oven at 325°F once brought to the boil, and cook for the same amount of time.

fried **rabbit** with mustard

This is Eliza Acton's recipe written in 1840, and adapted by Robin Weir and Caroline Liddell to include mustard, which I think is a great improvement. I have added a few tweakings of my own.

hind legs of 4 rabbits

homemade bread crumbs made from stale bread

1 1/2 tablespoons mustard powder

1 large egg or 3 egg whites, beaten

1/3 cup (3/4 stick) butter

1 1/4 cups white game stock

3 strips lemon rind

1 rabbit liver (optional)

1 tablespoon flour

2 tablespoons cream

juice of 1/2 lemon

salt, pepper, and cayenne pepper

Put the legs in a pan of unsalted, boiling water and simmer for 5 minutes; drain and cool. Mix the bread crumbs with 1 tablespoon of mustard powder and season with salt, pepper, and cayenne. Dip the legs in the egg and then the bread crumbs.

Melt two-thirds of butter in a frying pan, and gently fry the legs for 15 minutes, turning them once or twice during cooking. In a separate pan, simmer the stock with the lemon rind and rabbit liver (if you have it) for 5 minutes. Remove the liver and mash well with the remaining butter and flour to form a thick paste, then add it little by little to the stock, whisking as you go, (if you have no liver do this with flour and butter alone) until the sauce thickens. Take the remaining mustard powder and mix it with the lemon juice. Stir it into the sauce with the cream and let it bubble. Put the rabbit pieces, nicely browned, on a serving dish and pour the sauce over them.

rabbit brawn (head cheese)

I love a good brawn, and this is a Gloucestershire dish using rabbits which is an excellent use of them and very good as an appetizer or on a buffet table. I make my own setting agent using stock from pigs' feet which are very gelatinous, or use a leaf of gelatin, but powdered will do. This recipe serves 8–10.

3 rabbits, skinned, cleaned, and cut up

3–5 cups sharp alcoholic cider

2 carrots, sliced

1 onion, sliced

1 sprig of thyme

pinch of ground nutmeg

pinch of cloves

1 tablespoon cider vinegar or white wine vinegar

dash of Tabasco sauce

2 ounces leaf gelatin, or 8 1/4-ounce envelopes powdered gelatin

small bunch of parsley

2 hard-boiled eggs

salt and pepper

Cover the rabbits with the cider in a pan; if this doesn't cover them, make up the difference with water. Add the carrots, onion, salt and pepper, thyme, nutmeg, and cloves. Bring to a boil and simmer until the meat is tender—about 2 hours.

Remove the meat from the bones and chop into small pieces. Strain the stock. Add the tablespoon of vinegar, and the Tabasco sauce, and reduce by boiling to 5 cups.

Season to taste and mix with the gelatin. Arrange the rabbit pieces in a wetted mold, sprinkling with chopped parsley as you go; add slices of hard-boiled egg and the stock, and allow to set overnight. Turn out and serve.

rabbit in the dairy

Wild rabbit can have a strong taste, and the way the country people overcame this was to soak it in milk. This is probably the origin of this delicate dish. It is very good if you are feeling poorly or in need of comfort.

2 rabbits, cut up
2 ounces bacon rashers, chopped
2 onions, chopped (about *1/4–1/3 cup*)
mace or nutmeg
5 cups whole milk
salt and pepper

Preheat the oven to 350°F.

Wash and dry the rabbits and place in a flameproof and ovenproof casserole dish, or heavy pan for which you have a lid. Add all the other ingredients and cook, covered, for 1*1/2* hours. Remove the rabbits and reduce the sauce by fast simmering or thicken with a little *beurre manie*. Serve with a colorful vegetable, such as carrots or kale.

elizabethan rabbit

1/4 cup bacon fat or oil
2 rabbits, cut up
1 tablespoon flour seasoned with salt and pepper
3 sliced Jerusalem artichokes or uncooked artichoke hearts
1 onion, finely chopped
1/2 cup carrots, chopped
11/4 cups red wine
1/2 cup raisins
1 apple, finely chopped
faggot (bundle) of herbs
rind of 1 orange
2/3 cup stock
4 ounces seedless grapes, cut in half (about 3/4 cup)
salt and pepper

Preheat the oven to 350°F.

Heat the bacon fat or oil in a frying pan, dust the rabbit pieces with flour and fry until brown. Transfer to a flameproof casserole dish or other flameproof and ovenproof heavy pan for which you have a lid. Sauté the rest of the vegetables in the first pan and add to the rabbit. Pour in the wine, bring to a boil, and then reduce the heat.

Add the raisins, apple, herbs, and orange rind, and season with salt and pepper. Pour the stock in, cover, and cook in the oven for 2 hours; add the grapes for the last 30 minutes.

fife pie

The rabbit came late to Scotland and later across the Firth of Forth to Fife—I think this is one of the earliest Scottish rabbit recipes.

With my usual reluctance to buy meat when game is plentiful, I have made the forcemeat balls with rabbit not veal. If you have the rabbits' livers and they are clean, substitute them for an equal quantity of meat and fry them in a little butter first. Pies of this date included anything from oysters to cockscombs so let your imagination run riot! I make rough puff pastry dough from habit but use packaged puff for ease!

For the forcemeat balls:
meat stripped from 1 rabbit
an equal quantity of fatty bacon
1 anchovy, chopped
grated rind of 1/2 lemon
1 egg, lightly beaten
grating of nutmeg
8 ounces bread crumbs, made from stale white loaf (about 4 cups)
salt and pepper

Chop the meat and bacon and then finely mix all the ingredients together, binding them with the egg. Roll the mixture into small balls and set aside.

2 rabbits
1 pound pickled belly of pork (use unpickled if you must)
nutmeg
2 medium onions, chopped
1 1/4 cups game stock
2 tablespoons white wine
4 ounces rough puff pastry dough
1 egg
salt and pepper

Preheat the oven to 425°F.

Strip the meat from 2 rabbits and cut into 1-inch cubes. Slice the pickled pork thinly and season both meats with salt and pepper and nutmeg.

In a 2 1/2-quart deep greased pie dish, layer the meats with the forcemeat balls, sprinkling chopped onion on each layer as you go.

Pour in the stock and white wine. Cover with the pastry dough and brush the top with beaten egg. Bake in the oven for 15 minutes, reduce to 350°F and continue to bake until the pie is well risen and golden—about another 40–45 minutes.

rabbit with chocolate and tomatoes

This recipe, like the chocolate and tomatoes it contains, is believed to have been brought back to Spain by the Conquistadors. The rabbit is not native to South America, but the origins of this dish are reputed to have been for cooking chihuahua which were bred especially for the table. Whatever its origins, it is delicious.

1 large rabbit cut into 4, liver reserved

3 cloves garlic

2 tablespoons olive oil

1 onion, chopped

1 pound (about 3 medium) tomatoes, chopped, or 1 14$^{1}/_{2}$-ounce
  can chopped tomatoes

$^{1}/_{2}$ cup white wine

$^{2}/_{3}$ cup game stock

1 stale white bread roll, cut into small chunks

1 ounce unsweetened chocolate, broken into small pieces

6 almonds, roasted

small bunch of parsley (including the stalks), finely chopped

salt and pepper

Rub the rabbit pieces with salt and pepper. Peel and crush the garlic in a mortar with the liver.

In a large pan, brown the rabbit pieces in the oil, add the onion, and cook until colored. Pour in the tomatoes, white wine, stock, and the bread roll. Cook, covered, for about 30 minutes. Add the liver, garlic, chocolate, almonds, and the parsley leaves and stalks, and cook gently for another 2 hours, or until the rabbit is tender. Add a little water if the sauce appears to be drying out.

rabbit saltimbocca

This is a dish I made up when I was demonstrating at the Scone Game Fair. I took the ale from the lovely Heather Ale people, the bacon from Peter Gott, the sage from Scotherbs, someone shot the rabbit and away we went.

Per person:

2 rabbit fillets

1/4 cup (1/2 stick) butter

2 sage leaves

1 slice ham or Canadian bacon

1 bottle Heather Ale or other good ale (e.g., Sam Adams)

salt and pepper

Lay the rabbit between two bits of plastic wrap and flatten the fillets carefully with a meat hammer (or in my case, just lean).

Melt the butter in a heavy sauté pan or frying pan, lay 2 sage leaves and a slice of ham or bacon on one of the fillets, place the other fillet on top, and secure with toothpicks. Brown the rabbit in the butter, turning carefully. Season with salt and pepper, then pour in half a bottle of beer (what you do with the rest is up to you), cover, lower the heat, and cook, turning once, for about 10 minutes or until the rabbit is cooked.

rabbit with apples and cider

2 tablespoons oil or butter or bacon fat

1 large or 2 smaller rabbits cut into pieces

flour seasoned with salt and pepper

4 ounces Canadian bacon, preferably in a piece and cut into small cubes (about 2/3–3/4 cup)

4 onions, chopped

2 pounds sharp apples, peeled, cored, and chopped

2 1/2 cups alcoholic dry cider

salt and pepper

Preheat the oven to 325°F.

Heat the oil or fat in a heavy frying pan, dust the rabbit pieces with the seasoned flour and brown well. Transfer to a flameproof casserole dish or other heavy pan for which you have a lid.

In the first pan, fry the bacon and the onions until golden. Add the apples and cook a bit longer, and then transfer to the casserole dish with the rabbit. Season with salt and pepper and pour in the cider. Bring to a boil, cover, and transfer to the oven for 1–1 1/2 hours, or until the rabbit is tender.

rabbit with a piquant sauce

This is a curious dish that my mother used to make. The flavors combine very well and the crisp bread topping is rather comforting.

3 tablespoons flour seasoned with salt and pepper

1 rabbit, cut into pieces

1/2 cup (1 stick) butter

1 onion, chopped

1 tablespoon Tabasco sauce

1 tablespoon Worcestershire sauce

1 tablespoon dried mustard powder

1 tablespoon tomato ketchup

1 tablespoon brown or fruit sauce

1 bottle lager

crust of 1 small loaf of bread, torn into hazelnut size pieces

Preheat the oven to 350ºF. Dust the rabbit pieces with the seasoned flour. Melt three-quarters of the butter in a frying pan and brown the rabbit pieces.

Transfer the rabbit to an ovenproof dish, fry the onion in the frying pan until colored, and add to the rabbit. Put all the remaining ingredients except the bread into the frying pan and cook together. Pour the mixture over the rabbit, scatter the bread pieces on top of the rabbit and dot with the remaining butter. Cover with tinfoil and cook in the oven for 1 1/2 hours. If it appears to be drying out, add more beer and butter. For the last 15 minutes, remove the tinfoil to allow the bread to crisp up.

game fish

game fish

A tributary of the River Teviot runs through the farm in southern Scotland, its banks covered in mature alder trees and willows. These trees used to be coppiced a hundred years ago, with clogs for the workers in the nearby woolen mills made from the cut-off alder wood, and baskets made from the willow rods. It is an enchanting, peaceful place; the motion of the water is as soothing as its soporific mumbling sound, tumbling over shallows. In the early summer there are kingfishers and dippers, scudding just above the surface; mallard and duckling creep under the overhanging banks. Iridescent dragon flies dart here and there and bees drone among cow parsley, pink campion, and flowering wild garlic. I come down here with my old Sharpe's Parabolic, an $8^{1}/_{2}$-foot split cane rod designed by Cesar Ritz, the hotelier, and try roll casting for little brown trout that lurk in the shady pools. I know that my chances of catching anything are pretty remote—there are far too many herons—but like the $3^{1}/_{2}$ million other fishermen in Britain, I do love trying.

Angling is, like all other fieldsports, a vital part of the socio-economic fabric. Globally it is the most popular participant pastime, encompassing the whole spectrum of social backgrounds and every age, particularly children. In Britain alone, 6,000 people are employed by the fishing industry, with an estimated turnover of £$3^{1}/_{2}$ million. 36 million American anglers spend $34 billion, directly and indirectly on their fishing, supporting ancillary business that provide employment to 1 million people. Worldwide this figure must run into hundreds of billions and involve enthusiasts of every nation. Possibly no other sport induces such passion, fascination, and determination among devotees. I know any number of otherwise unadventurous people who think nothing of disappearing to the north of Norway

in pursuit of arctic char, sea trout in the Falkland Isles, enormous brown trout in New Zealand, bone fish in the Bahamas, wild rainbow trout in Alaska, steelheads in Patagonia or Michigan, cut-throat trout in Montana, or the silver goddess herself, the arctic salmon, in Iceland. I recently met a young bride, bitten by the fishing bug to such an extent that the proffered anniversary jewelery was rejected in favor of a classic Hardy Palakona split-cane trout rod.

I have seen a small boy about to leave on his first sea fishing trip, gazing in ecstasy at the heaving swell of a gray North Sea on an icy day in November. I have seen my own children spending hours at night trying to catch dog fish from the pier at Craignure on the Isle of Mull, off the west coast of Scotland. Enthusiasts will happily share a boat with the appalling stench of "rubby dubby"—shark bait made from rotting fish—in the hope of catching a nurse shark off the Florida Keys. Old men get eaten alive by mosquitoes trying to catch buffalo fish in the

Bayou Sara and small boys, too, trying to land a drum from the Red River. And all because of that indescribable buzz, the heart-stopping moment of excitement when a tentative tug on the line turns into a screaming reel and a quivering bent rod tip.

In the days when there were few domestic animals in Europe and the main food source was derived from virtually everything that swam, flew, or ran, fish were a vital component in the survival chain, and anything from a porpoise to a minnow was eaten. Coastal communities, with their off-shore fishing boats and fixed estuary nets, kept themselves supplied with fresh fish, and inland settlements with fish preserved in salt. Upriver, fish were netted, trapped, speared, and caught with bare hands. Wherever there was a principal building, be it palace, castle, manor, or monastery, moats were stocked and stew ponds dug. Carp were the most popular stocking fish as they are hardy, prolific and fertile. The monastic houses specialized in carp husbandry and considerable efforts went into selectively breeding bigger and better strains. Protecting fish in the inland waterways was of enormous importance and otters, the principal predator, were kept under control by otter hound packs. Their role was sufficiently significant to be recorded by a Royal Charter of King Henry II of England, appointing one Roger de Follo the "King's Otter Hunter," in 1175.

Rod fishing, as a sport, had been popular with the Egyptians, Greeks, and Romans. In Britain, the need for food was such that fishing as a recreational pastime scarcely occurred to anyone until well into the fifteenth century, although it had evidently become popular on the continent before that date. Possibly the earliest publication on fishing, *The Treatyse of Fysshynge with an Angle*, published in 1496, contained material of French origin. Descriptions of rods used—great cumbersome poles of willow and hazel topped with blackthorn, to which a line of nine-strand braided horse hair was attached—leaves one wondering how anything ever got caught.

Bait fishing is more credible than the descriptions of suggested flies for trout and grayling, colored tufts of wool and feathers, especially as these same flies were still in use a hundred years later when line and rod were both lighter and finer. The first real advances came in the seventeenth century. Fish were still of enormous economic importance in Britain. Fishing fleets were busier than ever and estuary netting was particularly lucrative, with licencees on rivers like the Bann in Northern Ireland, exporting thousands of tons of salted salmon a year to Europe and later, to the West Indies, as slave food. The massive growth in the popularity of rod fishing had much, I suspect, to do with Cromwell's Commonwealth. Hunting and

hawking were frowned upon by the Puritans as smacking of Roman Catholic Monarchist activities and the flood of seventeenth century fishing literature, Isaac Walton's *The Compleat Angler*, for example, was written during or shortly after that period. Rods were now becoming sophisticated enough for casting of a sort, lines were down to three strands of horse hair and by the end of the century, reels were commonplace. Fly making had become more scientific, varied, and realistic in attempts to imitate insects that attracted fish.

The majority of river, pond, and lake fish were still caught with bait and the fertile imagination of determined anglers was applied to improving bait recipes. Nicholas Cox, writing in 1679, devotes a considerable part of *The Gentleman's Recreation*, to the subject. For carp and tench, he recommends feeding ponds for a day or two by "casting in garbage, chicken guts, pellets of a honey and sugar mixture, livers of beasts, worms chopped in pieces, cow dung, or grains steeped in blood and dried." For the fishing itself, he recommends bait in the form of a paste made from bean flour, cat's flesh, and honey. Cox has a different recipe for each fish: cheese and honey for barbel, grasshoppers with their legs cut off for bream, Parmesan cheese mixed with saffron for chub, wasp larvae with their heads dipped in blood for dace, wire worms and earth worms kept in moss for twenty days for brown trout, minnows or lob-worms scented with oil of ivy berries for salmon. His recipes cover the whole spectrum of coarse and game fish, each different and most reflecting the brutality of the age.

Special inventiveness was reserved for pike, for whom all anglers had a ghoulish admiration, based on stories of monster fish attacking otters, dogs, cattle as they drank from pools,

and small children paddling. Attacks on humans were well documented—Cox knew of a maid who had been bitten in an extremely embarrassing part of the body, as he primly puts it, "she washed herself." A fish capable of such behavior needed a truly dramatic bait. Live frogs or a young duckling were Cox's suggestions, others favored a small puppy or a kitten tied to an inflated bladder to keep them afloat. William Lawson swore by a paste of powdered mummy and human fat. All recommended the heaviest tackle for these prehistoric creatures which, until fly fishing for salmon became the vogue in the nineteenth century, were indisputably the most exciting fishing experience available.

The early settlers, arriving on the East Coast of North America found estuaries, rivers, and the inshore, literally heaving with fish, and the tidal shores covered with every sort of edible mollusc. The city of Boston was built on the cod that was salted and sent back to Britain. As settlers pressed inland they would have used the great rivers and lakes as highways and would never have been far from an aquatic source of food. Fishing for these pioneers would be for survival and most fish were caught in nets or traps. There was little time for recreational fishing among colonists until the late 1700s. By the turn of the century, fishing as a sport was beginning to take off in what was to become a fisherman's paradise. There were brook trout in North Carolina, cut-throats in Montana, Atlantic salmon in the rivers of Newfoundland, monster chinooks in the Northwest, or sockeye salmon as far south as southern California, as well as any number of coarse fish—pike, perch, drum, catfish, suckers, bullheads, sturgeon, and zander. All that was needed was a decent rod.

Prior to about 1830, rods were cumbersome homemade affairs made of willow, elder, ash, or hazel, with perhaps a whale baleen tip to give it flexibility. Next came greenheart and some experimentation with sections of Calcutta bamboo, but it was a Pennsylvanian violin maker called Samuel Phillippe who, in 1845, revolutionized fishing by inventing a method of splitting bamboo into strips, then planing and tapering the pieces so that they fitted back together, to make a six-sided sectional rod of superb flexibility.

The first complete rod was made by Charles Murphy of New York in 1870 with Hiram Leonard, the gunsmith, developing machinery to bevel the new improved cane imported from Tonkin. Soon, rod makers were supplying fly rods, bait-casting rods, boat and surf rods as fast as they could, as recreational fishing in North America took off. One of the great makers who founded a business which was to become world famous and leaders in habitat conservation, was Charles Orvis. Some of the other great names in the history of North American rod making were employed by Leonard: Ed Payne, Fred Thomas, and Hiram Hawes, to mention only three. In Britain, rod makers who were to become famous, like Hardy, Grant, Farlow, and Sharpe, made rods on Phillippe's design. Today, most rods are made of carbon fiber, but there are still craftsmen making beautiful split-cane rods for aficionados like myself, who prefer natural materials.

With mechanization, a whole new industry in big game sea fishing developed with power boats taking fishermen out to try their luck for shark, barracuda, tuna, tarpon, and dozens of other exciting denizens of the deep. North America has more exciting varieties of fishing, whether coarse, game, or sea, than anywhere else in the world. As with all wildlife conservation, North America is a world leader in fish

stock conservation, particularly the endangered Atlantic salmon. Fishermen are the guardians of the world's waterways and the efforts of this generation will be the priceless legacy for those who follow.

Carving

All round fish are carved in the same way, whether they be the mighty salmon or the lowly tench. We'll use a salmon as an example, since most people make such a hash of it when a dressed one, appears as part of a buffet. The fish is presented from the kitchen skinned and lying on its side. Once the decorations have been removed, the division where the flesh joins at the spine is clearly visible. Simply run a fish trowel down this division from head to tail, pressing from side to side to ease the flesh. Starting at the head, where the flesh is thickest and on the opposite side from the belly, insert the trowel about $2^1/2$ inches down from the head, at right angles to the spine and work the trowel through the flesh over the ribs. Now use the trowel to press the flesh off the bones onto a fish fork. If the fish is properly cooked, the flesh will come away easily. Increase the size of each section as you move towards the tail and the body of the fish becomes narrower. Repeat on the other side and once the backbone is completely exposed, lift it free leaving the remain-ing fillets to be cut into sections and served.

Game Fish

Salmon

Curiously the advent of farmed salmon, which has so much diminished the fish in modern eyes, has returned it to a commonplace fish as it was in the seventeenth century when the London apprentices rioted when fed Thames salmon more than three times a week. After

World War II stocks declined and salmon became a luxury. I can still remember the excitement when some kind friend sent a salmon in its rush carrying bag, with bog myrtle to deter the flies, down by train overnight. But just when I decide I don't like salmon, someone gives me a wild, freshly caught one and again I declare it to be the finest of fish.

For perfect cold salmon: This is a lovely dish where the size of the fish dictates the cooking time. Clean and gut the fish, trim the tail, and leave the head on. Put it in a fish poacher and fill the pan with cold water, add a handful of salt. Bring to a boil and allow to boil for exactly two minutes. Turn off and allow to cool. Remove the fish to a dish, skin and decorate with slices of cucumber and lemon slivers, or as you like. I knew a Scottish doctor who used to surround it with laurel leaves as the king of fish. Gloomy and rather unattractive but *chacun à san gout*. For hot salmon: Rub the fish with oil, salt, and pepper and season the cavity. Put in some melissa (lemon balm) or lemon thyme or just half a lemon and a couple of teaspoons of white wine. Wrap in tinfoil and cook at 350°F for 12 minutes per pound.

In a dishwasher: Though I didn't invent this I think I was the first person to do it for television with my friend Sue Crewe, who was then writing *Jennifer's Diary*, and is now editor of *House and Garden*. You must first run your dishwasher through with the soap and rinse sections open to clear it. Rub your fish with oil, salt, and pepper and wrap in several layers of tinfoil. Put it on the top layer of the dishwasher, run on the glass wash and your salmon will be perfectly cooked.

Trout

When I worked for Rebeka Hardy, her husband and son would often come up from the lake with freshly caught brown trout, which is the food of the gods. Pan-fry them in butter or wrap them in foil and cook them in the oven at 350°F for 8 minutes per pound or, best of all, make a fire by your trout stream and cook them over the open fire on a twig skewer.

Coarse Fish

I have included this section for the thousands of lovely men of all ages who have asked me at fairs around the country, and for their long suffering wives who don't know what to do with the catch. In the Jewish community and in Europe, coarse fish are eaten much more and don't deserve
their name.

Carp

The fish of the Medieval stew ponds are part of the living larder complex. When I was a child in St. John's Wood our fishmonger, Mr Brown, always sold carp for the large Jewish community, as among other things it is an intrinsic part of gefilte fish. If your carp are in muddy water, take them alive and leave them with a running tap in fresh cold water for 24 hours.

Pike

The best of all fresh water fish and one which we totally ignore in the eating stakes. Until I went to the West Indies and learned how to fillet flying fish, which have the same three-banded bone structure as pike, I had terrible trouble fileting them but patience and a shape knife will work.

Zander (Pike Perch)

Zander were the first fish I caught in the Piskers' pond in Sussex and I could never persuade anyone to cook them for me, so I had to learn. Zander are much eaten in Scandinavia, Germany, and Switzerland where I had zander taken straight from the lake at Vevey.

robert may's **salmon**

The phenomenon of celebrity chefs writing cookbooks is not new. It dates back to Ancient Greece, but the advent of the Stuart Court in England saw a greater sophistication in cooking, and Robert May was on a par with the Gordon Ramseys and Marco Pierre Whites of his day. This is an excellent dish as seen on TV cooked by me in the second year of *Two Fat Ladies*, and I unrepentantly repeat it here. The darne is the cut of salmon at the thickest part behind the head.

2-pound darne of salmon
3 oranges, peeled and sliced
2 teaspoons nutmeg, freshly grated
red wine
juice 1 orange
salt

Skin the darne. In a pan large enough to accommodate the fish, spread a layer of sliced oranges. Place the fish on top and season with the salt and nutmeg. Put the remaining orange slices around the fish and on the top. Pour the wine and orange juice both inside and outside the cavity and bring to the boil. Cover and simmer for 15 minutes or until the salmon is just cooked. Serve with sippets of toast.

salmon and cabbage rolls

$1/8$ ounce dried cèps (porcini)
$1/2$ ounce dried chanterelles
$11/4$ pounds cooked salmon
2 ounces smoked salmon—about $1/3$ cup (optional)
$1/2$ cup whipping cream
2 tablespoons chopped fresh chives
1 cabbage
salt and pepper

For the sauce:
$21/2$ cups fish stock
$1/2$ cup light cream
pinch of saffron

Soak the mushrooms for 1 hour, sqeeze them dry, and chop them. Purée the salmon in a food processor, along with the optional smoked salmon. Add the cream, purée again, and transfer to a bowl and mix in the chopped mushrooms and chives. Season with salt and pepper.

Preheat the oven to 350°F.

Select 8 cabbage leaves and blanch them for a couple of minutes in salted, boiling water and then drain them. Spread the salmon mixture on the leaves, roll them up, and secure with string or toothpicks. Put in a greased ovenproof dish, pour some fish stock over them and bake in the oven for 30 minutes. Drain and keep the liquid.

In a pan, mix together the remaining fish stock, the pan juices, the cream, and the saffron. Bring to a boil and simmer to reduce by one third. Serve with the cabbage rolls.

salmon mousse with cheese

This is a very good way of using up cooked salmon that is lying about, and it makes a splendid appetizer or buffet dish. I usually make my salmon mousse with blue cheese but you already have that recipe from *Full Throttle*, so this is another good one.

6 ounces cream cheese (about $^2/_3$ cup)

$^1/_2$ cup sour cream

1 pound cooked salmon

1 shallot, finely chopped (if unavailable, use 1 tablespoon chopped mild onion)

2 ounces baby fava beans or petite peas (about $^1/_2$ cup)

1 envelope of gelatin

$1^1/_4$ cups cream

1 tablespoon summer savory or flat-leaf parsley, chopped

juice of 1 lemon

1 teaspoon dry sherry

2 gherkins, finely chopped

salt and pepper

Mix the cream cheese and the sour cream together and put the mixture in a large bowl. Flake the salmon and stir it in with the cheese and cream and the shallot. If the peas or beans are large, cut them into pieces. Dissolve the gelatin according to the instructions and mix in well. Add the remaining ingredients. Put into a wetted mold or molds and refrigerate for at least 2 hours. Serve with toast, oatcakes, or salad.

salmon fishcakes made with gnocchi

This is a dish I invented one day when I had some delicious cold salmon caught in a haaf-net on the Nith and for some reason some leftover gnocchi and decided to make some fishcakes. The gnocchi was commercial—no need to make your own for this—and gnocchi has, of course, already been mixed with eggs and flour. I preferred the texture to the usual mashed potatoes used in fishcakes—I hope you enjoy them, too.

6 ounces cooked gnocchi

8 ounces cooked salmon (about 1 cup)

4 scallions

1 egg

olive oil

salt and pepper

Reboil your gnocchi until it floats, then drain it and roughly mash it (you want to keep it textured). Flake the salmon and finely chop the scallions. Using your hands, mix all the ingredients except the oil together in a bowl and season well with salt and pepper. Form into patties.

Heat the oil in a heavy pan and fry the patties, don't turn them until they are cooked on the first side.

salmon as cooked at the golden aur

The Golden Aur is a wonderful fish and chip shop in Bala, Wales. I first came across it on a golden weekend with dear friends, when I discovered camping at the age of forty. We laughed all weekend in the rain when "gray were the skies over Cader Idris," and warmed ourselves up at the restaurant. On my second visit they were just closing, when Johnny, myself, and Steve Sclair, our series producer of the first *Clarissa and the Countryman*, arrived, but it was kept open just for us. On my third visit, the entire crew came as we had been thrown out of the dining room of a rather silly hotel for wearing jeans (not me!) at which we were the only guests! During the war, the only available fish were salmon from the River Dee. This is the only time I have had salmon deep fried in batter. It is very good.

Make a batter as for pigeon in the hole (see page 59). Cut the salmon into fillets, making each piece the size of an average cod fillet at your chippie. Season the fish and coat well with the batter and deep fry. Serve with pickled cucumbers and tartar sauce.

salmon with pine nuts

This is something different for your buffet or picnic table. You don't have to use a whole fish, as it makes a good summer dish with salmon cutlets, or even trout. This recipe serves 10–12 people.

10-pound salmon, cooked in tinfoil (juices reserved), skinned and backbone removed, and reassembled as a whole fish
1/4 white loaf of bread, crusts removed, soaked in water
14 ounces pine nuts (about 3 1/2 cups)
3 cloves garlic, crushed
juice of 3 lemons
3/4 cup olive oil
thin slices cucumber for decorating
salt and pepper

Squeeze out the bread. Purée the bread, pine nuts, garlic, lemon juice, salt, and pepper in a food processor, adding enough fish juices to make a sauce the thickness of mayonnaise. Cover the fish with the sauce and decorate with cucumber.

salmon with belgian endive and roquefort

I really like the combination of Belgian endive, Roquefort, and salmon, but if you don't have Belgian endive, use spinach and just lightly blanch it, and then make sure it is well wrung out.

3-pound salmon, skinned and boned
4 ounces Roquefort cheese (about 1 cup)
1/4 cup (1/2 stick) butter
juice of 1/2 lemon
1 head Belgian endive
puff pastry dough
egg for glazing
salt and pepper

Cut the piece of fish in half, lengthwise though the middle to open up 2 fillet pieces.

Mix together the cheese, butter, and lemon juice and season well with salt and pepper. Spread over one half of the fish and place the other piece of salmon on top. Cut off the bottom of the Belgian endive head and split it into leaves.

Preheat the oven to 475°F.

Roll out the puff pastry dough, spread a layer of Belgian endive leaves onto the dough and sprinkle a little salt and pepper over them. Place the salmon on top, and then place more endive leaves around and on top of the fish. Fold the pastry dough over, crimp the edge, and seal it shut with egg. Brush the top with egg and decorate as you like.

Bake for about 40 minutes, or until the pastry is golden brown. Serve with Hollandaise sauce (see page 112).

salmon cooked in goose fat

1 salmon fillet per person with the skin left on
¹/₂ cup canned or bottled goose fat
handful of fennel seeds
salt and ground black pepper

Heat a skillet and roast the fennel seeds in a little goose fat until they start to pop. Remove the seeds from the pan and mix with the remaining goose fat.

Season the salmon pieces with salt and pepper and then rub well with the goose fat mixture. Heat your skillet until it is good and hot and then place the fillets, skin down, on the skillet and then lower the heat.

Cook for about 10 minutes, depending upon the thickness of the fillet, and for the last 2 minutes, flip them over to sear the skinless side.

Serve skin side up—the skin should be golden and crispy.

trout in a cheese broth

This is a Swedish recipe which I found adapts very well to trout. Allow 1–2 trout fillets per person, according to the size of your fish. Swedish cherry wine is not like cherry brandy, but is quite a light wine, so unless you have access to it, use a light red wine. This can be served as an appetizer.

5 tablespoons butter
2 tablespoons flour
5 cups fish or chicken stock
1³/₄ cups light cream
12 ounces aged hard cheese (if unavailable, use cheddar)
4 trout fillets
2 eggs
¹/₂ cup cherry wine and 1 tablespoon kirsch
salt

Make a roux in a large saucepan by melting the butter and stirring in the flour; cook for 2 minutes. Add the stock and simmer until smooth. Add the cream and cheese and bring to a boil. Stir thoroughly and then add the trout fillets and reduce the heat. Simmer gently for 3 minutes. Whisk the eggs, wine, and kirsch together, add to the soup, and simmer for a few minutes.

TROUT FISHING

trout stuffed with confit

One year Johnny made some delicious *confit* from some geese that had not been sold before Christmas. It was a major labor of love and his friends got large jars. There comes a time when the contents are severely reduced and you want to finish it up. This is what I did and it is very good. Don't open a jar specially, but if you have some around and have caught some trout, I recommend it.

fat from a jar of confit
1 onion, finely sliced
1 clove garlic, crushed
1 tablespoon parsley, chopped
6–7 tablespoons confit, finely chopped
2 tablespoons bread crumbs
4 trout
1 lemon
salt and pepper

Take a couple of teaspoons of fat from the confit and fry the onion and garlic in it, until softened. Add the parsley and the meat from the confit and fry a little longer. Mix in the bread crumbs and season generously with salt and pepper.

Preheat the oven to 375°F.

Gut and clean the trout and dry them, inside and out. Divide the stuffing mixture in 4 and stuff each trout and then sew it up.

Cut 4 large pieces of tinfoil or baking parchment and grease them lightly. Lay 1 fish on each and squeeze on a few drops of lemon juice. Fold the tinfoil around each fish and secure. Bake for 35 minutes.

rainbow trout in red wine with tarragon

This is a Quercian dish which I acquired during a drunken visit to this lovely region of France. I begrudged the wine to the dish at the time, but it is a good dish and a useful way of cooking rainbow trout.

8 ounces mushrooms, finely chopped (about 2 1/3 cups)
2 shallots, finely chopped (or 2 tablespoons chopped mild onion)
1/4 cup (1/2 stick) butter
2 tablespoons homemade bread crumbs
4 sprigs of fresh tarragon or 1 teaspoon dried
4 rainbow trout
2 onions, sliced
2 carrots, sliced
3 slices fatty bacon, cut into pieces
2 sprigs of parsley
2 sprigs of thyme
2 bay leaves, crushed
1 bottle burgundy
1 tablespoon flour and butter mixed together
salt and pepper

Preheat the oven to 350°F.

Soften the mushrooms and shallot in the butter in a small pan. Add the bread crumbs and the chopped tarragon leaves, reserving the stalks. Season with salt and pepper, and stuff the mixture into the cavity of the fish, and secure with toothpicks. In a lightly greased, heavy ovenproof and flameproof pan arrange the onion, carrots, and bacon, and lie the fish on top. Add the tarragon stalks and the rest of the herbs, and pour the wine over them. Cover with buttered paper and bake for 35 minutes. Remove the fish to a dish and reduce the sauce over high heat by boiling. Thicken with little bits of butter and flour, whisking vigorously. Adjust the seasoning and pour the sauce over the fish.

quenelles of **trout** in a watercress sauce

When I worked for Rebeka Hardy at Danehill there was a trout lake on the property and, with both her husband and son as avid fishermen, I cooked a lot of brown trout. These quenelles are a very good dinner party appetizer and can even improve rainbow trout.

10 ounces brown trout

10 ounces smoked trout

3 egg whites

pinch of mace

1 1/4 cups heavy cream

salt and pepper

For the sauce:

2/3 cup dry white wine

5 tablespoons shallot, finely chopped (if unavailable, use onion)

2/3 cup pheasant stock

1 1/4 cups whipping cream

4 bunches of watercress

lemon juice to taste

1/4 cup (1/2 stick) butter

Put the fish, both sorts, into a food processor and blend until smooth. Add the egg whites, mace, and salt and pepper, and blend a bit longer.

With the motor running, pour in the cream and blend for no more than 20 seconds—the mixture must not be too thin. Chill for at least 30 minutes.

For the sauce, simmer the wine and shallot together for 15 minutes or more, until it forms a soft purée and the wine has almost evaporated. Add the stock and cream and boil until it has reduced by one-third and can coat a spoon.

In a separate pan, blanch the watercress for 2–3 minutes (using the stalks), drain, and refresh under a cold faucet. Squeeze out the excess water and purée in a food processor for 1–2 minutes until it is smooth. Pour in the hot cream and blend, adding the lemon juice and butter in small pieces.

Bring a pot of water to a boil and add salt. Make the quenelles of the fish by fully filling 1 soup spoon with the fish mixture and using a second soup spoon to shape it, and poach them in the water for 8–10 minutes. Remove them with a slotted spoon and drain on paper towels.

Put the quenelles on a warm dish, strain the sauce, and reheat it without boiling. Pour it over the quenelles and serve at once.

sea trout with cucumbers and cream

In the days of the Regency, salmon and sea trout were still very common but cucumbers less so. Here is a delicate dish which preserves the flavor of the sea trout.

1 onion, thinly sliced

1/2 cup (1 stick) butter

3-pound middle cut of sea trout

1 sprig of dill

1 pint light cream

2/3 cup water

3 tablespoons flour

1 cucumber

juice of 1 lemon and rind from half of it

salt and pepper

Preheat the oven to 400°F.

Butter an ovenproof dish and scatter the onion on the bottom of it. Smear the sea trout with half the butter, season well with salt and pepper, and place on the onion. Chop the dill and add to the cream, mix in the water, and pour it over the fish. Cover with tinfoil and cook for 25 minutes, or until the fish is cooked. Remove the fish to a warm serving dish.

Melt the remaining butter in a small pan and make a roux with the flour, letting it cook a couple of minutes. Pour in the liquid from around the fish. Cut the cucumber in strips and add them, and the lemon rind to the sauce. Adjust the flavor with lemon juice, season with salt and pepper, reheat, and pour it over the fish.

sea trout with chard and walnuts

This was inspired by the Filippino idea of wrapping fish in cardoon leaves—another good way of cooking it, however not for the delicate flavor of sea trout. I love chard and feel that people are often scared of it. This is a lovely dish.

1 pound Swiss chard, leaves and stalks separated

1/2 cup (1 stick) butter

3 shallots, finely chopped (if unavailable, use 3 tablespoons chopped mild onions)

3 anchovy fillets

6 ounces broken walnut pieces (about 1 1/2 cups)

juice and rind of 1 lemon

1 sea trout, skin removed

black pepper

Blanch the stalks of the chard in boiling water and refresh under a cold faucet. Do the same with the leaves, leaving them flat.

Preheat the oven to 400°F.

In a frying pan, melt three-quarters of the butter and fry the shallots. Add the anchovy fillets and allow them to melt. Add the walnuts and toss quickly, then add the lemon juice and rind and set aside. Spread half the chard stalks in the bottom of a lightly greased, ovenproof dish large enough to hold the fish, and then lay the flat chard leaves on top. Smear the fish with the remaining butter, and some black pepper on the outside, and sprinkle a little in the cavity, too. Lay the fish on top of the leaves.

Spoon as much of the walnut and shallot mixture as possible into the cavity of the fish. Fold the chard leaves over the top, place the remaining chard stalks on top, and pour the remaining walnut butter liquid over the top. Cover with tinfoil and cook for about 40 minutes, depending upon the size of the fish.

grilled **zander** with arugula, beets, and horseradish

A simple and delicious way of preparing this fish and one to be done at the lakeside.

2 medium beets, cooked
1/2 cup olive oil
juice of 2 lemons
4 ounces fresh horseradish
1 tablespoon cornstarch
oil for frying
1 zander (pike perch)
arugula
salt and pepper

Peel and thinly slice the beets with a cheese slicer. Combine the olive oil, lemon juice, and seasoning, and pour it over the sliced beets. Marinate them for 1 hour.

Cut three-quarters of the horseradish into matchsticks, and toss it in the cornstarch. Deep-fry the horseradish sticks in oil until golden brown and salt them lightly.

Grill the fish, skin side down. Heat some of the beet marinade in a small saucepan. Grate the rest of the horseradish and toss it in along with the arugula. Arrange the salad on individual plates, and put the fish on top with the sliced beets and horseradish sticks and drizzle the rest of the marinade over them.

zander fillets with chanterelles

This is a Swedish recipe, a country where both pike perch (zander) and chanterelles abound. People think of zander as too bony to eat, but in many parts of Europe it is a much sought after fish, and the flesh is very delicate and repays the effort. At the Weston Park Game Fair I was confronted by a young man with an English Midlands accent who declared it his favorite fish, both to catch and eat. I don't know his name but he will know who he is, and I hope he likes these recipes.

1 1/2 pounds zander (pike perch) fillets
8 small potatoes, peeled
8 ounces fresh chanterelles
1/2 leek, finely chopped
1/2 small onion, finely chopped
4 tablespoons (1/2 stick) unsalted butter
1 sprig of rosemary
3/4 cup dry white wine
3/4 cup fish stock
3/4 cup whipping cream
coarse salt and white pepper

Trim the fillets and remove the bones with tweezers. Sprinkle with salt and refrigerate. Boil the potatoes until tender. Blanche the chanterelles briefly and drain them; sauté them with the leek and onion in 1 tablespoon of melted butter. Add the rosemary spikes, wine and stock, and simmer for 5–10 minutes. Then stir in the cream and zap up the heat to reduce by a third. Transfer the mixture to a food processor, along with 3 tablespoons of butter, and purée until smooth. Season with salt and pepper.

Crush the potatoes and mix them with the puréed sauce. Pack into individual ring molds and keep warm. Grill the fish fillets, skin side down, and do not overcook—by the time the skin is crisp, the fish will be cooked. Season, and serve on each potato ring.

pike burgers

1¼ pounds pike fillets

dash of Tabasco sauce

pinch of paprika

1 cup light cream

3 eggs

2 ounces smoked salmon (about ⅓ cup)

5 ounces spinach leaves (2–3 large handfuls), blanched

4 ounces chanterelles

salt and pepper

Put the pike fillets in a blender. Add salt and pepper, Tabasco sauce, paprika, the cream, and the eggs one at a time, blending as you go. Add the smoked salmon, spinach, and chanterelles, and whizz again. Form into patties, chill, and then fry in butter on both sides until golden.

pike pudding with pumpkin

1¼ pounds pike, chopped

1¼ pounds grated pumpkin

3 tablespoons flour

⅓ cup fish stock

parsley

bread crumbs

butter

salt and pepper

Preheat the oven to 350°F. Combine the pike, pumpkin, flour, stock, and salt and pepper, and pour into a greased dish. Sprinkle with parsley and bread crumbs and dot with butter. Bake for 50–60 minutes until crisp and browned.

hecht smetena

Pike is the best of all freshwater fish and one which we totally ignore in the eating stakes. The Hungarians soak the fish overnight and then poach them like salmon, which dissolves the smaller bones. Poach the fish in *court-bouillon* (i.e. fish stock) rather than water. The Russians have a complicated dish where they remove the meat from the skin and then mix the flesh with butter, anchovies, nutmeg, and allspice before returning it to the skin to bake it. Here is a nice Viennese dish.

1 cup sour cream
4 pounds pike, cut into 2-inch lengths
3 onions, sliced
3 sprigs each of parsley, dill, and thyme
1 bay leaf
2 teaspoons capers
salt and pepper

Preheat the oven to 375°F.

Butter an ovenproof dish and pour in half the sour cream, add the fish and all the other ingredients except the capers to it. Bake in the oven for 15 minutes or until the fish is opaque.

Remove the fish to a warmed serving dish and keep hot. Strain the sauce and thicken it over a high heat. Add the second half of the sour cream together with the capers, reheat, and pour it over the fish. Serve with boiled potatoes.

carp stuffed with baked fruit

This is a dish that recurs throughout central Europe and the Levant and is a French-Jewish recipe from the celebrated Mme. Zette Guinadeau. It is very good and different. Get your fish vendor to scale, clean, and gut the fish and remove the backbone, but leave the head and tail on.

4-pound carp
2^1/$_2$ tablespoons cooked rice
4 ounces blanched almonds, slivered (about 1 cup)
1 teaspoon powdered ginger
1 teaspoon sugar
1 teaspoon cinnamon
^{1}/$_3$ cup clarified butter
1 pound pitted dates (about 3–3^1/$_2$ cups)
1 onion, chopped
2 ounces ground almonds (about ^{2}/$_3$ cup)
salt and pepper

Soak the carp for 15 minutes in water to remove any muddy flavor, dry well, and rub with salt and pepper. Mix the rice and the slivered almonds, and then add half the ginger, sugar, half the cinnamon, and 2 tablespoons butter. Stuff the dates with the rice mixture and stuff the fish with the stuffed dates and sew it up.

Preheat the oven to 350°F. Place the fish in a buttered ovenproof dish and add 1^1/$_4$ cups of water. Season with salt and pepper and add more ginger, the onion, and the remaining dates. Dot with the remaining butter and cook for 45 minutes, basting as you go.

Remove the fish and zap up the oven as high as it will go. Sprinkle the fish with ground almonds and the other half of the cinnamon, baste with butter, and return to the oven for another 25 minutes. To serve, remove the thread and place on a dish.

carp with cherries

This delicious recipe comes from Elana Molokhovet's *A Gift for Young Housewives*, a massive work in four volumes destined for the rising Russian middle-class, a sort of Mrs. Beeton for Russia; it sank without trace in the Revolution of 1917. The original recipe suggests keeping the carp's blood mixed with vinegar and adding it to the sauce at the roux stage. Get the fish vendor to clean and gut the carp for you.

4-pound carp

2 bottles beer (ale—not lager)

1 Hamburg parsley root (or bunch of flat-leaf parsley)

1 bunch of celery, chopped

1 leek, choped

2 onions, chopped

5–6 allspice berries

3–4 black peppercorns

2–3 cloves

2–3 bay leaves

crust from 1 loaf of bread

2 tablespoons vinegar

zest of 1 lemon

1–2 tablespoons butter

1 tablespoon flour

$^1/_4$ cup red wine

5–6 sugar lumps

4 ounces raisins (about $^1/_2$ cup)

juice of 1 lemon

15 marinated cherries

lemon slices from 1 lemon

Cut off the carp's head and set aside. Bring the beer to a boil and add the parsley root, celery, leek, onion, allspice, black peppercorns, cloves and bay leaves, bread, vinegar, and lemon, and boil for 30 minutes. Place the fish and its head in another pan and strain into it the boiled beer. Cook over a high flame for 20 minutes. While the fish is cooking, make a roux with the butter and flour, cook for 2 minutes, and then dilute the roux with some of the broth in which the fish is cooking. Add the wine, sugar, raisins, lemon juice, and cherries. Bring to a boil several times, but do not let it reduce too much. Arrange the carp (without the head) on a dish strewn with lemon slices and raisins. Pour the sauce over it and serve.

This is one of the great dishes of European Jewish cuisine and there are endless variations on the theme. In Russia in the nineteenth century they adopted the French style and added white wine, in Poland they didn't. Some cook the carp whole, some slice it—here is one for you to try. The European Jews make endless varieties of pickled cucumbers, I remember as a child going with my father into the cool dark shops his patients ran in the East End of London to taste them, but new green (half-sours) remain my favorite.

3^1/$_4$-pound carp

2 medium onions, finely sliced

1^1/$_4$ cups water

2^1/$_2$ cups white wine

peel of 2 lemons

juice of 1 lemon

2 bay leaves

1 sprig of thyme

small bunch of parsley

salt and pepper

Gut and clean the carp, leaving the head on. Lay the onions in a heavy pan, large enough for the fish and for which there is a lid. Place the fish on top of these and pour in the water and wine and add all the other ingredients. Bring to a boil, skimming as you go, cover, and simmer very gently until the fish is tender—about 1^1/$_2$ hours.

Lift the fish carefully and transfer to a dish, strain the stock, and pour it over the fish. Chill, and a delicious jelly will form from the stock. Serve with sliced, pickled cucumbers.

composite dishes
sauces & stocks

apician **crêpes**

I think it was Evelyn Waugh who said he never remembers the original dish but leftovers are lovely. This dish comes from the Roman cook Apicius and, I suspect, is the first recipe for lasagne, but it is made with crêpes. It is a curious dish, but very good for using up leftover game of any description. I usually make extra crêpes when I'm cooking, and freeze them for next time.

For the crêpes:

3 eggs

1²/3 cups flour

pinch of salt

¹/4 cup milk

¹/4 cup water

Make a batter by putting all the ingredients in a blender and whizzing for a minute or so. Let the batter stand for 1 hour in the fridge and make six crêpes, one at a time, using a little lard to grease a good frying pan and cook over a high heat.

1¹/2 pounds cooked game or salmon

3 eggs

2 tablespoons olive oil

¹/2 teaspoon celery seeds or lovage seeds (or use cumin)

2¹/2 cups stock

¹/4 cup white wine

¹/4 cup sweet sherry

flour

¹/2 teaspoon ground pepper

1 cup pine nuts or slivered almonds

butter

Mix the meat or fish with the eggs, oil, celery seeds, stock, and alcohol, and a little flour.

Butter a casserole dish and put a layer of the meat mixture on the bottom; sprinkle with pepper and nuts. Place a crêpe on top, repeat the layering, finishing with a crêpe layer.

Preheat the oven to 375°F. Pierce a hole in the last crêpe to let the steam out. Dot the top crêpe with a little butter and bake, uncovered, for 40 minutes, or until heated through. Sprinkle with pepper and serve with a salad.

stalker's pie

If lamb makes a shepherd's pie and beef makes a cottage pie, venison must equal stalker's pie. Shepherd's pie was a traditional use of the leftover Sunday roast on Tuesday, and the invention of the metal meat grinder in Victorian times made the dish more popular. My sister Heather first added port or Scotch to the white sauce with which she bound her version, and a great improvement it is.

2–3 large potatoes

butter

3 tablespoons flour

2 tablespoons butter

1 1/4 cups milk

1/2 cup port or Scotch (or other whiskey)

2 onions, chopped

1 1/2 pounds cooked venison, ground or finely chopped

handful of parsley, chopped

salt and pepper

Preheat the oven to 400°F. Boil the potatoes, drain and allow to steam until the steam has evaporated, then mash with a little butter and salt and pepper. In a large pan, combine the butter and flour to make a roux and cook for 2 minutes. Season with salt and pepper and add enough milk to make a very thick, smooth sauce; add the port or Scotch and more milk if necessary. In another pan fry the onion in a little butter until it is golden. Add the meat and parsley and cook, stirring well, for a few more minutes. Stir in the sauce. Transfer to a lightly greased ovenproof dish and put the mashed potato on top. Criss-cross the potato with a fork and brush with melted butter. Cook for 30 minutes in the oven until piping hot and nicely browned.

yorkshire christmas pie

I am always being asked for this recipe. Historically some of these pies were made to huge dimensions, and indeed one sent in 1832 to Lord Sheffield, the Lord Chancellor, broke the wagon with its weight! Make it with whatever birds you choose, I have started with a pigeon, building up to a goose. I usually make mine with puff pastry, but here is the original.

1 pigeon

1 partridge

1 pheasant

1 goose

2 pounds forcemeat (veal or pork)

4 cups hot water

2 pounds hot water crust pastry (see page 141)
  or puff pastry dough

salt and pepper

1 teaspoon nutmeg

Bone all the birds. Line a pie mold with the pastry dough and place a layer of forcemeat in it. Stuff the smallest bird with forcemeat and stuff the birds into each other according to size, seasoning as you go. Lay the birds in the pie, and fill in the spaces around it with breasts of pigeon, boned hare, or whatever you have, then pack tight with the rest of the forcemeat. Pour in as much clarified butter as it will take, about 1/2–3/4 cup (1–1 1/2 sticks). Cover with a pastry dough lid and brush with egg. Ornament it for fun. Preheat the oven to 325°F. Cover with buttered parchment paper and bake for 4 hours. When you serve it, break the crust in front of your guests and cut into thin slices. The pastry crust is not meant to be eaten.

game **paella**

Spain abounds with paella type rice dishes made with whatever the local ingredients are. It is also a great country for game. My mother and I once visited a place called Puebla Sanabria, northwest of Salamanca surrounded by a valley of hills with a lake in the midst of the dry land and a castle my mother yearned to buy. I always meant to go back but today looking at maps I see a motorway runs through it, so perhaps I'll just keep it in my head. It was a great region for game and there we had a paella made entirely from game. This is great fun for a party and a great user of the rather more battered contents of your game larder.

5 tablespoons olive oil

4 pounds mixed game: pheasant strips, partridge legs, rabbit pieces, roe deer chunks for example

3 ounces game sausage (about 1 or 2)

4 ounces raw ham or bacon (about 2/3 cup)

any available livers of game birds, any venison kidneys

3 cloves garlic, chopped

18 ounces paella (or risotto) rice, well rinsed (about 13/4 cups)

5 ounces frozen peas (about 3/4 cup)

1/2 tablespoon paprika

pinch of cayenne pepper

3 tablespoons puréed tomatoes

1 small sachet of saffron threads

5 cups game stock

1 cup white wine

2 red peppers, broiled and skinned (or a small can of pimento)

salt and pepper

Heat the oil in a paella pan or a large flat pan and fry all the meats until they color, finishing with the ham and then the organ meats. Then add the garlic, and continue cooking for a minute or two.

Add the rice, peas, paprika, cayenne, tomato, salt and pepper, and stir well. Soften the saffron in a little stock and add to the rice. Add half the stock and the wine. When the liquid is absorbed, add more. Cook for about 30 minutes on the stove or transfer the pan to the oven and cook at 350°F. Decorate the top with red pepper strips and any green herb that you have handy.

This is a splendid way of using up leftover meat or fish and gives quite a smart look to an ordinary supper of leftovers. The most famous Russian pie made with yeasted dough is *Koulbiaca* but that is of course because La Carème, returning from the court of the Czar, established it as Parisian Haute Cuisine. Properly made, it is a very complicated dish but this is its simpler country cousin. Remember that Siberia was not always a place you sent your prisoners to but a source of much game and wildfowl.

This dish can be made in any size you choose—individual ones are good for parties—but I find this size does more for appearance and succulence. The original recipe called for a few chips of ice to supply moisture but I have used butter or stock. The French have a variant on this theme made with 1 pound baked potato, a cup of flour, a little olive oil, and 1 egg made into a dough, filled with your stuffing and baked as below or fried in smaller cakes.

For the dough:

3 cups all-purpose flour

1 x 0.6-ounce cake compressed yeast

1 cup warm water or milk

1 tablespoon sugar

2 eggs, well beaten

1/2 teaspoon salt

3 tablespoons butter, softened

For the filling:

1 pound cooked fish or meat (about 3 cups)

1 medium onion, finely sliced and fried

1–2 tablespoons butter or jellied stock

pinch of whatever herbs go with the filling

salt and pepper

Sift the flour into a bowl and make a well in it. Gently crumble in the yeast with the liquid, mixing in gently. Cover and let it ferment for 15 minutes in a warm place. Add the rest of the ingredients and knead well. Divide in two, cover again, and let it rest and rise until it has doubled—about 20 minutes. Punch down the dough and roll out until it is 1/2-inch thick. Put half of the dough on a greased baking sheet and sprinkle with flour. Place the filling on it and cover with the other half of the dough. Seal the edges carefully. Leave for 30 minutes—the dough will continue to rise— then bake at 425°F for 40–50 minutes until golden.

You could try pheasant with cilantro, or venison with cumin, or salmon with coconut and red peppers. Have fun with it!

sauce for **pigeon** or **duck**

This is a variant on a Roman sauce; the original had mint and lovage seed but I like it better without them. This sauce can be served with pigeon or wild duck.

1 tablespoon olive oil

1 small onion, chopped

4 ounces pitted dates (about 2/3 cup)

1 egg yolk

1 tablespoon white wine

1 tablespoon vinegar

1 tablespoon honey

1 teaspoon anchovy essence

salt and pepper

Heat the oil in a pan and fry the onion until it colors. Transfer it to a food processor and add all the other ingredients. Blend well, return to the pan and heat through.

good **gravy**

This is how I make gravy and it is much enjoyed. The secret to good gravy is good stock, never mind the vegetable water or the stock cube, half a pint of good stock makes all the difference.

Remove whatever bird or beast you have roasted and pour off any excess fat—keep this for future cooking. Scatter in enough plain flour to absorb the pan juices (if your roasting pan isn't flameproof, transfer the juices to one that is), and stir in well with a wooden spoon, making sure no lumps remain. Scrape up any bits that have stuck to the bottom of the pan. When it is smooth, add a certain amount of stock and mix as it heats up, to absorb the flour.

Add the rest of the stock and let it cook gently. Season with salt and pepper, add a cup or so of red wine, and cook some more, then a half-cup of orange juice or a little red currant jelly. When your sauce tastes right, thin with a little vegetable water or let it cook to thicken—you can play about with it for some time. Make sure your sauce boat is scalding hot before you pour in the gravy. An Argyle is good for removing fat or if the sauce is greasy when made, ignite some brandy and pour into the sauce to burn off excess fat.

onion **sauce** vivien

This is so called because my friend Vivien Cassell and I concocted it in her kitchen. It is lighter than the usual and very delicious.

butter for cooking the onions, plus 2 tablespoons for the roux

4 onions, cut in half and sliced

3 tablespoons flour

1 bottle light beer

milk

salt and pepper

1 tablespoon crème fraîche (if unavailable, use cream or
 sour cream or a mixture)

Melt some butter in a pan and sauté the onions until pale gold. In another pan, melt 2 tablespoons butter and add the flour to make a roux, cook for a couple of minutes then add the beer, a little at a time to make a sauce. Add enough milk to make the right consistency—about 2 tablespoons. Add the onions, season with salt and pepper, and stir in the crème fraîche.

plum **sauce**

This is a good sauce for duck, goose, or most game and will keep well in the fridge. You can use preserved plums.

1 onion, chopped

1/2 teaspoon fennel seeds

1/2 pound plums or damson plums

2 tablespoons honey or mead

2 1/2 cups game stock

1/2 cup red wine

1 tablespoon olive oil or butter

1/2 teaspoon ground pepper

In a blender grind together the pepper, onion, and fennel seeds. Add the chopped plums and the honey (or mead), and blend quickly. Add the rest of the ingredients and whizz a bit. Transfer to a saucepan and simmer very gently for 30 minutes.

bread sauce

This use of stale bread in making a sauce is truly medieval. I love bread sauce, hot with white game, cold in sandwiches. There are many ways to make it—some like the onion cut up, some like it cooked whole and then mashed up before serving—I make mine in a double boiler. You can make it in advance, freeze it, or keep it in the warming drawer but this is what I do.

For about 2¹/₂ cups—enough for 4:

1 onion, liberally stuck with cloves

1 loaf white bread (crust removed), cut into cubes)

2¹/₂ cups whole milk

good pinch of ground mace or freshly grated nutmeg

1 bay leaf

²/₃ cup heavy cream

salt and pepper

Put the onion in a pan and arrange the bread around it, pour the milk over it, and season with salt and pepper, nutmeg, and bay leaf. Bring to a boil and reduce to a very low heat on a heat diffuser if possible. Simmer gently, partly covered for 2–3 hours, adding more milk if needed. The thickness of the sauce is your choice. Just before serving, discard the bay leaf, and do what you like with the onion—cut it up, mash it, or discard it. Add the cream and onion, if using, stir, and heat through.

green sauce

This is the traditional medieval sauce to be served with fish and game. It is sharp and if you find it too much, add a finely mashed yolk of a hard-boiled egg and a little olive oil. It is, I suppose, the precursor of mint sauce and probably came back from the Crusades. Use what herbs you have but let mint and parsley dominate.

12 sprigs of fresh herbs

2 ounces fresh fine white bread crumbs (about 1 cup)

2 tablespoons cider vinegar

1 clove garlic (or if available, tops of wild garlic, finely chopped)

salt and pepper

Finely chop the herbs. Sprinkle the bread crumbs with the vinegar and leave for 10 minutes. Crush the garlic in a mortar, add the herbs, bread crumbs, salt and pepper, and pound well. Add enough vinegar to bring to the consistency of thin bread sauce.

rowan jelly

4 pounds almost ripe rowan berries

5 cups water

3/4 cup sugar to every cup of juice

Strip the berries from the stalks. Put into a pot with the water, bring to a boil, and simmer for 15 minutes (do not exceed this time as the juice becomes bitter). Strain the fruit through a jelly bag, and be careful not to squeeze or poke the bag or the jelly will be cloudy. Measure the juice, return to a clean pot, and add the correct amount of sugar. Stir over low heat until the sugar is dissolved. Boil rapidly, stirring as you go and skimming when necessary. Test for setting on a cold plate. Pour into heated jars, cover with waxed paper, and let it set. Screw on the lid.

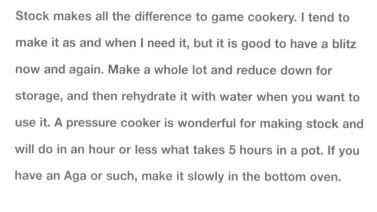

game stock

Stock makes all the difference to game cookery. I tend to make it as and when I need it, but it is good to have a blitz now and again. Make a whole lot and reduce down for storage, and then rehydrate it with water when you want to use it. A pressure cooker is wonderful for making stock and will do in an hour or less what takes 5 hours in a pot. If you have an Aga or such, make it slowly in the bottom oven.

2 pounds game meat

2 pounds game trimmings

about 4 quarts water

4 ounces onions, chopped and browned (about 1 cup)

4 ounces carrots, cut up (about 1 cup)

2 leeks, sliced

2 celery stalks, cut up

1 faggot of herbs (see page 202)

9 peppercorns

3 whole cloves

In a large pot, put the meat, trimmings and cold water, bring to a boil, and simmer for 1 hour. Then add the rest of the ingredients and simmer for 4 hours, skimming as you go. Strain through cheesecloth, let it to go cold, and remove the excess fat. Return to the pot and reduce by two thirds. Freeze in cubes in ice-trays, tip the frozen cubes into a bag, label, and use as needed, adding water as needed.

game fries

Some people serve chips with game—tut tut. Game fries are easy to make and even the best of potato chips don't measure up. For perfect game fries you must use floury potatoes, preferably bought from a farm shop so they haven't been irradiated and chilled like the supermarket variety, and when you have sliced them very thinly using a mandoline or a food processor or a very sharp knife, you must wash them well in running cold water to remove the starch. Dry them very thoroughly on paper towels or a lint-free dishtowel.

Heat your oil, vegetable not olive, in a deep fat fryer until it is very hot (about 400°F) and cook your fries in small batches to avoid sticking. I cook mine twice. To do this, fry each batch until they just start to change color, then drain them on newspaper or paper towels. Return the fries to the oil for 2–3 minutes to finish off.

You can be fancy and do this with parsnips or beets but cook them separately from the potatoes.

potato olad

This is a Russian dish from Belarus and a good way of using up leftovers. You can mix and match your ingredients until your heart's content and it makes a great supper dish; the Russians eat it with sour cream. You can add yeast and a beaten egg to make more of a cake at a ratio of 18 ounces potatoes to $1/2$ cup flour, with 1 egg and one package dried yeast mixed with $1/4$ cup warm water.

For the pancake:
4 large potatoes
2 tablespoons flour
$1/2$ cup (1 stick) butter
salt and pepper

Grate the potatoes, squeeze dry in a cloth, and season with salt and pepper. Mix in the flour using your hands. Heat the butter in a heavy frying pan and put half the potato mix in and form a flattened cake. Fry for a few minutes and then place a dollop of filling on top (see below). Cover with the rest of the grated potato and when the underside is crisp and well set, flip over and cook until the bottom side is done. Alternatively you can put it under the broiler to brown the top, but brush with oil or melted butter so that it doesn't burn.

Suggested fillings

Cooked pheasant with soft cheese and capers

Cooked venison with cranberries

Duck with marmalade sharpened with lemon juice

Salmon with blue cheese or macerated fruit (the sort you get given or win in a raffle, like peaches in brandy or some such)

stuffed onions

This is a perfect way to use up leftover game. Edward VII's favorite breakfast was onions stuffed with kidneys, cream, and brandy—delicious but perhaps not for breakfast. Stuffed onions make a great supper dish and you can stuff them in advance and stick them in the oven while having your bath. The onions can either be parboiled and then roasted, or raw and then braised.

4 large onions

1/4 cup (1/2 stick) butter

1 ounce bacon, finely chopped (about 3 tablespoons)

1 ounce fresh white bread crumbs (about 1/2 cup)

2 tablespoons chopped herbs (whatever goes with your filling) plus parsley for coloring

8 ounces game filling (see right)

salt and pepper

Carefully peel your onion and if parboiling, do so in boiling water for 10 minutes and let it cool until you can handle it. Cut off the root end to make a platform then cut a lid about 1/2-inch from the top and carefully cut out (and set aside) the insides leaving a 1/2-inch wall.

Preheat the oven to 375°F. Heat the butter in a frying pan, chop the removed onion innards and cook in the butter until golden. Add the bacon, bread crumbs, and the remaining ingredients and fry for a bit longer. Spoon into the onions and replace the lids. Put into an oven dish and paint the onions with olive oil to prevent them drying, or pour 2/3 cup stock over them. Cook in the oven for 40 minutes, and halfway through, cover with some tinfoil.

Suggested fillings, 1/4 cup per onion

Venison kidneys with cream, brandy, and mushroom

Pheasant with herbs, cream cheese, sherry, cayenne, and chili

Pheasant with wild mushrooms

Duck with bottled cherries or damson plums

Duck with green peas and mint

Venison with squares of beets (parboiled).

The options are endless!

beet pancakes

These eighteenth century pancakes make an attractive accompaniment to game and can be eaten hot or cold which make them a nice addition to a buffet table.

6 ounces beets, cooked and peeled (about 1–1 1/2 cups)

2 tablespoons brandy

2 tablespoons heavy cream

4 egg yolks

2 tablespoons flour

2 teaspoons sugar

1 teaspoon nutmeg, grated

clarified butter

Put all the ingredients except the butter in a food processor and blend well together to create a pancake mixture. Heat a little butter in a small frying pan. Make pancakes with the mixture but be careful as they burn quite easily. Turn them after a minute or two—they cook quite quickly.

gratin with leeks

This is another good leftover dish but to give it a bit of zip make your cheese sauce with half Stilton or another blue cheese and add a few capers and cayenne pepper. Use any leftover game you have, either singly or mixed for extra curiosity!

1 pound potatoes (about 3–4 medium), thinly sliced and washed to remove starch

2 teaspoons capers

1 pound cooked game, sliced (about 3 cups)

leeks or heads of Belgian endive, sliced into 2-inch pieces and blanched

2 1/2 cups cheese sauce, made with a good cheddar

salt, pepper, and cayenne pepper

Preheat the oven to 375°F. Butter an ovenproof dish and line it with a layer of potatoes. Sprinkle with capers and season with salt and pepper. Put on your slices of game and your leeks or Belgian endive, add another layer of potatoes and pour the sauce over it. Scatter some grated cheese on top, dot with butter, and bake in the oven for about 45 minutes.

meat suppliers

Game is increasingly available in grocery stores and meat markets. You can ask your butcher to order it for you or look in the *Yellow Pages* under "meats". Alternatively you can use mail order. Here are some suppliers that may be of help.

888 Eat Game
Tel: 888-EAT-GAME
www.888eatgame.com
Retail and wholesale meats from alligator to zebra

Broadleaf Venison USA, Inc.
3050 East 11th Street
Los Angeles
California 90023
Tel: 800-336-3844
www.broadleafgame.com
Wholesale and mail order
Large and small game, game birds, exotic game

Broken Arrow Ranch
P.O. Box 530
Ingram
Texas 78025
Tel: 800-962-4263
www.brokenarrowranch.com
Wholesale and mail order
Venison, wild boar, smoked meats, and sausages

D'Artagnan Inc.
399 St. Paul Avenue
Jersey City
New Jersey 07306
Tel: 800-327-8246
Wholesale and mail order
Large and small game, game birds, exotic game

Durham Meat Company
P.O. Box 26158
San Jose
California 95159
Tel: 800-233-8742
Wholesale and mail order
Large and small game, game birds, exotic game

ExoticMeats.com
Tel: 800-680-4375
www.exoticmeats.com
Large and small game, game birds and exotic game

Hills Foods Ltd.
109-3650 Bonneville Place
Burnaby
British Columbia
Canada
V3N 4T7
Tel: 604-421-3100
www.hillsfoods.com
Wholesale only
Large and small game, game birds, exotic game

Game Sales International
2456 E. 13th Street
P.O. Box 7719
Loveland
CO 80537
Tel: 800-729-2090
www.gamesalesintl.com
Large and small game, game birds and exotic game

Joie DeVivre
P.O. Box 875
Modesto
California 95353
Tel: 800-648-8854
Mail order
Duck , smoked duck, rabbit, geese, guinea hens, foie gras

MacFarlane Pheasant Farm, Inc.
2821 South U.S. Hwy. 51
Janesville
Wisconsin 53546
Tel: 800-345-8348
Wholesale and mail order
Pheasant, smoked pheasant, and other types of wild game

Mount Royal USA Inc.
3902 N Main
Houston
Texas 77009
Tel: 800-730-3337
www.mountroyal.com
Large and small game, game birds and exotic game

Musicon Farms
157 Scotchtown Road
Goshen
New York 10924
Tel: 914-294-6378
Wholesale and mail order
Kosher venison

Native Game
12556 WCR 21/2
Brighton
Colorado 80601
Tel: 800-952-6321
Wholesale and mail order
Large and small game, game birds, exotic game

Nicky USA, Inc.
223 S.E. 3rd Avenue
Portland
Oregon 97214
Tel: 800-469-4162
www.nickyusa.com
Wholesale and mail order
Large and small game, game birds and exotic game

Nightbird
358 Shaw Road
South San Francisco
California 94080
Tel: 650-737-5876
Wholesale and mail order
Large and small game, game birds and exotic game

Polaricia (Wholesale)/The Game
Exchange (Retail)
P.O. Box 990204
San Francisco
California 94124
Tel: 800-GAME-USA
Wholesale and retail
Large and small game, game birds, exotic game

Prairie Harvest
P.O. Box 1013
Spearfish
South Dakota 57783
Tel: 800-350-7166
Wholesale and mail order
Large and small game, game birds, exotic game

The Sausage Maker, Inc.
1500 Clinton Street, Bldg. 123
Buffalo
New York 14206
Tel: 716-824-6510
www.sausagemaker.com
Wholesale and mail order
Sausage-making supplies

Valley Game & Gourmet
P.O. Box 2713
Salt Lake City
Utah 84110
www.valleygame.com
Large and small game, game birds, exotic game

cooking glossary

Argyle A specially designed gravy boat, the idea of John, 4th Duke of Argyll, which allows the gravy to sink to the bottom and the fat to be poured off before serving it.

Bain marie or water bath Can be any deep pan or ovenproof container, half-filled with hot water, in which delicate foods are cooked inside their mold(s) or terrine(s), set in the hot water. The bain marie is put into a low or moderate oven. The food is protected from direct heat by the gentle, steamy atmosphere, without the risk of curdling. The term bain marie is also used for a similar container which holds several pans to keep soups, vegetables, or stews warm during restaurant service.

Barding Wrapping meat, game, or poultry which is low in fat with thin slices of bacon or pork fat to prevent it from drying out while roasting.

Barding fat Ask the butcher to give you this.

Basting Spooning roasting juices during cooking over meat to moisten and add flavor.

Beurre manie Paste mixture of flour and butter which is used to thicken sauces and stews.

Bouquet garni A small bunch of fresh herbs used to flavor stews, casseroles, stocks, or soups, usually consisting of parsley stalks, a sprig of thyme, perhaps a bay leaf and an outside stalk of celery. Remove before serving.

Bursa test The Bursa is a blind vent above the anus, the purpose of which is still really unknown; it closes completely when the bird reaches sexual maturity, so a toothpick inserted will tell all—it will go up $1/2$ inch in a young bird.

Carving other game birds Grouse, snipe, woodcock, teal, golden eye, partridges, quail, pigeon, etc., are always served whole, unless cooked as a salmis or stew. To take the meat of any of these delicious little birds, start with the legs towards you and your fork firmly fixed to the left of the breast bone. Begin just above the wing, working your way upwards towards the dividing breast bone. Once one side is clean of breast meat, turn and repeat on the other side. Cut or tear off the legs and wings, and eat them in the time honored way—with your fingers.

Caul fat Lacy membrane that surrounds the organs in the abdominal cavity of the pig. It melts away during cooking and imparts richness to the ingredients.

Clarified butter Butter cleared of impurities and water by melting slowly. Remove the salty skin with a spoon. The clear butter is the clarified butter; discard the liquid at the bottom.

Coarse fish Freshwater fish other than members of the salmon family.

Coffyn Simply means a box in Medieval English; in culinary terms it refers to a thick pastry dough box, with or without a lid, in which things were cooked and served direct to the table.

Confit Meat, especially goose and duck, preserved the French way, in fat—delicious!

Crop Pouch in the esophagus where undigested food is stored in a bird. It needs to be removed when cleaning and gutting the brid.

Cutting a bird in quarters Pull the leg away from body. With a sharp knife, cut through the skin joining the leg to the body, pull the leg away further and cut through more skin to free the leg. Bend the leg outwards and back forcing the bone to come out of its socket close to the body. Cut through the flesh between the end of the thigh bone and the carcass to remove the leg. Split the carcass along the breastbone, cut through the ribs on each side to take away the fleshy portion of the breast.

Cutting a hare/rabbit in quarters Use a sharp knife to sever the fore end just below the shoulder blade. Then divide the saddle by cutting down the center of the back bone.

Cutting a bird in two Use a sharp knife to cut right through the flesh and bone, just on one side of the breastbone, open out the bird and cut through the other side immediately next to the backbone. Then pull the backbone away from the half to which it remains attached.

Darne The cut at the thickest part behind the head of a fish.

De-glaze To dilute pan juices in a pan in which meat has just been cooked, by adding wine, cream, or stock to make gravy, scraping all the bits for flavor.

Drawing To clean out the intestines from poultry.

Dressing To pluck, draw, and truss poultry or game.

Drumstick The tibia of a bird.

Dusting Sprinkling lightly with flour, sugar, spice, or seasoning.

Faggot of herbs A bundle of herbs.

Fillet of rabbit The section along the backbone below the shoulders.

Flank Side of an animal from the ribs to the thigh.

Forcemeat Meat (usually pork or veal but can be game) chopped finely and heavily seasoned. It can be used as a stuffing or made into balls.

Freezing All game freezes very well. Bag whole birds separately or cut the game into pieces; remove from the bone or finely chop. Remember to label what you freeze or you get interesting mixtures. I reduce my game stock down as much as possible and freeze in ice cube trays, then pop out the cubes and bag them so that I can just take out one or two as I need them. Do remember to use your frozen game throughout the year, shooting wives are forever sorting out the bottom of the freezer in September to make room for the new season's crop, and like all things that freeze, they are better used within 6 months.

Game fish Freshwater fish of the salmon family with the exception of grayling.

Game trimmings Accompaniment for the roast game birds: game fries, bread sauce, gravy, and red currant jelly. It can also refer to the wings, liver, cleaned gizzard, heart. neck, etc. of birds that make a tasty stock.

Giblets Edible internal organs of poultry and game including the liver, heart, gizzard, neck, pinions, and often in days gone by, the feet and cockscomb.

Gizzard The stomach of birds in which the food is ground.

Glaze A glossy finish applied to food by brushing with milk, beaten egg, sugar, syrup, or jelly after cooking.

Gnocchi Small dumplings made from semolina, potatoes, or choux pastry dough.

Gutting To remove the inards from a fish, poultry, or game, and clean thoroughly ready for cooking.

Hanging Wild game is often dry and tough. By hanging it after shooting to remove blood, the meat is tenderized. The longer the hanging time, the more gamey the flavor, and the greater the change in the molecular structure of the meat. Older game tends to need longer hanging than young animals. To describe game as high implies a very strong gamey flavor.

How Long to Cook Game It is traditional to eat most game rare, the exceptions to this is pheasant or partridge, and even they should be slightly underdone or they will dry out. Some people like grouse very blue (personally I prefer mine rare—still red but not bloody), others prefer them more cooked but they should always be slightly red. Where not otherwise indicated, the cooking times in the recipes are for medium rare and if two sets of time are given, the shortest is for rare and the longest for as long as is acceptable without drying the meat out.

Venison, when roast, should be pink like lamb as it will become too dry if cooked any longer.

Fish should always be slightly underdone. Remember there is nothing you can catch from undercooking game or fish, and pheasant, unlike chicken, is not subject to salmonella when undercooked.

Joint To divide meat into individual pieces, separating it at the joints.

Jugged Meat dishes stewed in a covered pot.

Lard Natural or refined pork fat.

Larding Threading strips of fat through lean meat using a specially designed needle. This stops the meat from drying out when roasting.

Lardons Small pieces of thick-cut bacon, sold ready-chopped. As an alternative to lardons, thick slices of bacon can be cut lengthwise into strips and then into small pieces.

Marinade Blend of oil, wine or vinegar, herbs and spices. Used to make the meat more tender to add flavor.

Mead An alcoholic drink made by fermenting honey with water, often flavored with spice.

Offal Edible internal organs of meat, poultry, and game. Also called organ meats or variety meats.

Paella A traditional Spanish recipe. Dish of saffron rice, chicken or shellfish, named after the traditional pan in which it is cooked.

Parson's Nose The piece of fatty flesh at the tail end of the bird.

Paunching To remove the guts of an animal, the paunch being the prominent portion of the abdomen.

Pinion The wing, and in particular, the last joint of the wing of the bird, or it can be used to describe the outermost flight feather on the wing.
Pluck To remove the feathers from a dead bird.

Polenta Cornmeal, made from maize (corn) dried and ground.

Primary feathers The longest of the flight feathers on the wing, and furthest away from the body.

Raised Pie Usually made with hot water crust, and containing meat and stock which forms a jelly.

Ratatouille Mediterranean stew of eggplants, onions, peppers, and tomatoes cooked in olive oil.

Reducing Concentrating a liquid by boiling and evaporating excess liquid.

Roux A basic liaison of equal parts butter and flour which is used as a thickening agent.

Quenelles Usually poached, these are forcemeat dumplings often made of fish, and occasionally chicken and veal.

Saddle Butcher's cut including a part of the backbone with the ribs.

Salamander A hot metal plate for browning meat.

Salmi A ragoût of previously cooked game or other meats.

Seasoned flour Flour seasoned with salt and pepper.

Sewing up Use a needle with some strong thread and sew up any meat. Remove thread before servng.

Singe To quickly flame duck or geese to remove all traces of feathers and down after plucking. A taper is very useful for doing this.

Sippet Morsel of bread, often eaten with soup.

Skirt Midriff of meat.

Smoking Curing meat or fish by exposing it to warm or cold wood smoke over a period of time.

Skinning game birds To save plucking, you can skin your birds; this is really only successful with pheasant as duck and goose skin is arguably the nicest bit. Remember to remove the leg sinews from an unplucked bird. If you are using any of the casserole recipes for pheasant, just skin them. There is an interesting way to remove the breast from a whole pheasant: lay the bird on its back on the floor, put your feet on either side of the bird firmly on each wing, grasp the legs and pull upwards and your pheasant will come in half leaving the breast to be cut off the wings. If you pull the sinews before starting this then you can just skin the legs as well and devil them or make confit with them.

Skinning, jointing, and paunching hares and rabbits You can paunch them after they are skinned. Sever all 4 legs at the first joint, then cut through the skin of the hind legs halfway between the leg joint and the tail. Peel the skin from the hind legs. Tie them together and hang over a bowl containing a little vinegar to catch the blood. Pull the skin over the body and forelegs. I remove the head but you can skin it and keep it on. Cut it up the middle, but don't cut into the gall bladder. Tip the blood from the rib cage into the bowl. Paunch it by discarding the guts, keeping the liver. Rinse in cold water and dry with paper towels. Remove the blue membrane.

Spur Claw-like projection at the back of a bird's leg.

Spatchcock With a sharp knife, cut lengthwise down the middle of the bird and spread the two halves out flat.

Suet Fat around beef or lamb kidneys.

Supreme The breast from poultry or game—that is, including some of the wing by cutting it off at the first joint.

Tendons Bands of fibrous tissue, attaching muscles to the bone; in game birds they can be annoying and are best removed to make the leg meat totally edible. Put the foot of the bird over a suitable hook and pull gently down, twisting as you pull. The tendons should come out and remain with the foot.

Trivet A metal plate placed in a pressure-cooker to raise the food to be cooked off the bottom of the vessel.

Trussing Tying a bird or joint of meat in a neat shape with skewers and string before cooking. Butchers should do this for you.

game calendar

The game calendar in North America varies from state to state and year to year. It is decided by each state Fish and Wildlife Department who monitor speices numbers before making their decision for the season dates and bag limits. Like in all other countries the game season is determined by the immature species becoming adult—you don't shoot anything before it is big enough to eat.

Find out from your local state Fish and Wildlife Department for the dates of each season (website addresses pages 204-5) .

website addresses

International websites

www.asafishing.org
American Sportfishing Association

www.basc.org.uk
British Association of Shooting and Conservation

www.bds.org.uk
The British Deer Society

www.sportsmenslink.org
The Congressional Sportsmen's Foundation

www.countrysideireland.com
Countryside Ireland

www.ducks.org
Ducks Unlimited

www.face-europe.org
Federation of Fieldsports Association of European Union

www.fga.net.au
Australia Field and Gam

www.gct.org.uk
Game Conservancy Trust

www.fedflyfishers.org
International Game and Fish Association

www.igfa.org
International Game Fish Association

www.hunt4land.org
International Hunting Land Association

www.pheasantsforever.org
Pheasants Forever

www.qu.org
Quail Unlimited, Inc.

www.trcp.org
Theodore Roosevelt Conservation Partnership

www.salmon-trout.org
Salmon and Trout Association

www.wingshooters.co.za
South African Wingshooters Association

www.fws.gov
US Fish and Wildlife Service

www.whitetailsunlimited.com
Whitetails Unlimited, Inc.

North American websites

www.shootata.com/atahome.cfm
Amateur Trapshooting Association

www.statesportsmenslink.org
Assembly of Sprotsmen's Caucuses

www.aurorasc.org
Aurora Sportsmen's Club

www.backcountryhunters.org
Backcountry Hunters and Anglers

www.boone-crockett.org/index.html
Boone and Crockett Club

www.bowhuntermaxx.com
BowHunterMaxx

www.bowhuntersofwyoming.com
Bowhunters of Wyoming

www.buckmasters.com
Buckmasters A.D.F

www.crpa.org
California Rifle and Pistol Association California

www.calwaterfowl.org
Waterfowl Association

www.ccfsa.com
Clinton County Farmers' and Sportsmen's Association

www.buckfax.com
Commemorative Bucks of Michigan

www.pawco.org
Conservation Officers of Pennsylvania

www.biggame.org
Dallas Safari Club

www.ecfnaws.com
Eastern Chapter of FNAWS

www.elcr.org
Equestrian Land Conservation Resource

www.fedflyfishers.org
Federation of Fly Fishers

www.firearmsalliance.org
Fire Arms Alliance

www.furtakersofamerica.com
Fur Takers of America

www.gcfng.com/index.html
Greene County Fish & Game Association

www.hilltopsportsmansclub.com
Hilltop Sportsman's Club

www.scihouston.org
Houston Golf Coast SCI

www.hunterspro.com
Hunters Pro

www.hunting101.com
Hunting 101

www.ifhd.net
Illinois Federation of Hunting Dogs

www.ibo.net
International Bowhunting Organization

www/iowadeer.com/index.shtml
Iowa Deer

www.kishelscents.com
Kishel's Scents & Lures

www.alligatorfur.com
Louisiana Fur and Alligator Advisory Council

www.marylandsportsmen.org
Maryland Sportsmen's Association

www.massbowhunters.net
Massachusetts Bowhunters Association

www.michiganbowhunters.org/index.html
Michigan Bow Hunters Assn.

www.mcrgo.org/mcrgo/
Michigan Coalition for Responsible Gun Owners

www.midha.org
Michigan Duck Hunters Assn.

www.michigan-outdoors.com
Michigan Sportsmen's Web

www.mnbowhunters.org
Minnesota Bowhunters Assn.

www.mntrappers.com
Minnesota Trappers Association

www.montanahoundsmen.com
Montana State Houndsmen Association

www.montanatrappers.org
Montana Trappers Association

www.nbef.org
National Bowhunter Education Foundation

www.nssf.org
National Shooting Sports Foundation

www.nationaltrappers.com
National Trappers Association

www.nwtf.com
National Wild Turkey Federation

www.nhtassoc.org
New Hampshire Trappers Association

www.njsportsmen.com
NJ Sportsmen

www.nodakoutdoors.com
NoDak Outdoors

http://visitors.fishingclub.com/
North American Fishing Club

www.naweoa.org
North American Wildlife Enforcement Officers Association

www.ncbha.com
North Carolina Bear Hunters Association

www.ncbowhunter.com
North Carolina Bowhunters Association

www.nwtf.org
NWTF National Capital Area Chapter

www.ohiobass.org
Ohio B.A.S.S. Chapter Federation

www.ducks.org
Ohio Ducks Unlimited

http://web.tusco.net/ohiohuskiemuskieclub/index.htm
Ohio Huskie Muskie Club, Inc.

www.orpa.net
Ohio Rifle & Pistol Association

www.qdma.com
Quality Deer Management Association

www.rabbitsunlimited.org/web/main_site_folder/site
Rabbits Unlimited

www.robinhoodarchery.org
Robinhood Archery Club

www.firearmsalliance.org
Shooters' Alliance for Firearm Rights

www.sportsmansweb.net
Sportsmans Web

www.stepoutside.org
Step Outside

www.archerysociety.org
The Internet Archery Society

www.mdwildlifeprotection.org
The Wildlife Conservation Enforcement Fund

www.unifiedsportsmenpa.org
Unified Sportsmen of Pennsylvania

www.bowsite.com/ubc
United Bowhunters of Connecticut

www.unitedbowhuntersofkentucky.org
United Bowhunters of Kentucky

www.westleyrichards.com
Westley Richards Gunmakers

www.wcsarenovo.org
Western Clinton Sportsmen's Association

www.wildlifeforever.org
Wildlife Forever

Fish and Wildlife Agencies

Alabama Division of Wildlife and Freshwater Fisheries
http://www.dcnr.state.al.us/agfd/

Alaska Department of Fish and Game
http://www.adfg.state.ak.us/

Arizona Game and Fish Department
http://www.gf.state.az.us/

Arkansas Game and Fish Commission
http://www.agfc.state.ar.us/

California Department of Fish and Game
http://www.dfg.ca.gov/dfghome.html

Colorado Division of Wildlife
http://wildlife.state.co.us/

Connecticut Department of Environmental Protection
http://dep.state.ct.us/

Delaware Division of Fish and Wildlife
http://www.dnrec.state.de.us/fw/index.htm

Florida Fish and Wildlife Conservation Commission
http://floridaconservation.org/ http://georgiawildlife.dnr.state.ga.us/

Hawaii Department of Land and Natural Resources
http://www.state.hi.us/dlnr/

Idaho Game and Fish Department
http://fishandgame.idaho.gov/

Illinois Department of Natural Resources
http://dnr.state.il.us/

Indiana Department of Natural Resources
http://www.state.in.us/dnr/fishwild/index.htm

Iowa Department of Natural Resources
http://www.iowadnr.com/

Kansas Department of Wildlife and Parks
http://www.kdwp.state.ks.us/

Kentucky Department of Fish and Wildlife Resources
http://www.kdfwr.state.ky.us/

Louisiana Department of Wildlife
http://www.wlf.state.la.us/apps/netgear/page1.asp

Maine Department of Inland Fisheries & Wildlife
http://www.state.me.us/ifw/index.htm

Maryland Department of Natural Resources
http://www.dnr.state.md.us/sw_index_flash.asp

Massachusetts Division of Fisheries and Wildlife
http://www.mass.gov/dfwele/dfw/

Michigan Department of Natural Resources
http://www.michigan.gov/dnr

Minnesota Department of Natural Resources
http://www.dnr.state.mn.us/index.html

Mississippi Department of Wildlife, Fisheries, and Parks
http://www.mdwfp.com/

Missouri Department of Conservation
http://www.conservation.state.mo.us/

Montana, Fish, Wildlife & Parks
http://fwp.state.mt.us/default.html

Nevada Department of Conservation and Natural Resources
http://dcnr.nv.gov/

New Hampshire Fish and Game Department
http://www.wildlife.state.nh.us/

New Jersey Division of Fish and Wildlife
http://www.state.nj.us/dep/fgw/

New Mexico Game and Fish Department
http://www.wildlife.state.nm.us/

New York Department of Environmental Conservation
http://www.dec.state.ny.us/

North Carolina Wildlife Resources Commission
http://www.ncwildlife.org/

North Dakota Game and Fish Department
http://www.state.nd.us/gnf/

Ohio Division of Wildlife
http://www.dnr.state.oh.us/wildlife/default.htm

Oklahoma Department of Wildlife Conservation
http://www.wildlifedepartment.com/

Oregon Department of Fish and Wildlife
http://www.dfw.state.or.us/

Pennsylvania Fish and Boat Commission
http://sites.state.pa.us/PA_Exec/Fish_Boat/pfbchom2.html

Pennsylvania Game Commission
http://www.pgc.state.pa.us/

Rhode Island Division of Fish & Wildlife
http://204.139.0.230/programs/bnatres/fishwild/index.htm

South Carolina Department of Natural Resources
http://water.dnr.state.sc.us/

South Dakota Game Fish and Parks Department
http://www.sdgfp.info/index.htm

Tennessee Wildlife Resources Agency
http://www.state.tn.us/twra/index.html

Texas Parks and Wildlife Department
http://www.tpwd.state.tx.us/

Utah Division of Wildlife Resources
http://www.wildlife.utah.gov/

Vermont Department of Fish and Wildlife
http://www.anr.state.vt.us/fw/fwhome/index.htm

Virginia Department of Game and Inland Fisheries
http://www.dgif.state.va.us/

Washington Department of Fish and Wildlife
http://www.wdfw.wa.gov/

West Virginia Division of Natural Resources
http://www.wvdnr.gov/

Wisconsin Department of Natural Resources
http://www.dnr.state.wi.us/

Wyoming Game and Fish Department
http://gf.state.wy.us/

index

Andalucian doves, 57
Antelope. See Venison
Apician crêpes, 182

Barbel, 158
Beans
  pheasant with peanut butter,
    tomatoes, and flageolet beans, 27
  potato and white bean cakes, 115
  venison chili with lemon, beans,
    and a tomato sauce, 116
  wild boar with red beans and sour
    plums, 128
Beet pancakes, 194
Belgian endive
  partridge with Belgian endive, 21
  salmon with Belgian endive and
    roquefort, 164
Bollocks to Blair, 113
Bread sauce, 190
Bryn-y-pys hare terrine, 136
Burnett's woodcock, 68
Buttered Barley, 195

Cabbage
  goose with red cabbage and
    treacle, 93
  salmon and cabbage rolls, 160
Calabrian pheasant with macaroni, 52
Canada goose stuffed with olive and
  prunes, 93
Caribou.Ssee Venison
Carp, 159
  carp à la juive, 179
  carp stuffed with baked fruit, 175
  carp with cherries, 176
Carpaccio of grouse, 50
Cheese
  moose carpaccio with cheese and
    ligonberry compôte, 121
  quail stuffed with feta and
    fenugreek, 40
  roast pheasant with truffled
    cheese, 34
  salmon mousse with cheese, 162
  salmon with Belgian endive and
    roquefort, 164
  trout in a cheese broth, 166
Chestnuts
  mallard with sausage and chestnut
    stew, 83
  partridges stuffed with chestnuts, 16
Circassian pheasant, 31

Claypot pheasant, 30
Coarse fish, 158, 159
Cumberland boar pie, 131

Deer, 98–101
  venison recipes. See Venison
Dove, 54, 55
  aging, 55
  Andalucian doves, 57
  dove bistalia, 62
  dove in the hole, 59
  dove with rice and eggplant, 60
  doves from Emilia Romana, 58
  doves with raisins, 59
  drawing, 55
  Egyptian dove with green
    wheat, 63
  hanging, 55
  jellied dove, 57
  plucking, 55
  roasting, 55
  Yorkshire Christmas pie, 183
Duck, 80
  aging, 80
  carving, 80
  cold duck salad with Lucy's
    dressing, 91
  duck Allan Jarrett, 82
  duck casserole, 81
  duck pizzas with caramelized
    pineapple, 87
  duck with gin-soaked sloes, 83
  hanging, 80
  mallard with port, 84
  mallard with sausage and chestnut
    stew, 83
  orange and herb duck, 81
  pochard with parsley and
    blackberries, 84
  roast mallard with quinces, 88
  roasting, 80
  salmis of wild duck, 88
  teal with oranges, 91

Egyptian dove with green wheat, 63
Elizabethan rabbit, 146
Elk. See Venison

Fife Pie, 149
Fish, 156–159. See also Salmon,
  Trout, etc.
Fruit quail, 37

Game fries, 192
Game paella, 184
Game stock, 191
German roast venison with Brussels
  sprouts and walnuts, 113
Goose, 92
  aging, 92
  Canada goose stuffed with olives
    and prunes, 93
  goose with red cabbage and
    treacle, 93
  hanging, 92
  plucking, 92
  roast goose with dumplings, 94
  roasting, 92
  salmon cooked in goose fat, 166
  trout stuffed with confit, 167
  Yorkshire Christmas pie, 183
Gravy, 187
Green sauce, 190
Grouse, 42–45
  aging, 45
  buttered grouse, 46
  carpaccio of grouse, 50
  casseroled grouse with marmalade,
    49
  drawing, 45
  grouse duntreath, 52
  grouse in a rye crust, 53
  grouse pie, 49
  grouse pudding, 52
  hanging, 45
  hazel grouse in a Russian style,
    50
  plucking, 45
  potted grouse, 46
  roasting, 45

Hare (jackrabbit), 134, 135
  baron of hare, 137
  Bryn-y-pys hare terrine, 136
  hare swet, 137
  jugged hare, 138
  lagas stifado, 138
  raised hare pie, 141
Hazel grouse in a Russian style, 50
Hecht smetana, 175
Horseradish
  grilled zander with arugula, beets
    and horseradish, 173
  pheasant with noodles and
    horseradish cream, 32
Hungarian bartash with eggplant, 35

Issy's pheasants, 34

Jackrabbit. See Hare
Jellied dove, 57
Jugged hare, 138

La Mancha, 32
Lagas stifado, 138
Leeks
  gratin with leeks, 194
Lemons
  broiled partridge with garlic, oil,
    lemon, and cayenne, 15
  partridge with lentils and pickled
    lemons, 15
  Thessalian quail, 39
  venison chili with lemon, beans
    and a tomato sauce, 116

Mallard. See Duck
Moose. See Venison
Mushrooms
  hazel grouse in a Russian style,
    50
  salmon and cabbage rolls, 160
  venison with wild mushroom stew,
    104
  zander (pike perch) fillets with
    chanterelles, 173

Norwegian venison with sour cream,
  109

Onion sauce Vivien, 188
Oranges
  loin of wapeti with spiced blood
    oranges, 118
  orange and herb duck, 81
  Robert May's salmon, 160
  teal with oranges, 91
Partridge, 10–13
  aging, 13
  drawing, 13
  broiled partridge with garlic, oil,
    lemon, and cayenne, 15
  hanging, 13
  Hungarian bartash with eggplant, 21
  La Mancha, 18
  partridge in a pilaf, 16
  partridge with Belgian endive, 21
  partridge with lentils and pickled
    lemons, 15
  partridges for Lady Lucy, 19

partridges stuffed with chestnuts, 16
partridges with cockles on a cataplana, 19
partridges with peppers and tomatoes, 18
plucking, 13
roasting, 13
Yorkshire Christmas pie, 183
Perch, 158
Persian meatballs, 124
Pheasant, 22–25
aging, 24
Calabrian pheasant with macaroni, 32
carving, 25
Circassian pheasant, 31
claypot pheasant, 30
drawing, 25
hanging, 24
Issy's pheasant, 34
pheasant chitarnee, 29
pheasant terrine with pickled walnuts, 26
pheasant with Cremona mustard, 29
pheasant with noodles and horseradish cream, 32
pheasant with peanut butter, tomatoes, and flageolet beans, 27
pheasant with saffron and bread soup, 26
pheasant with sauerkraut, 30
plucking, 24–25
roast pheasant with truffled cheese, 34
roasting, 25
Yorkshire Christmas pie, 183
Pies
Cumberland boar pie, 131
Fife pie, 149
grouse pie, 49
raised hare pie, 141
sage cobbler, 122
snipe in a pie, 71
stalker's pie, 183
Wapeti ciste, 116
Yorkshire Christmas pie, 183
Pigeon. See Dove
Pike, 159
hecht smetana, 175
pike burgers, 174
pike pudding with pumpkin, 174
Pike perch. See Zander
Plums
plum sauce, 188
wild boar with red beans and sour

plums, 128
Pochard with parsley and blackberries, 84
Potatoes
Burnett's woodcock, 68
gratin with leeks, 194
potato and white bean cakes, 115
potato olad, 192
Quail, 36
fruit quail, 37
quail cooked in clay, 40
quail's eggs, 37
quail stuffed with feta and fenugreek, 40
Thessalian quail, 39
Quenelles of trout in watercress sauce, 169

Rabbit, 142, 143
Elizabethan rabbit, 146
Fife pie, 149
fried rabbit with mustard, 145
rabbit brawn (head cheese), 145
rabbit in the dairy, 146
rabbit saltimbocca, 152
rabbit stew, 144
rabbit with a piquant sauce, 152
rabbit with apples and cider, 152
rabbit with chocolate and tomatoes, 150
Raised hare pie, 141
Robert May's salmon, 160
Rowan jelly, 191

Sage cobbler, 122
Salmis of wild duck, 88
Salmon, 158
Robert May's salmon, 160
salmon and cabbage rolls, 160
salmon as cooked at the Golden Aur, 163
salmon cooked in goose fat, 166
salmon fishcakes made with gnocchi, 162
salmon mousse with cheese, 162
salmon with Belgian endive and roquefort, 164
salmon with pinenuts, 163
Sauce for pigeon or duck, 186
Sausages
duck Allan Jarrett, 82
mallard with sausage and chestnut stew, 83
venison sausages, 124
Siberian shangii, 186
Snipe, 70
snipe curry, 71
snipe in a pie, 71

snipe pudding, 72
snipe with lettuce and capers, 72
Stalker's pie, 183
Stock, game, 191
Stuffed onions, 193

Teal with oranges, 91
Texas hash, 102
Thessalian quail, 39
Tomatoes
partridges for Lady Lucy, 33
partridges with peppers and tomatoes, 32
pheasant with peanut butter, tomatoes, and flageolet beans, 15
rabbit with chocolate and tomatoes, 150
venison chili with lemon, beans and a tomato sauce, 116
Trout
brown trout, 158
quenelles of trout in a watercress sauce, 169
rainbow trout in red wine with tarragon, 167
rainbow trout, 158
sea trout, 158
sea trout with chard and walnuts, 170
sea trout with cucumbers and cream, 170
trout in a cheese broth, 166
trout stuffed with confit, 167

Venison
antelope meatloaf, 122
antelope stewed with blackcurrants, 121
bollocks to Blair, 113
Caribou pot roast, 125
Caribou as Sauerbraten, 126
carving, 101
flank of moose stuffed and rolled, 115
German roast venison with Brussels sprouts and walnuts, 113
Moose Carpaccio with cheese and ligonberry compote, 121
Norwegian venison with sour cream, 109
Persian meatballs, 124
red wine venison burgers, 106
saddle of wapeti with anchovies, 119
sage cobbler, 122
stalker's pie, 183
Texas hash, 102

venison chili with lemon, beans and a tomato sauce, 116
venison hotpot, 109
venison liver with puréed peas, 106
venison pastie, 107
venison sausages, 124
venison with beets, 104
venison with wild mushroom stew, 104
wapeti ciste, 116
wapeti glazed and stuffed from Cremona, 119
wapeti loin with spiced blood oranges, 118
white-tail fillet benedict, 110
white-tail with fresh pear chutney, 110
white-tail with red onion marmalade, 110
west country venison with cider, 102

Walnuts
German roast venison with Brussels sprouts and walnuts, 113
pheasant terrine with pickled walnuts, 26
sea trout with chard and walnuts, 170
Wapeti deer. See Venison
White-tailed deer. See Venison
Wild boar, 128
Cumberland boar pie, 131
wild boar from the Haute Savoie, 130
wild boar with red beans and sour plums, 128
wild boar with red wine and coriander seeds, 131
Wildfowl, 76–79
Woodcock, 64, 65
aging, 65
Burnett's woodcock, 68
drawing, 65
hanging, 65
plucking, 65
roasting, 65
woodcock with polenta, 66
woodcock with truffles, 69
Wood pigeon. See Dove

Yorkshire Christmas pie, 183

Zander (Pike perch), 159
grilled zander with arugula, beets, and horseradish, 173
zander fillets with chanterelles, 173

picture acknowledgements

Page 1 and Page 13: Old English Sports and Pastimes; Shooting , Cecil Charles Windsor Aldin (1870-1935)Private Collection/Bridgeman Art Library/The British Sporting Art Trust

Page 6: Still shows: James Mason and Patrick O'Connell in The Shooting Party; Edenflow/The Kobal Collection (1984)

Page 7: Maximilian I hunting deer, Tyrolean Manuscript, (16th century) Bibliotheque Royale de Belgique, Brussels, Belgium/Bridgeman Art Library

Page 10: Detail showing Two Partridges from a Fourth Century mosaic floor in the Crypt of Basilica of Aquileia, Corbis

Page 15: Patridge Shooting, Henry Alken Senior (1785-1851), The Tryon Gallery incorporating The Malcolm Innes Gallery

Page 23: 'The First of October', Edith Hayllar (1860-1948) Private Collection/Bridgeman Art Library

Page 31: Pheasant Shooting, Henry Thomas Alken (1785-1851) Yale Center for British Art, Paul Mellon Collection, USA/Bridgeman Art Library

Page 32: Driven Pheasants, George Lodge (1860-1954), The Tryon Gallery incorporating The Malcolm Innes Gallery

Page 35: An Autumn Shoot, Bernard Boutet de Monvel (1881-1949) Stapleton Collection, UK/Bridgeman Art Library

Page 36: Quails, Italian School, (14th century), Osterreichische Nationalbibliothek, Vienna, Austria, Bridgeman Art Library / Alinari

Page 37: Quails, Booah Malacca, Boorong Poo-eeoh, from 'Drawings of Birds from Malacca', c.1805-18, Chinese School, Royal Asiatic Society, London, courtesy of Bridgeman Art Library

Page 42: Going North, George Earl (1824-1908) Science Museum/Science & Society Picture Library

Page 43: Coming South, George Earl (1824-1908) Science Museum/Science & Society Picture Library

Page 44: Grouse and Chicks, George Lodge (1860-1954), The Tryon Gallery incorporating The Malcolm Innes Gallery

Page 53: Grouse in Flight, Archibald Thorburn, (1860-1935), The Tryon Gallery incorporating The Malcolm Innes Gallery

Page 55: Wood Ingraving 'Shooting Wild Pigeons in Iowa', Corbis

Page 65: Woodcock on Snow, Colin Woolf

Page 69: Woodcock, George Lodge (1860-1954), The Tryon Gallery incorporating The Malcolm Innes Gallery

Page 70: Snipe, Roland Green (1890-1972), The Tryon Gallery incorporating The Malcolm Innes Gallery

Page 77: Buying the Goose in a street market in Normandie, unnamed artist in Le Petit Journal, 27 Dec, 1907, Mary Evans Picture Library

Page 78: Pink-feet geese, Richard Barrett Talbot Kelly (1896-1971), The Tryon Gallery incorporating The Malcolm Innes Gallery

Page 80: Mallard Getting Up, Winifred Austen (1876-1964), The Tryon Gallery incorporating The Malcolm Innes Gallery

Page 82: The Game Stall, Beuckelaer or Bueckelaer (c.1530-1573), The Bridgeman Art Library

Page 99: Hunting at the Saint-Jean Pond in the Forest of Compiegne, Jean-Baptiste Oudry (1686-1755), Giraudon/Bridgeman Art Library

Page 107: Frieze of deer, 15000BC, Caves of Lascaux, Dordogne, France, courtesy of Bridgeman Art Library

Page 112: Young Ghillies with Stag, Ronald Robert Mclan, The Tryon Gallery incorporating The Malcolm Innes Gallery

Page 125: A Male Caribou Watches Females Swim across the River, E. Calawell in The Encyclopedia of Sport, Mary Evans Picture Library

Page 130: Devonshire Hunting Tapestries, Boar Hunt, probably Arras, 1425-1450, Victoria & Albert Museum, courtesy of Bridgeman Art Library

Page 134: Hunting hares, Comte Gaston Phebus de Foys, Livre de la Chasse (begun 1387), Bibliotheque Nationale, Paris, France, courtesy of Bridgeman Art Library

Page 143: Tapestry valence showing hunting scenes, Sheldon, early 17th century, Victoria and Albert Museum, London, UK, courtesy of Bridgeman Art Library

Page 144: Huckleberry Finn Holding Up a Rabbit he has Just Shot, illustrated by E. W. Kemble, 1888 edition of Huckleberry Finn by Mark Twain, published by Frontispiece, Mary Evans Picture Library

Page 153: Rabbit Man Sells Dead Rabbits for Food and Fur, The Cries of London, Drawn from Life Publishing in 1823, Mary Evans Picture Library

Page 156: The Last Trout, Henry Mayo Bateman (1887-1970), Estate of H.M.Bateman, UK, courtesy of Bridgeman Art Library

Page 159: Angler on the Seine, Monnier, from 'Les Francais', 1850, Mary Evans Picture Library

Page 163: Gaffing the Salmon, Richard Ansdell (1815-1885), The Tryon Gallery incorporating The Malcolm Innes Gallery

Page 166: Fishing for Trout in Rapids, Canada, Frank Feller, c. 1905, Mary Evans Picture Library

Page 169: American Winter Sports: Trout Fishing on Chateaugay Lake, pub. by Currier & Ives, 1856, Arthur Fitzwilliam Tait (1819-1905) Private Collection/Bridgeman Art Library

Page 174: Salmon Netting, Loch Awe, Hamilton Macallum (1841-1896), The Tryon Gallery incorporating The Malcolm Innes Gallery

Page 176: Still Life, John Russell, Senior, (1820-1893), The Tryon Gallery incorporating The Malcolm Innes Gallery

Page 182: The Market Place, Victor Gabriel Gilbert (1847-1933), Private Collection, courtesy of Bridgeman Art Library

Page 188: Leadenhall Market, Andreas Scheerboom (1832-1880), Guildhall Art Gallery, London, courtesy of Bridgeman Art Library

Page 195: Gamekeeper with dogs, Richard Ansdell (1815-85), Bury Art Gallery and Museum, courtesy of Bridgeman Art Library